The Great Atlantic Air Race

Also by Peter Bostock
Incurable Wanderlust

THE GREAT
ATLANTIC AIR RACE

The Adventure and Its Lessons

by Peter Bostock

WILLIAM MORROW & COMPANY, INC.

NEW YORK 1970

Contents

List of Illustrations

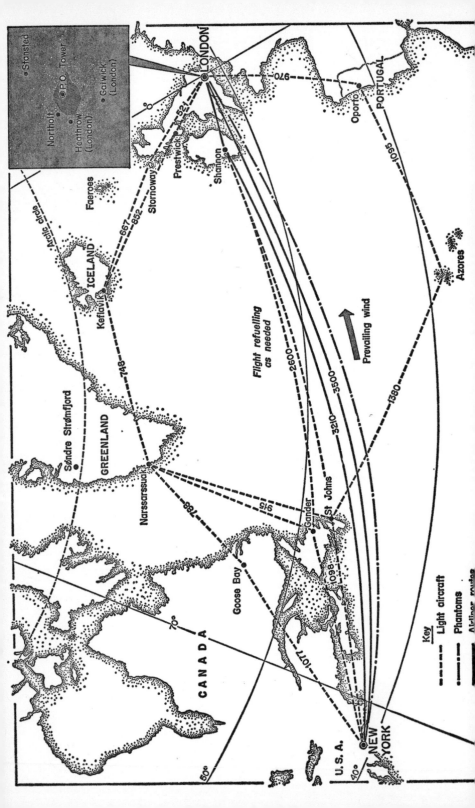

Chapter One

ELEVENTH-HOUR DRAMA

*'There is always satisfaction in being the first to
do anything, whatever it may be.'*

Sir John Alcock, 1919

THURSDAY, 1ST MAY 1969, looked like being one of the blackest
days in the peace-time history of the Royal Air Force. For on that
day, in utmost secrecy, an order to kill the planned participation of
the RAF's revolutionary Hawker Siddeley jump-jet Harrier in the
Daily Mail Transatlantic Air Race had reluctantly been prepared.
It was the last thing in the world the RAF wanted to do; but at that
moment circumstances demanded that an order be prepared to
put into reverse all the months of preparation that had gone into
getting the Harrier ready for its sensational début. All it needed
was a signature. It was less than seventy-two hours before the
start of the eight-day event, which was to set an irrepressible
international cavalcade of competitors racing either way
between check-in stations atop London's Post Office Tower
and New York's Empire State Building, in search of £60,000
($144,000) in prizes, to commemorate the fiftieth anniversary of
the first non-stop flight across the Atlantic by two British
aviators, Captain John Alcock and Lieutenant Arthur Whitten
Brown.

Scrapping the Harrier entry, after its pre-Race publicity build-
up, would not only be harmful to Britain's national pride—and
how badly that needed a fillip—it would also be a cruel blow to
Service morale, which was already badly flagging under the effects
of five years of defence cuts. The prospect of Atlantic-hopping
Harriers, using their unique ability to operate without runways,

lifting off or setting down with the ease of helicopters in the heart of London and of New York had already excited the interest of people around the world. News of their intended participation had for months been bandied around by the world's press, radio and TV. In America the New York authorities had quickly, and magnanimously, given special permission for the Harriers to operate less than a mile from the Empire State Building.

Underlying the RAF's participation was the sure knowledge that success would inevitably bolster the Harrier's prospects of landing much-needed export orders which could ultimately top the £100 million ($240 million) mark, and at the same time show Britain's Far East allies how quickly aid could reach them in an emergency. The Service, and the manufacturers, Hawker Siddeley, saw the Air Race as a unique shop window for displaying the revolutionary virtues of this single-engined fixed-wing aircraft to a captive world audience. No secret was made of the fact that one of the two participating Harriers would stay on in America to give strategic demonstrations to U.S. Air Force and Marine chiefs to tempt them into buying the jet.

In preparation for the Race one Harrier had already been positioned in America to fly the eastbound leg, even as the baffling saga of Whitehall incompetence was being played out. For some extraordinary reason, one of the key Ministers stubbornly refused to give permission for the Harriers to operate from Central London even though state-owned British Rail had offered the RAF the use of an abandoned coalyard close by St Pancras Railway Station. The Board of Trade – responsible for civil aviation matters – had already 'washed their hands' of the project and said someone else could bear the responsibility for the safety aspects of such an unconventional flight.

Fretfully, a small group of key RAF personnel waited on that Thursday for the fateful decision, as last-minute attempts were made to get permission for the Harrier to operate out of the heart of London. Ironically, almost all of the British Defence Ministry, including the Minister, Denis Healey, and the Chiefs of the Air Staff – backed wholeheartedly by the Admiralty Board – were totally behind the project, as were the rest of the Service right down to the WRAF typists at the Harrier base at RAF Wittering, who had spent months preparing documentation for the big event. But they were powerless to act without the go-ahead for the flight being given.

For several days there had been some anxious, nerve-tingling moments of utter despair and frustration within the Ministry of Defence building, sited on the banks of the River Thames under the shadow of Big Ben. But the RAF were still determined not to be beaten, and a round of bitter negotiations forced the objectors to capitulate just before the Friday withdrawal deadline was reached. With utter relief, the success signal was flashed – 'EXER-CISE BLUE NYLON to go ahead'. At last the Harrier could show its paces to the world.

Unsigned, the order to kill the Harrier's participation in the Air Race was filed away as the RAF organization, responding to a complex series of Air Staff telephone calls and signals, moved swiftly into action to prepare for the Air Race. Stations where the Victor tankers were based had to be alerted, as did radar tracking stations. RAF Wittering was one of the first to hear the good news. They started preparing the first Harrier, piloted by Squadron Leader Tom Lecky-Thompson, for its flight into St Pancras on Saturday in readiness for the start of the Race. Because of a desire not to disturb the Sunday quiet, Monday, Day Two of the Race, was the prime target date.

Who finally brought the bumbling British bureaucratic machine to its senses is still a closely guarded secret – and likely to remain so. But from the inception of the Air Race the clammy hand of unimaginative officialdom had been all too evident, though often this was due more to a desire not to be involved in extra work or to set policy precedents than to deliberate obstruc-tiveness. What troubled the objectors and the Board of Trade was the idea of the single-engined Harrier landing in and taking off from the heart of built-up London: with no reserve engine or low glide ability, they did not think it safe! Finally they succumbed to the argument that taking off from a deserted coalyard and flying out over a railway track was a reasonable risk.

Ironically, as the RAF battled to get their London go-ahead another drama, unknown to them, involving the Harrier was being played out on the other side of the Atlantic.

For in New York the Indian Government almost succeeded in wrecking the RAF's plans to land the Harrier in the heart of Manhattan on the United Nations East River pier. The trouble began in mid April, when Air India had asked permission to land an Air Race competitor on the United Nation's Headquarters garden. The request was turned down, whereupon the airline got the Indian Ambassador to protest to U Thant about the RAF using the United Nations East River pier. The Secretary General immediately ordered permission to be withheld. After a 'touch and go' late-night session, U Thant had finally agreed that the RAF plan could proceed. Everyone, including the RAF, believed the problem had been overcome.

But the Indians don't give in that easily. National pride was at stake, or so it seemed, and on 30th April back came the Indian Government with another protest, this time demanding that the Air India contestants be allowed to use the same site as the RAF. This time the *Mail* Air Race Bureau decided not to tell the RAF – a fortunate decision in view of the London troubles – but made direct representations to U Thant, pointing out that to grant permission to Air India would be unfair to all other competitors outside the special military categories. It was a delicate problem, for while the United Nations controlled the actual site only the New York City authorities could authorize its use by aircraft or helicopters, and their go-ahead for the Harrier was never in question. The London office of Air India were horrified to learn of the protestations on their behalf. But by the time they were alerted to the troubles, the difficulty had been resolved. For with perfect diplomacy, U Thant accepted the organizers' submission, overruled the Indian objection and gave the all-clear for the Harrier.

Such sensitivity and purposeful thinking was so often lacking in British circles. This was evident at one of the earliest meetings called by the Board of Trade to thrash out some of the problems presented by the *Daily Mail* Race. It would be difficult to single out definite instances of obstructionism, but there was an undercurrent of obvious resentment at the trouble the whole 'stunt' (their word) would cause. They failed to grasp, at the outset, that here was an opportunity to examine in detail some of the problems afflicting passenger and civil aviation generally, and to try out experiments which could be invaluable to British airports in preparation for the jumbo-jet era, which would ultimately result in nearly five hundred people at a time tumbling off a single jet-liner. The Board of Trade, charged with upholding the interests of the British public in civil aviation, chose to ignore this opportunity for experimentation with helicopters operating from Central London – indeed, only by a very determined stand on the part of the organizers were the Board of Trade prevented from com-pelling the RAF and the Navy to observe the very restrictive heli-copter landing regulations imposed on civil operators, although they are not required normally to observe them.

Fearful of Parliamentary critics and public protests about noise, the Board of Trade were unyielding on the use of helicopters by civilian operators, although existing regulations allowed them to make special 'exemptions' for suitably equipped helicopters to land in the heart of London. Several building sites were available, and helicopters could easily have landed on the new Euston Station, a mere short run away from the Post Office Tower, or put down on one of the nearby playing fields. But the Board of Trade refused to grant permission for their use. They also banned the use of winches to get competitors into and out of helicopters, refused to allow descents from trailing rope ladders, and issued a flat instruction that helicopters, gliders or aircraft would not be per-mitted to 'take off or land either at ground level sites or on the top of any building or structure near to the Post Office Tower'. The only exception was the River Thames. These same regulations had been applied ten years before, during the *Daily Mail*'s London to Paris Air Race. Though the decade had brought vast advances in helicopter development and techniques, the authori-ties stubbornly refused to take notice of them. By refusing to grant the exemptions the law allowed, they were in fact making special restrictive laws for the period of the Race.

In their bid to curb the daring and daffy adventurers who might like to drop on to the top of the 620-foot-tall Post Office Tower, or let down on one of the tall blocks of offices under construction near by, this government department succeeded in inhibiting legi-timate attempts to advance the use of helicopters within Central London. British helicopters were not to be allowed to be as flexible as their opposite numbers in New York, who could scurry in and out of Manhattan like hummingbirds.

A bitter disappointment was the point-blank refusal of the Ministry of Public Building and Works to allow competitors – civil or military – to use the royal parks, particularly Regent's Park, just a brisk walk away from the Post Office Tower. Regent's Park was the obvious site for a temporary helicopter pad from which to fly out the Harrier – in complete comfort instead of in a cloud of coal dust. You could even set up a landing strip for the new breeed of short take-off and landing aircraft without endangering the public. But they were adamant. Nobody was to be able to take advantage of the public amenity – at least not for airborne purposes. They wouldn't even allow British Army parachutists to drop into Regent's Park – but neither would the New York authorities allow them to drop into Central Park, so on that score they were in step with the Americans. Such bickering was typical of the lack of an imaginative approach to the Air Race by the British civil aviation authorities, and some sections of the airports authorities, as well as some of the world's plane makers, British, American and European. Mostly they failed to grasp the significance of what was being attempted, and to appreciate the mood of the public.

But apart from predictions and shrewd guesses by the organizers, who insisted there would be between 300 and 500 competitors, there was nothing factual to present to the authorities. For even three days before the 18th April deadline for entries was reached only 40 actual entry forms had been handed in to the organizers. That another 350 entry forms would cascade in, in less than seventy-two hours, seemed unbelievable.

Yet they did so, to unleash on a tired world a flood of resourceful exploits which ranged from the bizarre to the immensely practical, and introduced such extrovert characters as New Jersey's uncrushable Ben Garcia who – after ending a solo flight attempt upside down in a Pennsylvania chicken farm – switched to regular airline flights and gimmickry and stole the headlines, and peak TV spots, with a series of zany performances that would have been worthy of any show-biz comedy star. With three days stubble of beard on his chin, he arrived on roller skates, creating pandemonium at the top of the Tower as he hurtled towards the final check-in station with a hunk of his unfortunate aircraft's fuselage rolled up under his arm. On the way, he created more fun and friends than any of the 390 cavaliers of the air could ever have dared hope for when, weeks before, they paid their £10 ($24) entry fees for the Race.

Together with a couple of dozen other flamboyant competitors – including Tina the chimpanzee and a U.S. naval commander with his head in a hood – Garcia added a touch of spice and irreverent unpredictability to balance the tensions created by the world-record-breaking dashes of the three Royal Navy Phantom supersonic jets and the revolutionary antics of the RAF's Harriers. To highlight the drama, there was Britain's Sheila Scott adding four more transatlantic records as she flew from London to New York in her Piper Comanche 260 which she fondly calls *Myth Too*. And four Army parachutists dropped from a helicopter after racing over the Atlantic in a military VC 10, just to prove a point. Certainly the majority of the entry forms were submitted by people captivated by the sheer delight of taking part rather than dedicated to winning a share of the £60,000 ($144,000) prizes. That's why some, like Mira Slovak in his powered glider, didn't mind taking 175 hours 42 minutes and 7 seconds to complete the race – he was not the slowest – and several late starters signed up 'for the hell of it', waiving their rights to any prize money as a penalty for entering after the 18th April deadline.

All helped to turn the *Daily Mail* Transatlantic Air Race into the greatest aviation show of all time – a spectacular, staged on two continents, which provided not only enjoyment and entertainment but pointed up lessons to help the 261 million passengers a year who take to the air on commercial airline services. Along the way, competitors punched holes through some of the more frustrating and outmoded government air regulations, while immigration and customs officials smoothed out their 'ferocious faces' and entered into the fun of it all, getting competitors cleared in times everyone believed were quite impossible.

The gargantuan task of getting the event off the ground might have been easier if the *Daily Mail* Air Race Bureau and all the outside officials could have foreseen that the eight days in May would prove so much of a riotous success that competitors would travel more than 1,250,000 miles to make 349 magnificent Race attempts. Together they provided a rainbow of colour arcing across the Atlantic, dropping one end of it slap bang in the middle of grey old London and the other into the crock of gold that is New York.

Unfortunately, when the hard bargaining round of negotiations began in the closing months of 1968, all thought of such support was only a fondly fostered twinkle in the eye of the organizers.

Chapter Two

A TIME FOR BOLDNESS

*'We applaud bravery and initiative and feel
strongly that any minor inconveniences to
other citizens that this [Daily Mail] race
may involve can be excused on this score.'*

Motor Sport, December 1968

EVEN IN THEIR post-war heyday of the '40s and early '50s, news-papers would not tie up £100,000 in a promotion just for the sheer hell of it. There is a business side to every spectacular event – and in the case of newspapers, the inevitable incentive is the bait of attracting new readers or consolidating a reputation for dynamic exploitation to convince the ever-watchful advertisers that their product is being viewed in pages of the press by a suitably alert public.

Getting the right response from any given promotion is a difficult task and it takes a lot of personal courage to embark on a major scheme, particularly when every newspaper department is fighting for a share of the economic cake. But sitting in a fifth-floor office at Harmsworth House, just off London's Fleet Street, was Brian Harpur, a flamboyant, persuasive character of great integrity, with a flair for picking winning ideas and possessing the dogged determination necessary to see them through to fruition. Brian Harpur, a mercurial 51-year-old director of Harmsworth Publications Ltd – owners of the *Daily Mail, Daily Sketch* and London *Evening News* – made the first tentative plans for the Transatlantic Air Race back in 1965.

Primarily devised as a *Mail* circulation booster at a time when its publication future was the subject of a great deal of unhealthy, and misinformed, speculation, the 1969 Race was also aimed at upholding a long-standing tradition of pioneering aviation support which began with a model aircraft competition in 1907; and which resulted in the *Daily Mail* handing out a total of £75,000 ($180,000) in prizes over the years for its first eighteen aviation events, culminating with the sensational London–Paris race in 1959, held to commemorate the first cross-Channel flight by Blériot in 1909.

Brian Harpur conceived the idea of the Transatlantic Air Race as something more than a mere time-trial which the military would inevitably win. He saw it as a chance to put the fun back into flying before the jumbo and supersonic jets reduced flying to a numbers game where passengers lose all their identity in the mass of humanity being shuttled remorselessly at high speeds across the heavens. He set out quietly to assemble a group of co-sponsors with the idea that the prize money would be split up in such a way that everyone got a fair chance of taking a major prize, whether civilian or serviceman.

Inevitably, critics abounded. In January 1969, answering an interviewer's particularly savage dose of carping criticism that the Air Race was nothing more than 'a publicity stunt of the old style which is a bit old-fashioned now', he retorted:

This is the following through of a great tradition of aerial enterprise pioneered by the *Daily Mail*. It sets out to make three points. Firstly, to commemorate a great all-British achievement, the first non-stop crossing of the Atlantic in June 1919 by Alcock and Brown, made in response to a £10,000 ($24,000) *Daily Mail* challenge thrown out in 1913 by Lord Northcliffe.

The second object is to dramatize the growth of inter-continental travel over the last fifty years. Whilst the third point is to test the belief that this large-scale operation. involving people from every walk of life, will prove, quite conclusively, that the bureaucracy and the strictures and regulations which tend to hinder, rather than ease, our day-to-day commuting between city centre and city centre can, in fact, be revitalized to bring about an urgent speed up of total travelling times.

Though it took four years for the original idea to be brought to fruition, it was not until 25th April 1968 that the first public announcement of the event was made. With due ceremony before an invited audience of government, civic and aviation dignitaries, the *Daily Mail* project—with prizes already totalling £45,000 ($110,000)—was announced at a reception given high above London's West End at the Martini Terrace. Almost a mile north-wards, from that vantage point, could clearly be seen the Post Office Tower, lit up like a fanciful, illuminated cocktail stick reaching expectantly skywards from amid a morass of stubbly buildings.

With the publication of details of the first nine sponsors' prizes, it became clear that the objective of obtaining a broadly based competition had been achieved. The *Mail* was offering £10,000 ($24,000) to be divided equally for the fastest time in each direction. Vickers—who had manufactured Alcock and Brown's Vickers Vimy biplane—added an extra £1,000 ($2,400) to the *Mail's* £5,000 New York to London prize; and the British Aircraft Corporation added another £1,000 to the *Mail's* £5,000 prize for the fastest London–New York crossing.

Following the example of the Ardath Tobacco Company, who had put up prize money for some of the earlier aviation attempts in the early 1900s, Rothmans of Pall Mall contributed £8,000 ($19,200), awarding £4,000 ($9,600) prizes for the fastest time by subsonic means from London to New York and New York to London.

Quite predictably, Britain's state-owned national flag-carrier BOAC willingly offered a £5,000 ($12,000) prize for the fastest time using an ordinary scheduled airline passenger flight from New York to London—there was no attempt to insist that com-petitors use BOAC aircraft.

Less predictable was the decision of Aer Lingus–Irish Interna-tional Airlines to put up a £5,000 ($12,000) prize for anyone using ordinary scheduled passenger flights between London and New York stopping at Shannon. There was certainly the his-torical connection of Alcock and Brown having landed in Ireland at the end of their historic 15-hour-57-minute flight from St

John's, Newfoundland, but this in itself would not have been enough to galvanize the airline into action.

The Irish Airline was desperately seeking ways in 1968 to project Aer Lingus-Irish International as a transatlantic jet carrier in a British market that knew Aer Lingus mainly as a cross-channel airline flying Viscount turbo-props. The task was not an easy one. But when Douglas Kelly—not an Irishman, despite the name— the airline's Publicity Manager in Britain, first heard of the *Daily Mail* Transatlantic Air Race, he decided, even at a distance of fourteen months, that 'it would offer a publicity vehicle of unprecedented scope, duration and impact for the British market'. He persuaded the head office in Dublin to put up the £5,000.

It was a brave decision. He knew that BOAC could swamp him with their publicity machine and that many competitors would be confused by the sheer number of categories and believe, wrongly, that Shannon-routed flights would be competing against direct London–New York services, though in fact the latter were eligible only for the Rothmans' prize. To counter this problem, Douglas Kelly launched a unique advisory service to attract competitors to the Aer Lingus and the paralleled *Daily Sketch* category. Starting in September 1968 he despatched a total of ten special bulletins, plus maps, to would-be competitors, covering everything from passports to hotel accommodation, airport procedures and alternative means of ground transportation. They were so comprehensive that the final bulletin, issued just before the start of the Race, ran to forty pages. The plan worked. When the official entries closed on 18th April 1969, in their own words 'Aer Lingus had a healthy surprise'. BOAC, the national carrier, and eligible for at least five categories, had attracted bookings from sixty competitors. Aer Lingus had achieved forty-one bookings from competitors—double their original estimate. But there were a lot of anxious months to go before this.

Lined up with Aer Lingus on the London–New York route via Shannon was the *Mail*'s sister paper, the *Daily Sketch*, which offered a £2,500 ($6,000) prize to anyone making a personal attempt. The *Sketch* put up an additional £2,500 ($6,000) prize for the fastest time from New York to London, thus complementing the one offered by BOAC. But the *Sketch* prize could not be won by anyone who had the official backing of an organization, the armed services or any government department.

In keeping with the decision that speed should not be the only criterion for winning a prize in the Air Race, Robert Butlin, chairman of Butlins Ltd, holiday camp pioneers, came forward with a £5,000 ($12,000) prize for the most meritorious and ingenious non-winning entry by a Briton. The final prize announced at the reception on 25th April had been decided upon only that afternoon, when John Gold, the editor of the London *Evening News*, agreed to put up £5,000 ($12,000) in prizes for competitors using light aircraft.

Within days other sponsors joined in to broaden the scope of the Air Race. An executive jet category was sponsored jointly by the Castle Britannia Group of Unit Trusts (London–New York) and the *Financial Times* (New York–London), each offering £2,500 ($6,000). The American publisher Ziff-Davis came forward with a £5,000 ($12,000) prize for the most meritorious non-winning entry by an American. And *Blick*, a Swiss newspaper, put up a £1,000 prize for the fastest time achieved by a Swiss national. By the end of May 1968 the prize money stood at £56,000 ($134,400) broken down into 18 different categories. So that there would be no particular advantage for those travelling eastwards with the predominant following wind, prizes were offered in each direction.

Competitors had to combine any form of ground and air transportation to get from the top of London's Post Office Tower to the top of the Empire State Building—or the other way round. Basic requirements included a £10 ($24) entry fee, an insistence that the Atlantic be flown, and attempts had to be within the law though full advantage could be taken of any tolerance shown by the civic authorities.

There was an immediate flood of inquiries and by September 1968, when the inquiries had topped the 2,000 mark, I found myself plummeted into the fray to carry out the day-to-day organization of the Race and handle the press and public relations for the event. Since I had been for three years the Air Correspondent of the *Daily Sketch*, it was thought that my 'expertise might be useful'.

The formula was already set and the Royal Aero Club in Britain, and the National Aeronautic Association in America, were providing sound advice, and had accepted responsibility for the technical supervision of the Race and the vetting of entries. Thrust into the most exciting venture of a lifetime I had hardly time to catch my breath before the first organized dummy runs took place to test out the organizational system and give some clues to what we were to expect during the actual eight-day race period.

Chapter Three

TRY-OUT

'Heroes of accomplishment as well of daring.'
New York Sun, June 1919

JUST BEFORE 10 A.M., white-helmeted American actress Susan Oliver frantically forced her way through the smoothly opening doors of the high-speed elevator at the top of London's Post Office Tower and raced for the cocktail bar, pursued by a one-armed man. For a second it looked like an episode of a TV drama, and Susan's grim face could have misled you into thinking it was. In fact the episode was the climax of a real life drama: together with Richard Slawsky, the one-armed Ziff-Davis publisher of *Airline Management and Marketing,* Susan (remembered in Britain as Ann Howard of 'Peyton Place'), was out to shatter the 8 hours, 27 minutes and 30 seconds it had taken Ohio millionaire Paul Vaughan to race from the Empire State Building to the Post Office Tower four days before, in a September try-out for the Air Race.

In a moment of excited panic Susan overshot the check-in machine standing on the bar counter. As she plunged headlong into the crowd only three steps from the elevator she was turned back by frantic calls from the spectators and a TV crew. Spinning on her heel she banged into Richard, and with a chorus of yells in their ears he shot a sharp arm back to press the yellow button which froze the Omega timing clock. It registered a satisfying 7 hours 13 minutes and 3 seconds from the time they had checked out of the 86th floor of the Empire State Building.

They would have clipped more off the time if it hadn't been for an unwarranted seven-minute immigration delay at London's

15

Heathrow Airport. The officer had insisted on repeatedly reading their passports from cover to cover. Until that point everything had moved with precision. They had reached Kennedy Airport in a fast 28 minutes and 10 seconds by using a helicopter. Then, in spite of bad weather, their BOAC VC 10 jetliner arrived at Heathrow Airport 16 minutes ahead of schedule. As the giant jet taxied towards the terminal helpful cabin staff pulled back the doors, allowing Susan and Dick to leap on to the waiting ramp before the VC 10 had rolled to a complete stop. After their frustration at clearing immigration the couple took only 23 minutes and 30 seconds to reach the foot of the Post Office Tower on the back of Army motor-cycles, provided by a Chelsea-based reserve unit of the Royal Corps of Signals.

When finally they had paused for breath and a celebratory sip of champagne, Dick handed over a letter from Mayor John Lindsay of New York to the Leader of the Greater London Council, Desmond Plummer which expressed the hope that: 'this epic two-way event will encourage yet greater goodwill and offer opportunity for valuable exchanges between New York and London.'

Responding, Desmond Plummer announced that the Greater London Council would throw a gala reception on 1st May as a tribute to the Air Race enterprise.

But even more than sparking off an exchange of messages, the Oliver-Slawsky effort had raised some important issues that needed resolving before the race got under way less than eight months later. The most important need was to iron out the problems at Heathrow to prevent immigration snarl-ups—this proved amazingly easy and the co-operation meted out by both immigration and customs during Race Week was, in most instances, a text-book example of how flexible a somewhat frighteningly formidable system can be when it is operated by sympathetic officials. As one over-awed competitor announced with nervous relief after arriving at the Post Office Tower on the second day of the actual race—'Gee, I could have kissed your immigration boys they were so helpful. But I didn't have time to stop.'

Of more significance was the lesson learned from the overcrowding which resulted from the press, radio and TV turn-out to welcome Susan and Dick. It underscored the need for more space for the actual event. From that moment it was decided to switch the London check-in station venue from the cocktail lounge on the 35th floor to the public observation platform two floors below.

Filmco President Paul Vaughan's time had not been as spectacular as that achieved by Oliver–Slawsky, but his trial had an added point. For Vaughan, voted Ohio businessman of the year in 1967, had made his run in response to a challenge by British property millionaire Edward Drewery, who had chartered a jet and assembled a team of more than a hundred export-minded British businessmen to take part in the Race. His challenge was made to any similar business group competing. The idea was irresistible to Paul Vaughan, who immediately upon hearing about it cabled Drewery that he would accept.

During all the pre-Race period dedicated competitors were Atlantic-hopping, scurrying between the Post Office Tower and the Empire State Building, while others simply polished up their performances on the ground sections at either end. For it was obvious from the outset that with today's modern 600-m.p.h. jets —and given the fact that several competitors could be travelling in the same aircraft—prizes would be won or lost on the ground. Painstaking efforts went into discovering the best route through the snarl-up of one-way streets around the Post Office Tower. Motor-cycles busied themselves 3,500 miles away with ferreting out the easiest way to Kennedy Airport and slide-rule-hugging enthusiasts staked out the most suitable helicopter landing spots on the River Thames as soon as it became known that the Port of London Authority had thrown open the river for use by competitors.

But in one set of categories, even though the fastest times would win, getting to and from the airports was not all that critical. This was the light-aircraft class.

The most formidable problems confronting the enthusiasts flying twin- and single-engined aircraft, all weighing well under 12,500 pounds, would be not a mile-long traffic jam on some carbon-monoxide-filled motorway, but the ice building up on slender wings as, fighting against gusting head-winds, they navigated their island-hopping way across the lonely Atlantic Ocean. The light-aircraft contingent battling the elements in May 1969 would be flying in conditions similar to those experienced by pioneers like Alcock and Brown, United States Navy Lieutenant-Commander Albert Read who piloted the Curtiss NC–4 Navy flying-boat in stages across the Atlantic in 1919, Charles Lindbergh and Amy Johnson. There is a world of difference between flipping around the English countryside or down the west coast of America in a busy little light aircraft and trying to fly it across the Atlantic—even with a cabin packed with every modern navigational aid.

As a curtain raiser to this true pioneer flying Stephan Wilkinson, Managing Editor of *Flying*, breezed into my London office just before Christmas and announced casually that he was shortly setting off on a ferry flight in a factory-fresh, British-built eight-seater Beagle 206–S twin in order to test the Transatlantic Air Race route. He was to accompany Jim Kieffer, a 47-year-old ex-Coast Guard pilot whom Miami Aviation Corporation—Beagle's United States distributor—employed to do all its Beagle ferrying. The next day, after checking out from the Post Office Tower he headed for Gatwick, where Kieffer and the Beagle were waiting to take off for Shannon. There extra fuel tanks were fitted in the cabin, and they flew on towards Iceland.

Describing his first glimpse of it Stephan recalls: 'Iceland slides into sight unnoticed at first, for the range of mountains and glaciers glistens so whitely in the sun that they seem to be more like clouds.'

Dogged by electrical and mechanical faults which had to be fixed en route and which caused them to slip hours behind schedule, they left Iceland with Stephan at the controls hoping to make Labrador non-stop, rather than putting down in Greenland's vast icy wastes. Stephen described Greenland, when it came into view beneath them, as the 'merest bit of icy, rocky shoreline, sliding silently past a break in the clouds'. By that point they had decided to over-fly Greenland and they pressed on through a grey world of cloud and sky brittle with cold towards the Canadian Airfield at Goose Bay. After stopping overnight at Goose Bay they finally arrived at La Guardia, where Stephan hurried to a taxi and headed for the Empire State Building.

In spite of the technical problems that more than quadrupled the expected time, *Flying* magazine announced that it would present an appropriately engraved trophy to any light-aircraft competitor beating Stephan's time of 97 hours 58 minutes and 7 seconds.

In the April issue of the magazine Wilkinson added a rider to the offer, printed at the head of the article about his flight. He wrote:

> Lest this seem a sweeping, last-one-in-the-Pond's-a-chicken invitation to mass disaster, let it be known that we consider this not a game for casual lightplane drivers but a near-professional test of skill for serious pilots.

These sentiments were shared by others. Having heard talk of a Vickers Vimy, a Puss Moth and a 1936 Stranraer flying-boat being possible contestants, concern about the type of light-aircraft entrant that could be attracted into the Race was felt also by the Royal Aero Club, America's National Aeronautic Association and departments of the Air Forces of Britain, Canada and America involved in Atlantic rescue operations. Bound by a common desire to eliminate unnecessary risks to competitors they were brought together, at the turn of the year, by the Flight Safety Division of the Board of Trade, and the U.K. representative of the U.S. Federal Aviation Authority in a confrontation with the organizers.

The issue was one of some delicacy and the *Mail* had tactfully to choose a path between buttoning up the regulations so tightly, in order to pacify the official bodies, that they ruled out the capable enthusiast who had never before dreamed of flying across the Atlantic, but who had the same verve for adventure that inspired pioneers like Alcock and Brown, and, on the other hand, encouraging every crank seeking instant glory in an ill-equipped plane and inviting disaster from the moment he lifted off the runway.

The problem was compounded by the fact that the British, American, Canadian and European Governments each had different regulations and often recommended totally incompatible radio equipment, safety aids, etc. As a rule of thumb guide, it was agreed initially that if an aircraft was given an airworthiness certificate by its own country and cleared for flying the Atlantic by that authority, then there was no reason for an application to be refused by the *Mail*.

The trickiest question was the carrying of air-sea rescue locator beacons which send out signals to guide rescue aircraft to the spot of a downed pilot or aircraft. The British authorities and the British, American and Canadian Air Forces were vehemently in favour of making the carrying of such equipment a condition of acceptance as a race competitor. This was turned down by the *Mail*, partly because of strong contrary opinions in America. The general feeling there, among officials of the NAA and other American aviation organizations, was that 'no attempt should be made to try to impose regulations where regulations do not already exist'. While keen that contestants' attention should be drawn to the desirability of carrying air-sea rescue aids—and also to the fact that if they touched down in Canada, Canadian law required such equipment to be carried—it was felt that the *Mail* should not impose its own special Air Race rule. 'The FAA does not require it and neither should the Mail', was the popular sentiment, though the majority believed that most flyers taking off from the United States would carry them for their own protection anyway.

Survival time for a ditched pilot in the icy North Atlantic wastes is something around the minute mark unless he manages to scramble into a survival dinghy, which can be a herculean task in the numbing cold. The cost and difficulty of launching a full search and rescue operation are almost prohibitive, and even if a downed aircraft is correctly equipped with special survival locator beacons the rescue bill could be between £60,000 ($144,000) and £100,000 ($240,000). One of the problems was that many probable competitors might not possess adequate radio equipment, let alone locator beacons and survival kits, which should include self-inflatable dinghies, flares and emergency food supplies. In fact one would-be solo flier, the indomitable Ben Garcia, had as his 'survival kit' for the planned 4,000-mile Atlantic crossing only half a dozen cans of peanut butter and a dozen packets of soda crackers. He also took a do-it-yourself navigation book to 'mug up' techniques on the way during the lonely hours, and to cap it all he worked out that because his 108 horsepower, single-engine, fabric-covered Piper Colt hadn't the fuel reserves to make the 699-mile hop from Iceland to Shannon he would glide* for 99 miles if the hoped-for extra push from following winds didn't enable him to make good the distance!

Fortunately, at the time of the meeting with the authorities no one knew of Garcia's plans. The tough problem was reconciling the desire to get as many light-aircraft entries as possible with the need to reduce risks to the minimum. Playing it very coolly, and deftly turning aside the most harrowing official predictions of impending disaster, it was decided to wait and see who actually entered before imposing special strictures, that could result in their being vetoed.

During the talks with the authorities it was not possible to quote an accurate figure as to the numbers of attempts that could be expected by contestants using light aircraft. The initial response to direct mailings had been luke-warm, although over three hundred British flying clubs had been circularized. With nearly two hundred leaders of British industry using their own company aircraft, for the most part ranging from a £5,000 ($12,000) twin-seater, single-engine aircraft to a £55,000 ($132,000) eight-seater Beagle 206-S, and with some 10,000 qualified private pilots in Britain capable of flying the 1,000 light aircraft registered with the Board of Trade, it seemed not unreasonable to expect about twenty of them to enter the Race. American interest was totally unpredictable, particularly because the Race was basically a British show. Another adverse factor was the uncertain economic cycle which by January had already resulted in five major corporations dropping plans to enter the race for fear of upsetting their shareholders. In the end a figure of 30–40 light-aircraft entries was put forward as a basis for discussion.

Even more perplexing was the failure, by February, of the executive jet categories, sponsored by the Castle Britannia Group of Unit Trusts and the *Financial Times*, to attract support. The inherent weakness was the lack of a handicap system to even out the

---

* From the maximum height he could reach without oxygen equipment on board Garcia's plane could in fact have glided only about 20 miles.

widely differing characteristics of the 500-mph-plus pure jets and the 250-mph turbo-prop aircraft.

Prompted by Handley Page, manufacturers of the new £180,000 ($432,000) British Jetstream, an approach was made to the Royal Aero Club, who worked out a system of handicapping which, while not perfect—it was never intended to be so—gave a whole range of business jets a chance to win. Another factor against the category was that it cost almost £4,000 ($9,000) to make the return Atlantic crossing and the top prize obtainable was £2,500 ($6,000) because the rules prevented more than one prize being won by each competitor. A survey of business jets in Britain, in January 1969, showed that only 12 were registered compared with over 700 pure jets registered in the U.S. None of the Handley Page Jetstreams had been delivered and the response from direct mailings was abysmal.

It was just as well that, at that stage the *Financial Times* and the organizers were not aware of a few short sharp exchanges which took place at a sales conference at Hatfield, just north of London, for the men whose job it was to sell the Hawker Siddeley 125 executive jet. When questioned about the advisability of entering the 125 in the Race the overwhelming opinion was that it could do nothing to help sales. Far from it, it was believed that to highlight its performance capabilities, in direct competition with rival business jets, could well have a damaging, rather than a helpful, effect on sales. The salesmen argued that while a handicap system would probably give an edge to the Hawker Siddeley 125, as far as the Race placing was concerned, the handicap would not alter the fact that compared to many American executive jets the 125 long-range performance was poor; it was not designed for Atlantic hopping.

Ironically, at about the same time as the Hatfield session took place, a top Lockheed executive was putting out feelers to see if a Grumman Gulfstream or a Fan-Jet Falcon had been entered. They feared that if either were to compete, the Jetstar's performance figures would not be shown in a good light.

Another unforeseeable element, which was to remove one of the 'certain' entries, was the pending management reshuffle in the PAN AM division controlling the marketing organization for the

Fan-Jet Falcon 70. Together these facts spelt doom for the executive jet categories. But early in 1969 there was no sign of the refusal of the manufacturers to support this particular race category. In any case, it looked certain that Handley Page would take up the suggestion that Winston Spencer Churchill Junior should co-pilot one of the Jetstreams—a fair publicity coup if it came off.

If the business-jet men were dragging their feet, the same couldn't be said for Aer Lingus publicity man, Douglas Kelly. In between sending off informative circulars to his closely guarded group of would-be competitors he had been puzzling over the best way to highlight the Aer Lingus category. Breaking any transatlantic air journey at Shannon is hard to justify and to attract the press, radio and TV services into covering a dummy run over that route was decidedly difficult.

'Look, fella,' he said, with his blue eyes giving a disarming and distinct twinkle, 'we have got to get together on this. How do we set about it?' Taking advantage of his height of 6 ft 4 in., he leant over the lunch table and pointed a reprimanding finger at me. 'You, by that I mean the *Mail*, the *Sketch* and the *Evening News*, are ignoring Aer Lingus's part in the Air Race.' It was said with a half concealed grin, but the point was taken.

What he didn't know was that only that morning I had been working on the same problem and I was ready for his challenge, though it came forty-eight hours earlier than I should ideally have liked.

'It's simple. The *Mail, Sketch* and *Evening News* each send a reporter racing against one another from London to New York on an Aer Lingus flight,' I said.

His eyebrows raised and the furrows in the brow beneath the healthy mop of light hair slowly straightened out.

'Go on, I'm listening.'

'Just to keep you happy and give it an historical flavour I thought we might take along Captain John Alcock, brother of Sir John . . .'

Before the sentence could be completed Douglas cut in, 'You wouldn't be kidding me, would you?'

'Do I look as though I am?'

'You're damn right you do. But now you've got me

interested.' He cocked his head in expectation of more details about the brother of the man who, with Whitten Brown, made the first non-stop flight across the Atlantic.

By the time the lunch session was over the details were thrashed out, and he agreed that the BBC TV team, who had already been assigned to cover the actual Air Race, should go along too. The dummy run was important for several reasons. First, it would encourage the group newspapers to take a more active interest in the Air Race. Secondly, it would firmly commit the BBC to the Race—not that they needed much convincing. Thirdly, it would allow both Doug Kelly and me to examine the set-up on the other side of the Atlantic. Finally, by taking Captain Alcock along, it would underscore the *Mail*'s desire to commemorate the achievement of his brother. It also presented an unrivalled opportunity to be able to illustrate dramatically the changes that had taken place in fifty years of Atlantic flying.

It was all part of the essential build up to the Race for at the time, in late February, when the decision to hold the trial run was made, only 20 actual entry forms had been received with another 73 people saying they would definitely enter. Hardly re-assuring. So a lot depended upon the Trial Run.

Chapter Four

A TOUCH OF THE IRISH

'We landed in the softest part of Ireland . . . a bog!'
Captain John Alcock, 1919

'Now, LET'S GET this straight,' said chief *Sketch* photographer Geoffrey White, as he leaned a patronizing arm over the back of one of the office chairs and looked at Andrew McEwen and Roger Bamber of the *Mail* and Peter Roe of the *Evening News*. 'I don't want this turning into a cut-throat race. Don't forget, compared to you youngsters I'm an old man.' His handlebar moustache dropped appropriately low over his lip.

The others nodded. It suited me. We didn't want any of them to set unbeatable times, for fear of scaring competitors away. 'Now I'm off. There is some shopping to do before tomorrow's trip. See you all at Aer Lingus' office at ten tomorrow for the briefing?' With that, he got up, threw a weary wave of a hand and disappeared.

So much for Geoff's plea not to turn the trial run into a cut-throat competition. When he turned up at the briefing meeting he was dressed in a light blue flying overall with a luminous orange over-jacket, and sported a white crash helmet, while on his feet, to give him extra running power, he had the latest-fangled rubber-soled racing shoes.

Disarmingly, he announced to his astonished newspaper rivals: 'You didn't think I was going to leave anything to chance?'

He wasn't, either. Teamed up to take him to London Airport was champion racing motor-cyclist Bill Ivy.

Besides Captain Alcock and the four men representing the group's newspapers, the BBC team led by John Mills arrived for

a

the briefing at Aer Lingus's Special Air Race Control Centre. So did Clement Freud, making the run for London's Thames Television, and Mike Wooley, the runner for Britain's *Travel Trade Gazette*. There was also a strong Irish contingent, but they were only headed for Ireland.

Aer Lingus were using the trial as a test for their elaborate Race set-up, and for the occasion had replaced their turbo-prop Viscount with a Boeing 720 jetliner. Because the first leg of their flight is considered a domestic service, there are no immigration or customs formalities at London's Heathrow Airport—they are carried out at Shannon. As a result, Aer Lingus hit on the idea of assembling all the Race competitors at a pavement rendezvous just by the new Heathrow domestic terminal and taking them directly to the aircraft in specially authorized cars. In that way they were able to separate Air Race competitors from regular passengers and allow them to board the aircraft a few vital minutes later than would normally be permitted. In theory it looked fine. But the trial run was needed to highlight any problems that might obstruct the smooth running of the actual event.

A frightening object lesson of what might happen during Race week came, surprisingly, just before the count-down began for the start of the dummy run from the 35th floor of the Post Office Tower. As the party arrived, one of the two elevators went out of action, with the result that the remaining elevator had to cope with the Post Office engineering staff working on the majority of the Tower's floors; the public, who paid their four shillings to travel to the 33rd floor public observation platform; and the restaurant clientele. An additional problem was a gusty wind scurrying around the Tower, forcing a half-speed reduction in the normal 1,000 feet per minute speed of the elevators. It all added up to a 90-minute wait to go up and a 30-minute wait to get down. What chaos!

Because of these delays, the special Omega timing device only just reached the starting point as the first man, Mike Wooley, left. He was headed for the Aer Lingus terminal to complete a baggage check, like a regular passenger, for he wanted to establish how long the ground section would take for competitors without the aid of motor-cycles or helicopters. After the time-table had been revamped the others got away to a fine start, led by Captain

Alcock in the Rolls Royce. It became clear that the later you left your departure from the Post Office Tower the better the time you could make—provided, of course, you didn't miss the plane by arriving too late at the airport!

Since time was not the most important factor, Captain Alcock and I, cushioned in the Rolls, left well ahead of everyone else with the exception of Mike Wooley. Predictably, on arrival at the airport we found that everyone, with the exception of Clement Freud, had reached the aircraft. Freud turned up seconds later, to be followed up the steps by the BBC TV team, who had been filming the arrivals. Shortly after, the doors closed and we were Ireland-bound aboard our Boeing 720 jet. With just time for a cream-topped Irish coffee, we changed at Shannon to an intercontinental Aer Lingus Boeing 707.

Pushed onward by an unusual following wind we cut an hour off the scheduled flight time, only to find that this caused chaos in New York. Everyone was caught on the hop, though we were not to know this until we had passed through the barrier of uniformed officials blocking the way to America.

Hurried off the aircraft at top speed, we expected the pre-alerted U.S. immigration authorities to wave us through as all our visas had been double checked. But no. There was the humiliating 'black book' procedure to go through—a pitiful introduction to American hospitality as the officials leisurely thumb through a constantly changing list of undesirables to see if you are a desirable alien. The clinical atmosphere was broken when one of the party yelled out: 'We're in a hurry. We're taking part in the Air Race.'

'We ain't,' came back the laconic reply.

What was shaping up to be a difficult passage was suddenly transformed into farce when the television crew who had come with us arrived in the immigration hall with lights blazing and cameras turning. To baffled yells of 'They're filming, they're filming. It's an immigration area—they can't do that here!' the cameras whirred.

'What's going on? Who's in charge?' rang out the cries of bewilderment as a bevy of uniformed bodies hustled to investigate. Their attention distracted, the immigration officials quickly stamped our passports. Finally we got through—and luckily the BBC didn't have any problems, in spite of the fracas they caused.

At customs the airline's ploy of 'post entering' our baggage paid off and we were able to pass right on through the control point, just checking out our hand baggage and leaving the rest to be cleared later by an agent and delivered to the hotel.

The system worked well and Captain Alcock and I, easily identifiable by Aer Lingus armbands, were heading for the exit when a small, navy-blue-raincoat-clad man appeared at a side door and beckoned us to join him. Without a second's hesitation we followed him through the door, out of the building and into his waiting car. 'You're too early. Everything's gone crazy this end,' he volunteered. 'Nothing's ready and the police won't let you park.' Just as we were about to draw away Geoff White and a man I recognized as Henry Thody, the *Sketch* correspondent in America turned the corner, rushed to the car and squeezed in beside us. Barely had the door closed when the car lurched urgently forward.

Only when we flashed by the tail sections of a row of parked giant jetliners did I realize that we were not headed towards Manhattan. Seeing my concern, Henry just grinned. The car screeched to a halt. He and Geoff bolted. Before I could ask the driver where they had gone, the throbbing of helicopter blades and the flurry of newly stirred-up dust told me they were on their way to the Empire State Building.

A less fortunate getaway was attempted by *Mail* photographer Roger Bamber. Racing for another helicopter with his cameras banging about his chest, he got an unexpected turn-down from the pilot, who refused to let him on board. 'I'm not going to take any photographers on board this flight,' he announced. There was no arguing. Roger got left behind whilst the whirlybird lifted Andrew McEwan skywards.

There was nothing wrong with Roger. He was simply getting the ricochet from an incident that occurred during the Dick Slawsky-Susan Oliver dummy run. On that occasion an accompanying photographer, jumping into the helicopter, sat on something which cut the power as he struggled to take in-flight photographs. It nearly resulted in the whole caboodle falling into the Hudson River. Quick action by the pilot averted a disaster. But then, as they reached Kennedy airport, the same photographer jumped out so fast before the 'copter hit the ground that it soared back in the air again because of the weight loss. Frightening moments which obviously the helicopter pilot wasn't going to risk happening again, so out went Roger.

As for the crestfallen Captain Alcock and me, we returned to the terminal to wait almost an hour for our London taxi. Unbelievably, it had been parked waiting for the regular arrival time of the Aer Lingus jet, the driver never thinking, or checking, that the flight could be an hour early. It didn't matter. It gave Doug Kelly and me time to examine the arrival arrangements with an eye on the forthcoming Race. Neither of us was satisfied and we left realizing the need to stir up more interest in New York as far as the sponsors were concerned. There were no Air Race directional signs or line-ups of stewardesses to propel anxious competitors through the labyrinth of passageways that bedevil every airport user.

When finally Captain Alcock and I reached the 86th-floor check-in point at the Empire State Building, everyone else had arrived, including Mike Wooley, who turned in a Race Time of 10 hours 20 minutes 48 seconds.

Over a welcome drink in the Empire State Building bar we discovered an elated Geoff White celebrating his victory. He had got from the top of the Post Office Tower to the top of the Empire State Building in 9 hours 8 minutes and 52 seconds, beating second place Peter Roe by 10 minutes. Third home was *Mail* reporter Andrew McEwen in 9 hours 24 minutes and 44 seconds.

Close behind came Clement Freud. He recorded a time of 9 hours 37 minutes and 44 seconds. At the outset he arrived at the Post Office Tower for a pre-trial lobster and champagne send-off before setting out on what he announced as 'One of the most splendidly pointless trips that I have ever taken.' Then he clocked out, rushed down the Tower, jumped on to the back of a motorcycle and headed for Heathrow Airport, carefully calculating his strategy for the actual Race. When he arrived at the Empire State Building, he shunned the celebratory festivities. He turned round instead and went back to London on the next flight. His eyes were already gleaming over his prospects of winning the £5,000 ($12,000) Aer Lingus prize. He had worked out all kinds of wrecking gimmicks, such as employing an army of children to sabotage the lifts at both ends and a variety of unmentionable 'gamesmanship' ploys to tear the heart out of any frustrated rival. But Clement's lips were sealed as to his exact May strategy as his motor-cycle sped him back towards Kennedy Airport.

Reaching New York gave me the opportunity of linking up directly with Jeffrey Blyth, the chief of the *Daily Mail* New York Bureau and man responsible for organizing the American end of the Air Race. Though we had never met before, we had exchanged hundreds of telex messages, letters and telephone calls over the preceding months as we ironed out problems connected with the Race.

Arriving as I did with Captain Alcock, who is the most energetic 67-year-old I've ever met, gave me a competitor's eye view of the Empire State Building. Although I had made many previous visits there, never before had my mind been working out ways of shaving seconds off my time-table.

From the narrow circular confines of the Post Office Tower I found myself in the lofty spaciousness of the Empire State Building, Eighth Wonder of the World, a self-contained city of ceaseless activity where the choice of elevators and street level entrances is baffling, the elevators are sickeningly swift and the opportunities for getting lost disquieting. Accustomed to the error-defeating exactness of the twin elevators at the Post Office Tower, which would spill competitors directly out on to the 33rd floor less than a dozen strides from the London check-in station, I now found myself in the marbled entrance hall of the New York skyscraper. With my mind racing back frantically to the advice that I needed two elevators to reach the American check-in station, I suddenly froze, baffled as to which of the battery of lifts I should take. At that point an alert polo-sweatered giant of a man, breaking from a party of people being disgorged from an elevator, beckoned us over. He was Andrew Davey, an off-duty New York 'speed cop', who had whisked Geoff White from his helicopter pad to the Empire State Building early that evening. Under his friendly guidance we grabbed an express elevator to the 80th floor—which took a 1 minute and 2 seconds—and dashed to a second elevator to reach the 86th floor. As the doors opened there was a moment of minor panic over the direction to take before Captain Alcock and I sprinted the last yards up a few steps to the check-in point.

Because of our hour's wait for the taxi, most of the others had disappeared for a celebratory drink, and when Captain Alcock and I joined them we found to our delight that the reception room was swarming with RAF and Navy men who were in New York, drumming up co-operation from the U.S. Navy and New York City authorities for the participation of the Harriers, V-bombers and Phantoms in the Race. For above all else the Services realized that success depends upon planning. In that they were not alone, for planning sessions were going on in America and Britain and at strategic points all over the world.

Chapter Five

GIMMICKS GALORE

'PERSON WITH TITLE and initiative required by American based company to enter Daily Mail Air Race competition—fastest time, London to New York in commercial air passenger category. All expenses paid. Give full particulars in first letter, which will be treated in strict confidence.

So RAN A 23rd June 1968 advertisement in the Personal column of the London *Sunday Times*. Immediately, twenty-five titled European men and women from five countries decided to trade on their titles for a free trip to New York and answered the anonymous challenge. They found that the advertisement had been placed by a cheerful, cherubic-featured American, Alan 'D Caston, President of Murray-Allen, the largest importer of European biscuits and confectionery in the United States. As soon as he became aware of the Race, Caston decided it would provide a unique opportunity for publicizing his operations provided he could think up the right gimmick.[*] It didn't take him long. He hit on the idea of 'blue-blooded nobility'.

Originally looking for only one aristocrat to carry the Murray-Allen colours, Caston was so delighted by the response to the advertisement that he promptly chose two 'top drawer' Britishers. Heading his list was Lord Montagu of Beaulieu, owner of one of Britain's leading 'Stately Homes' located in vast acres of Hampshire not far from the bustling seaport of Southampton, and inter-

---

[*] Known for their creative and unusual marketing efforts, Murray-Allen imported 'The World's Largest Cough Drop' in 1967.

nationally known as a lover of vintage cars. For the other, he chose a charming British European Airways traffic girl, Lady Hermione Thompson, second daughter of the Earl of Verulam, owner of a prize elkhound, expert gemmologist and linguist. Lady Hermione's immediate reaction was that the Race was 'a challenge demanding ingenuity and offering excitement and adventure', but she was 'scared stiff' of having to learn to ride on the back of motor-cycles which would speed her between the airports and the check-in stations. Speed was not quite so import-ant for Lord Montagu, since he had opted for a vintage motor-cycle to take him stylishly to Heathrow Airport on 7th May, the day before Lady Hermione was to make her record-breaking effort.

Murray-Allen were not the only company to resort to provoca-tive announcements in the personal columns of newspapers. An intriguing one appeared on Tuesday, 12th November 1968 in *The Times*. With captivating bluntness it said:

> TWO NUTS (in reasonably sound mind) wish to hire Twin Cessna, or Comanche with long-range tanks, de-icing, and masses of lovely radio/navigation equipment, for three weeks next Spring to fly across the Pond and back. Anyone interested please write with details of charges and any other snags.

Though strict anonymity was adhered to it was a portent of things to come.

Another intriguing proposition arrived the same month from Patrick Watson of Heirloom Airlines of Toronto. He was figuring out ways and means of entering what he believed was 'the last existing Stranraer flying boat—designed by Mitchell of Spitfire fame'. A check showed that the two-step hulled plane, of 1935 vintage, was still in flying trim. Designed as a long-distance reconnaissance bomber the twin-engined biplane, capable of carrying an eight-man crew, could cruise for 1,000 miles at 160 mph. The thought of its being able to land on the River Thames below Tower Bridge caused immediate excitement.

Then, almost in the next post, came news that a New Zealander living in Canada, Neil Stevens, was hoping to take part flying solo in a much earlier plane, either a '1928 De Havilland Gypsy Moth of the type used by Sir Francis Chichester for his solo flight from England to Australia in 1929–30, or a DH 80A, as used by Amy Johnson and Jim Mollison in their record flights of the early '30s'.

He couldn't be serious! Or could he? There was no telling. He might have been an absolute madman or a veteran aviation enthusiast. Certainly a check with John Blake of the Royal Aero Club produced nothing about him from their comprehensive records, and the National Aeronautic Association in America had no record on Stevens.

Theoretically, you could fly the Atlantic in either of the aircraft, but to do so would be just about as sensational as Alcock and Brown doing their flight all over again. Yet the letter, in regimented handwriting, appeared intelligent enough. Stevens wrote: 'Both are in New Zealand at this time and both require modifications to enable them to make the trip.'

So at least he wasn't going to try hopping across the Atlantic unprepared, in a plane whose successors were more usually to be found doing bone-shaking landing and take-off flights with raw student pilots aboard rather than droning their way over icy cold, lonely stretches of forbidding Atlantic ocean.

In a second letter he confirmed his eagerness to take part:

If the DH 60 is used I will be flying via Greenland and Iceland—this aircraft is currently airworthy and flying. The DH 80A Puss Moth is located in a barn and is not currently flying.

However, it has the advantage of being able to fly direct from St John's, Newfoundland, to London with the addition of a large fuel tank as used by Jim Mollison. An estimate on the cost of modification etc. is being made at present, and should these prove reasonable the Puss Moth will be used.

The whole idea is very exciting and stimulating, and nothing will give me greater pleasure than completing the Race in a British machine and competing against our friends across the border with all their big money and Lear Jets by the score.'

Then, referring to one of my earlier replies, he added 'Your usage of the word "intrigued" is perhaps a very subtle and diplomatic way of saying I'm crazy, and on reflection at times I would be inclined to agree with you. No doubt those reflections will increase as Sunday May 4th draws closer!'

After a letter like that he just had to be genuine.

He was. But it was months before the truth was revealed. Neil Stevens was too busy preparing for the trip to be really worried about the impression his imaginative plans were creating. In February he returned to New Zealand, only to find that he couldn't get a reconditioned Gypsy Moth engine for less than £1,300. Undeterred, he decided to ship the plane to Los Angeles where Mira Slovak—who also entered the Race—had promised to help prepare the plane. Then the New Zealand Government refused to grant the essential Certificate of Airworthiness to the aircraft without its engine, thus effectively blocking Stevens from sending it to America; for there was not enough time available before the Race began to start from scratch with the series of inspections and examinations needed to obtain an American Airworthiness Certificate after the engine had been fitted, in California.

Dejectedly, Stevens went back to Vancouver convinced that he 'would have to cancel'. But when he reached Canada the old determination returned and he decided on one last throw. Originally he had gone to Canada with the hope of landing an airline pilot's job, for which he was fully qualified. But none of the companies were hiring so he had started up a successful business importing biplanes into North America.

It was recalling one of these deals that put him back in the Race. For on returning to Vancouver he remembered that just the right aircraft, a Tiger Moth, was sitting down across the American border at Bellingham, Washington. The snag was that he had already sold it to Clay Henley of Kellogg, Idaho. But a telephone call, and Henley agreed to let Stevens have it. In nine days the tiny aircraft was converted for its transatlantic role. New fuel tanks were fitted and radio equipment and navigation instruments installed in readiness for 4th May. After months of painstaking preparation, Neil Stevens was able to send off his entry form.

There were many other competitors who spent months preparing for their participation in the event. Mostly the preparations involved technical considerations, but for *New York Times* travel editor Paul Friedlander—the first American to submit his entry—the forward planning was of a more personal nature. When his daughter asked if she could get married in May '69, he told her: 'You have my blessing—as long as you don't set the date between May 4th and 11th.' She didn't, and Paul made two trips in the Race.

Right from the outset Ted Drewery had been captivated by the Air Race idea, and he busied himself with collecting together a planeload of businessmen who could combine the fun of being associated with the Air Race with a week's hard selling in America. He brought them together under the umbrella of the British Export Sales Team—BEST for short—issued them with a Union Jack symbol, which graced special team notepaper and the tie which was part of the standard uniform for all the 120 members of of the party, and then Drewery chartered a BOAC VC 10 to have 'the best chance of taking a prize'. The BEST set included underwriters, insurance brokers, accountants, foreign exchange brokers, lawyers, dress manufacturers and even a dentist. The group was to cause a near riot when it arrived in New York. For they were all wearing identical pin-stripe trousers, black jackets, and bowler hats and carried umbrellas in one hand and their business samples in the other.

Not all would-be competitors were having such a smooth passage as the bowler-hat brigade. In America the company who had hoped to use the 'James Bond' type Jet Packs★ to get their man from the top of the Empire State Building to a waiting helicopter hit snags—including the prohibitive cost of insurance—and had to drop the idea altogether. Even sadder news came in from Raymond Selkirk, the Secretary of the Sunderland Flying Club in England. In February, he reported dejectedly that the De Havilland Rapide—an aging biplane—which he was to have navigated in the Race and delivered to an American who had

---

★ A jet-powered manpack unit which can be strapped to an infantryman's back, allowing him to jump over obstacles and buildings and travel several hundred yards in one hop.

bought it, had hit troubles. 'While a pilot was being checked out, the brakes failed, and the aircraft ran off the end of the runway and was very badly damaged,' he related forlornly. 'Do you know anyone who wants a qualified co-pilot or navigator?' he pleaded.

Luck ran out too for 28-year-old Jackie Paul of Slough, Bucks., who planned to enter in a coffin; the self-styled 'only true white fakir in the world' aimed to check out at the Post Office Tower before settling comfortably in the coffin as the lid was screwed down tight. Pall bearers and a funeral car—carrying *Daily Mail* Air Race stickers—were to take him in solemn procession to the Embankment, whereupon the coffin would be floated up the Thames on its way to Heathrow Airport. Carried across the Atlantic in the freight hold of a commercial jet to Kennedy Airport, Paul, entombed in his coffin, did not expect to appear in public again until the lid was lifted at the Empire State Building check-in station. According to Paul, who has made several TV appearances, he would put himself into 'suspended animation' in a bid to win the £5,000 ($12,000) offered by Butlin's for the most meritorious non-winning entry. But he was destined never to get off the ground, for BOAC, like several other airlines, refused to carry him in his coffin. All thought the idea was too macabre—and so did the organizers.

Over in America the New York office received a request for an entry form from a firm in Alaska called the Dead Horse Transportation Company, and in London three Italians wrote to ask if they could run all the way between the check-in stations and the airports. Other would-be competitors, like newly qualified pilot Rodney King of the London School of Flying, were looking for sponsors to help them enter the Race; Rodney hoped to use the prize money to pay off some of the costs of his commercial airline pilot's course. In America Hobey Vance of Tucson, Arizona, turned himself into a company—Hobey Inc.—and sold $10 units of stock to local well-wishers with the promise that any prize would be returned by way of a dividend share-out. A variation of the sponsorship scheme was thought up by Donald McNab of Haven Green, London, who set out to prove that 'anybody wishing to travel and sell products to the U.S.A. can do so by using their own initiative and without using existing capital or established contacts'. Ignoring all his friends' help, he promised to 'leave the top of the Post Office Tower without a penny in my pocket and apart from sleeping at my home, shall raise the money by providing a service to individual companies or people'. As a rider to his self-appointed challenge McNab pointed out that to raise £100 ($240) in four days would be the equivalent of earning £9,000 ($21,600) in a year.

In sharp contrast to the go-getting ambition of such individualists as Rodney King, Hobey Vance and Donald McNab, the attitude of some of the airlines was sickeningly disappointing. British European Airways (who like to preen themselves with the questionable title of 'First in Europe') just didn't want to know about the Air Race—not even when they were reminded of the tremendous effort they had put into the *Mail*'s London to Paris Air Race ten years before when their team, led by Public Relations Manager Bill Simpson, made a lasting contribution to aviation by showing how to cut the total travelling time by a third, using regular transportation, and ended up with a special prize. It was left to Lady Hermione Thompson and BEA Steward Peter Palmer of Oxshott, Surrey—who managed to make one crossing for only £18 ($43.20), which included the £10 ($24) entry fee—'unofficially' to uphold the reputation of state-owned BEA.

Britain's independent airlines were not showing much enthusiasm, either. Whilst non-scheduled American carriers like Capitol International Airlines were getting excited about the promotion prospects of the Race, their British rivals for the lucrative North Atlantic charter market, British United Airways and Caledonian Airways, were showing little inclination to get on the Air Race publicity 'bandwagon' that was even taxing the imagination of Japanese Airlines, QANTAS and Air India, as well as ALITALIA and TWA.

Stewart Hulse, BUA's bustling Public Relations Manager, tried hard enough. He hit on the idea of sponsoring pioneer aviator and current pilot licence-holder Wing Commander R. H. McIntosh who was made a life member of the 'Quiet Birdman Club' of the U.S.A. in 1927. Stewart saw in Mac—who had flown Lawrence of Arabia, Anthony Eden and a galaxy of stage and film stars, including Charles Chaplin and Mary Pickford—a potential 'show stopper' who could be exploited (with his full co-operation) to attract coverage of the airline and its associated Bristow Helicopter Company, and to publicize the advantages of BUA's base, London (Gatwick) Airport. But the Board of Directors turned the idea down.

Within weeks of their doing so the British Post Office picked the sprightly Wing Commander to be one of the key contestants to be featured in a full-length film they decided to make about the Race and the carriage of special Race mail; a film destined to be given world-wide distribution as well as being shown in cinemas throughout Britain.

Airline employees, of course, had a distinct financial advantage over other competitors. One of the 'perks' of their job is their ability to get reduced rate fares on their own and some other airlines. It meant that many of them were able to make a number of exploratory trips to either check-in station to beat traffic problems and work out ideal city centre to airport solutions. The comings and goings of would-be airline entrants became pretty routine. That is more than can be said for their questions, which were often complex and sometimes so demanding that it was clear that they assumed the organizers had encyclopaedic knowledge of every aspect of air transportation and of the road and rail arrangements between the check-in stations and the airports. There were many times when, without an aviation background, I should have been stumped, or led into dangerous commitments, regarding interpretation of customs and immigration and airport and Air Traffic Control regulations, such as the rights of passengers to board or leave aircraft at points other than the official ramps.

Others, like Pan American co-pilot Richard W. Selph of Sandy Hook, Conn., were comparatively trouble-free, though their questions could still be difficult ones to answer. But in return they would feed me with information which helped to iron out many difficulties of non-airline folk. From the outset I reckoned Richard Selph would be close up with the leaders. Tall, alert yet slightly studious, he had that quietly confident approach which breeds success. In the early days he had the airline right behind him. But towards the 18th April entry deadline, I got the impression that things were not going so well. Therefore it came as no surprise when he wrote to break sad news:

> To bring you up to date, PAN AM has turned thumbs down on any support or sponsorship, so I'm on my own. This limits my options somewhat but I have decided to go ahead with my entry as an individual. Unfortunately, the round trip idea appears to be too risky (I might miss the westbound flight and it is the best one of the week). I could still do it, if there were some particular incentive, but there does not seem to be any.

So PAN AM wrote off one of their best prospects of capitalizing on one of the hottest competitors to have emerged during the long months of pre-Race planning.

The same type of dejected feelings that must have possessed Richard Selph when he wrote that letter were, for different reasons, troubling Captain John Wilsey of the Royal Military Academy at Sandhurst (Britain's equivalent to West Point).

Captain Wilsey had represented Sandhurst ten years before, when he was a cadet, in the London–Paris race, dropping into London by parachute. Largely through his enthusiasm he got General Philip Tower, Director of Sandhurst and former Army Public Relations Chief, to agree to entering three cadets in the 1969 Race, two flying on commercial jets and one piloting a light aircraft. They would be backed by fifty fellow cadets providing communications, transport and administration in Britain, while in America they would be supported by cadets from the United States Military Academy at West Point.

But, and this was the rub, the most perplexing problem was getting sponsors to cover the £3,500 ($8,400) costs of the operation. In theory this was a not altogether impossible task; indeed, the cadets got off to a good start. Lord Litchfield, who was a Sandhurst Cadet with John Wilsey in 1959, immediately agreed to help, as did Northern Executive Aviation Ltd and the Three Counties Aero Club. Distressingly, though John Wilsey wrote to hundreds of companies and organizations in Britain and made personal calls on dozens more, he got the polite brush-off: usually, 'It's the government squeeze, old chap. If it wasn't for that we would love to help.'

In desperation the elegant, slim young Captain turned to America to raise support. But the excuse there was, 'The new administration in the White House has made the business future so uncertain there is no spare cash.' John Wilsey returned to Sandhurst disappointed. Less than half the money was accounted for, but he decided to go ahead and try to solve the financial crisis at the Race end. Neither Mark Fraser nor Simon Langdon, who were entered in a scheduled passenger jet category, nor the light-aircraft pilot David Wynne-Davies, was let into the secret of the parlous state of their Race fund finances. John didn't want them to be put off by worrying about where the money was going to come from. He wanted no distractions for them in their bid to win a prize and uphold the reputation of the Academy.

The Cadets were not the only ones suffering under a crushing financial burden. One of the early light-aircraft enthusiasts, C. C. Russell Vick of London, who put in hours of painstaking effort was finally defeated by the economics of taking part. In thanking the fifteen people who had each magnanimously offered him £50 sponsorship, he explained why he had made the firm decision not to enter:

The cost of taking part has beaten me; all I can say is that I never quite appreciated the business acumen or rapaciousness (whichever you care to call it) of the modern world! With the single exception of my own Flying Club, Air Touring Club at Biggin Hill, largely run by Bob Cleary, I have not had one single offer to reduce the cost of work on the aeroplane that I needed to have done. I took her over to Paris on Wednesday and have just heard that Sud Aviation, who built the Horizon, are unwilling to install the long-range tank (which they have lying in their hangar) for a moderate or nominal charge. This was the final straw.

You might be interested to know that I found out that the cost of the trip would have worked out as follows:

D

Hire of aeroplane at £7 10s 0d per hour for 60 flying hours	..	..	..	..	..	£450
Petrol	..	..	..	..	..	100
Fitting of Air Direction Finder		..	..	..		85
Fitting of H.F. (and hire at £7 per day)			..	..		350
Life Insurance at 25 shillings %		..	..	..		125
Insurance of the plane at 6% on £8,000			..	..		480
Sud Aviation to fit long-range tank ..			.	..		300

£1,890
($4,536)

I now know what the word escalation means!

It was in the hope of overcoming the type of problems that Russell Vick faced that the mysterious 'TWO NUTS' advertisement had appeared in the personal column of *The Times* on 12th November 1968. The 'TWO NUTS (in reasonably sound mind)' turned out to be 33-year-old Gloucester solicitor's wife Mrs Julia Turner, a busy housewife with three kids and a large home to run, and her one-time pupil pilot Vivian Wales. Unfortunately *The Times* advertisement did not bring the response anticipated and only one written reply was received—from the sixth Form at a Girls' School!

However, they managed to locate a Piper Comanche Twin PA 30A with long-range tanks at Oxford; and the Cheltenham College Junior School (attended by two of the Turner children and one of Wales's) launched a T.W.T.W. Supporters' Club—(Turner-Wales To Win)—to provide the pair with a tape recorder. In spite of the lack of sponsors, they decided to go ahead planning a 3,765-mile journey—the longest over-water leg being 920 miles between Greenland and Canada.

The news about the lack of response to *The Times* personal column advertisement didn't make me feel so upset about the refusal of *The Times* to take this one:

WANTED

ADVENTUROUS TYPES TO SHARE COST (ABOUT
£10 EACH) OF ENTERING THE *DAILY MAIL* TRANS-
ATLANTIC AIR RACE IN MAY. ACTUAL COM-
PETITOR SELECTED BY BALLOT. OTHERS WILL
ORGANISE GROUND LEGS BETWEEN AIRPORTS
THE POST OFFICE TOWER AND EMPIRE STATE
BUILDING. ANY OF THE £60,000 PRIZE MONEY
WON TO BE SHARED. CONTACT ADVENTURER,
BOX NO.....

They did not know when Cyril Higgs went along to their
offices to insert it that he was in fact trying to place it on my behalf. What triggered off the thought of a *Times* ad. was the news
that several groups had been set up throughout the country,
functioning on similar lines. John Smith, the landlord of the Royal
Oak pub at Charlton, Andover, in Hampshire, had gathered a
team of customers together; Peter Hammond had already been
chosen to represent the Green Diamond Club, and a syndicate of
travel clerks had put forward Jeffrey Dearden of Harlow, Essex,
as their representative. I met representatives of one syndicate in
America as they were sizing up the New York traffic situation.
Part of a ten-man, 'strictly no girls' team from BOAC's Motor
Transport Traffic department, they had been together since May
1968, chipping in weekly contributions and raising additional
money through competitions. Their runner was to be Robert
Taylor, and one of the rivals they would be competing against was
another BOAC driver, Clem W. Whitlock, a member of a rival
syndicate.

Another group, the Taunton (Somerset) Round Table, saw the
Daily Mail Air Race as offering 'the opportunity to participate in
the excitement with a real chance of adding a worthwhile sum
to our Disaster Fund'. They got the help of Hounslow Round
Table—also affiliated to the 960-strong British organization—at
the London Airport end, and Taunton, Massachussetts, Jaycees to
cope with the New York arrangements. To them, the Race was
'an imaginative scheme lending a little light and colour to a rather
drab and uninteresting decade'.

Certainly the Air Race—even before the 4th May start—was anything but uninteresting. But to give it that extra zing and punch we needed to get someone to prevent a walk-away victory by the Royal Air Force. None of the foreign Air Forces would pick up the challenge—I tried them all, including the NATO allies, as well as the Russians, the Australians and the French, whose Chief of Staff wanted to enter but was over-ruled by de Gaulle.

At one point, I got so carried away that I wrote off to the Republic of Malawi, only to receive a deserved but polite reprimand:

'I am directed to advise that Malawi has no Air Force and therefore regrettably cannot take part in the Race.'

The United States Air Force just wouldn't look at the event. There was no reason for the Americans not to take part, even if not with supersonic combat aircraft. Just like the Royal Air Force, the USAF have regular troop transport shuttle services between America and Britain, and even if they felt that they were too stretched in Vietnam to participate with front-line jets, they could have sponsored at least one team to commemorate the event—after all, Whitten Brown's parents were Americans. In any case, the USAF were flying regular training sorties to Europe during the period of the race, so the Vietnam argument looked like a diplomatic get-out.*

But there was not a peep out of the Pentagon. The nearest the U.S. military got to participation was when the U.S. Navy not only decided to have a crack at the Race, but they went as far as preparing two 1,400-mph North American supersonic Vigilantes. Plans had reached the stage of the aircraft being made race-ready with a complete overhaul. They were even polished—to get every last bit of speed out of them—and helicopter details were tied up in America and Britain, when an eleventh-hour veto ruled them out of the Race. It was inspired by the Public Relations department, who advised the new Secretary of State for the Navy that to take part would leave him open to accusations that he was being 'frivolous' at a time when a war was being fought in Vietnam, and at a period of economic uncertainty.

* On the Search and Rescue side, the USAF were wonderful, and specially located a long-range search aircraft in the light-aircraft area in case it was needed.

Still, as a compensation a couple of U.S. Navy boys did take part as individuals, helped by the RAF and Royal Navy. One of them, Commander Bill Martin, made the race blindfolded by a hood to prove his powers of extra-sensory perception, and in doing so did more to foster goodwill for the American Services than many of the high-flown 'goodwill programmes' which cost a small fortune to mount, and too often end up souring relationships with the people they were intended to impress. Some day, somewhere, some public affairs officer will learn there is no appeal more compelling than an individual 'having a go' at something interesting or worthwhile—that is the natural way to make friends. And Bill Martin did exactly that as his fascinating attempt and explanation were projected into millions of homes by television. Instinctively, he knew more about influencing people than all the high-powered public relations advisers on the Staff of the Secretary of State for the U.S. Navy.

With all hopes of the participation of a foreign military team ended, it was left to the Royal Navy to prove that its flying sailors could challenge the Royal Air Force, even though the Fleet Air Arm was under sentence of death because of the Government's decision to scrap the carrier-borne force in 1971.

But the Royal Navy were in no hurry to commit themselves, as was made clear at an informal gathering in the Directors' dining-room on the sixth floor of Harmsworth House.

Chapter Six

THE CHALLENGERS

'Not once or twice in our rough island story,
The path of duty was the way to glory.'

Alfred Lord Tennyson, 1809–92

CAPTAIN RAY LYGO was not a man to be dragooned into committing himself before he was quite ready. And on Thursday, 13th February, he was not ready. Stoically, the dynamic, small, alert-eyed, 44-year-old Naval Captain, who was shortly to take over command of the Carrier H.M.S. *Ark Royal,* refused to be drawn. From behind his champagne glass he acidly turned aside all the goading questions, the waspish comments, the appeals to patriotism and the honeyed words of naval praise designed to talk him into giving his blessing for naval participation in the Air Race. For as his tall, jovial companion, Admiral Derek Empson, Assistant Chief of Naval Staff for Operations and Air, pointed out, 'Ray is the project officer. It's up to him to make his recommendations. Until he does so we can't take things a stage further.'

It was logical but infuriating. For on that February evening everyone was exceedingly anxious to tie the Navy down. A firm commitment from one of the Services was needed to give point to a Press Conference that had been called in New York on 18th February. It had been automatically assumed that the RAF would be able to announce participation of the Harrier. But following the experience of the London Press Conference on 29th January, when the RAF had tried to delete reference to any official entry at all, that could no longer be taken for granted. The get-together on 13th February was, therefore, by way of being a softening-up operation; but the Navy—in the person of Ray Lygo—had no intention of being softened up.

Talkative? Certainly. Appreciative of the film, which was the official reason for the get-together? To a degree. But he didn't give a passing hint about his recommendations regarding the participation of the Royal Navy in May.

It had been hoped that the showing of the film of the 1959 London to Paris Air Race would inspire the Navy with enthusiasm—particularly the sequences of their entry—and remind them of the vow they had made, afterwards, that never again would the Royal Navy allow the RAF to triumph over them: for on that occasion the Navy had treated it more casually than the RAF, who were in deadly earnest. The 214-mile race, from London's Marble Arch to the Arc de Triomphe in Paris, had been won in 40 minutes 44 seconds by Squadron Leader Charles Maugham. The RAF also took third place, the second being filled by a civilian. The Navy just couldn't make the list of prize-winners and their morale suffered a hurtful blow.

Ray laughed boisterously at the antics of those of the 167 competitors shown on the screen, but remained tight-lipped afterwards about the Navy plans, if any, for the 1969 event. He was in no hurry. I liked him instantly. From beneath his blond bushy eyebrows he looked deep into your face, as though searching out signs of weakness or hints of deception. One got the faintest impression that perhaps inwardly he was laughing at everything that was going on. He came under pressure not only from the organizers but also from many of the civilians who attended the select gathering.

Like the Naval party, they had come along to see the London–Paris Air Race film to alert them to some of the problems which, being indirectly involved in the event, they would face. People like Tom Gibson, Central London Telephone Manager, who was responsible for the Post Office Tower, were present, so were Roger Croxford, from the Flight Safety division of the Board of Trade, Commander Paul Satow of the Port of London Authority, who was responsible for allowing helicopters to use the River Thames, together with Chinchen of Immigration and Veale representing Customs and Excise. The occasion also gave many of them their first opportunity to meet the Managing Director of Harmsworth Publications, Duke Hussey, whose faith in Brian Harpur's judgment had not only enabled the Air Race to be mounted but had also been largely responsible for the other two group newspapers, the *Daily Sketch* and the London *Evening News*, joining the *Mail* as co-sponsors of the event.

It was an interesting gathering from the Navy's point of view, for the majority of those present had not been aware that the Royal Navy possessed any aircraft capable of challenging the Royal Air Force. This was part of the legacy of the decision to axe the fixed-wing element of the Fleet Air Arm, scrap the aircraft carriers by 1971 and subordinate the remaining helicopter service to the Royal Air Force.

The bitter fight which had taken place to retain the carriers, culminating in the resignation of the First Sea Lord in 1966, had left the Navy shattered, and created a great rift between it and the Royal Air Force, who were given the go ahead to order the fifty American F111's (they were later cancelled). As a result of the economy cuts Royal Naval recruiting had suffered and many men, who would normally have signed on for further terms of service, were quitting in disgust at the end of their engagements.

It was against this background that the Navy had to judge their entry into the *Daily Mail* Race. It would undoubtedly be the last occasion on which they would be able to show their paces as an air Service in their own right. But would it do more harm than good? Would it open up old wounds? Or would it simply be a waste of public money? These were some of the problems occupying Ray Lygo on that February evening. In fact, he was well on his way to giving the go-ahead, but he gave no clue.

As far back as June 1968 the Royal Navy Air Station at Yeovilton had been given the task of studying the possibility of entering the Race with British-engined, American Phantom supersonic jets of 892 squadron.

As soon as Captain Lygo took over the planning in January 1969 he set as his target 'the task of producing the fastest man to cross the Atlantic' between the check-in stations. He would accept no less. But being a realist he was completely aware that a lot would depend upon the supersonic entries that were received from abroad.

With meticulous care the Navy worked out a whole range of comparative statistics of the types of supersonic aircraft that might conceivably be entered in the Race. Rough approximation showed that most military aircraft, capable of flying the 3,500 mile distance at above Mach 1, the speed of sound,* would have overall flight times within 45 minutes of each other. Another key fact was the need for all of them to be refuelled in the air as they crossed the Atlantic, a manœuvre requiring a high degree of navigational accuracy and airmanship.

Also providing a highly competitive factor would be the non-stop subsonic aircraft like the RAF Victor V bombers, whose range enables them to take every navigational advantage— including seeking out tail-winds which could dramatically increase their speed. Following on from these findings was the conclusion that the critical factor would be 'good terminal arrangements'—getting the competitor to and from the check-in points. As a result Ray Lygo was convinced that the race would be won by minutes rather than, as one might think in the Concorde era, by hours.

Initial research convinced the Navy that if they were to enter, the Phantoms, capable of Mach 2, should make the New York–London crossing. First, because they could expect favourable tail-winds in May (in fact that didn't happen), and secondly because to race in both directions would have needed 'unjustifiable support'. That decision made, the next most important factor was the question of getting the Phantoms refuelled in mid air.

One popular idea was to use Buccaneer aircraft as tankers to keep the race a Naval affair from beginning to end. But to do so, one of Britain's three carriers would have had to be positioned in mid Atlantic to be ready to receive the Buccaneers when they themselves ran out of fuel after topping up the Phantoms. The cost of diverting one of the carriers to mid Atlantic would have been enormous and probably politically unacceptable. But more than anything else it would have had the pro-carrier lobbyist

* The speed of sound, Mach 1, at sea level is 760 mph and 675 mph at 40,000 feet. At Mach 1 the sound barrier is broken.

howling for them to be retained after the 1971 deadline. On these scores the idea was dropped.

As the Navy had no tanker aircraft other than the Buccaneers they were left with two possibilities. They could either seek the tanker facilities from the U.S. Navy or ask the Royal Air Force to help. In fact both were approached and both willingly offered assistance. At the time of the *Mail* film show Ray Lygo was anxiously awaiting approval for the RAF to be given permission to refuel the Navy Phantoms from Victor tankers.

Meanwhile negotiations were under way with the U.S. Navy for help at the New York end. Eagerly they offered full facilities of the U.S. Naval Air Station, New York. But the most critical hurdle to overcome was obtaining Air Traffic clearance for the Phantom, which to fly supersonic speeds has to be above 40,000 feet (nearly 8 miles high), but also has to be able to descend to refuel in flight at least three times during the Atlantic crossing. Only by operating within strictly controlled limits would they be able to avoid causing havoc with the high-density civil airline traffic over the Atlantic and within the overcrowded New York area. To get aircraft travelling at over 1,000 mph in the precise position to meet a much slower refuelling tanker can be done only under strict radar control. That meant carrying out the first two refuelling rendezvous under American and Canadian radar surveillance. As there was no land station capable of monitoring the third refuelling operation far off the west coast of Ireland, it would be necessary to position the frigate H.M.S. *Nubian* to carry out the critical task.

Obviously, Royal Navy participation would be dependent upon the assistance of the RAF, the U.S. Navy and American and Canadian radar teams: a real co-operative exercise on a grand scale if it came off. But to predict the outcome on what was gleaned from Captain Lygo at the get-together on 13th February was impossible. I suddenly began to realize what people meant when they talked about 'the silent service'.

Another 'silence' gave cause for immediate concern. This time it was the RAF. For shortly after the get-together with the Navy, Brian Harpur had been promised a statement from them in time for the New York press conference. He had flown over to

America fully believing the last snags to the announcement of the Harrier participation had been ironed out, and that the news would provide the punch for the American press conference. But along the line someone made a miscalculation. Secretary of State for Defence Denis Healey was in the middle of preparing his policy-setting annual Defence White Paper. He had not got around to giving his 'blessing'. Consequently there was not a ripple of information from the RAF about exercise Blue NYLON— the code word for the Air Race, with NY standing for New York and LON for London.

The telephone rang with unusual urgency as I stepped into the office after a Monday lunch appointment. It was New York on the line.

'What's the hold up with the RAF announcement?' demanded Brian, troubled at finding things had not turned out as expected, and with an anxious Jeffrey Blyth at his elbow wondering what to put in the press handout.

'They still haven't got approval from Healey but they are working at it,' was my lame excuse.

'Just how much can we tell them over here?' crackled back the response.

'I'll cable you,' I said before the line faded completely.

A telephone call—the twentieth in seventy-two hours—to Air Commodore Peter Brothers, our most enthusiastic ally, and Director of RAF Public Relations, found him working frantically to clear the announcement. It had been further delayed because the Chief of Staff was away with 'flu.

'Don't worry. We'll clear it,' his cheerful voice assured me, and within a few hours, at 6.40 p.m., he was back on the line.

'We are in, boy. In a big way. I told you to rely on the RAF,' he assured me. 'Tell Brian it's all right.'

Immediately I cabled Jeffrey Blyth:

YOU CAN RELAX RAF TONIGHT SIGNALLING WING
COMMANDER PARKER* FULLEST DETAILS OF THEIR
ANNOUNCEMENT FOR THE PRESS CONFERENCE AND
ORDERING HIM TO BE PRESENT TO TAKE QUESTIONS STOP
PARKER WILL BE ABLE TO ANNOUNCE THE HARRIERS

* Wing Commander Parker was based at the British Embassy in Washington.

PARTICIPATION STOP THE NEWS WILL BE RELEASED
IN UK IN EVENING OUR TIME OR FEB 18 FOR USE IN
MORNING PAPERS OF FEB 19 TO COINCIDE WITH YOUR
CONFERENCE STOP
  THE HAWKER SIDDELEY HARRIER IS THE WORLDS
FIRST FIXED WING VSTOL (VERTICAL/SHORT TAKE
OFF AND LANDING) WEAPONS SYSTEM AND MORE THAN
60 HAVE BEEN ORDERED FOR THE RAF. IT LOOKS
LIKE A CONVENTIONAL FIGHTER BUT CAN LAND AND
TAKE OFF VERTICALLY LIKE A HELICOPTER STOP
  THE FIRST DEVELOPMENT HARRIER FLEW ON AUGUST
31 1966 AND WAS SUCCESSOR TO THE P1127 WHICH
FIRST FLEW IN 1960 STOP IT IS THE PLANE THAT
BRITAIN HAS BEEN TRYING HARD TO SELL TO THE US
MARINES AS IT CAN BE FLOWN OFF SHIPS
HELICOPTER PADS AS WELL AS OPERATE FROM
FORWARD AREAS WITHOUT THE NECESSITY OF A
PREPARED AIRSTRIP STOP

It was great news. Details of the Harrier participation—and
that of the Victor V bombers also announced by Air Chief
Marshal Sir John Grandy, Chief of the Air Staff—would have
made a bigger impact in Britain if it hadn't been for the fact that
news of an Arab attack on an Israeli airliner broke—just on the
edition times for the television news and some newspapers.

Apart from the bare announcement of its intention to take part
the RAF were very guarded about their actual strategy. The
reason became clear only later. Although they had received the
approval of Secretary of State for Defence, Denis Healey, for two
Harriers and four V bombers to take part, the details, particularly
the landing site for the Harrier, still had to be fully approved.
That was to take weeks of frustrating negotiations which in the
case of the Harrier nearly ended in an eleventh-hour calamity.

Group Captain Peter Williamson, the Commanding Officer of
the Harrier base at RAF Wittering, was made team manager. He
immediately set about the task of finding a site, not only for the
Harrier but also for the helicopters which would be used to get the
V-bomber men to and from their aircraft. Immediately the RAF
came up against the Board of Trade who, far from being enthusiastic over the prospect of selling the Harrier abroad, were obstruc-
tive. Repeatedly they refused to help the Services to obtain special
landing and take-off facilities. They would bring no pressure to

bear on the Ministry of Public Building and Works to allow the Royal Parks or the Horse Guards Parade to be used. In fact they wanted them to be treated like every other competitor, denied normal Service advantages. To prevent further problems a letter was sent to the RAF and Royal Navy to say there was no question of the organizers requiring them to observe the same restrictions as those imposed on civilian competitors, and that the categories had been so drafted that the Services would not normally be competing with civilians. That seemed to help, and the RAF went ahead with investigating suitable sites for the helicopter.

Ever since it had been mooted that they should take part, key RAF personnel, including Peter Williamson and Squadron Leader 'Olley' Crooks, had been examining every conceivable landing site for their helicopters, which, with their twin engines, presented no safety hazard when flying directly over Central London. They wanted to get as close to the Post Office Tower as possible and thus avoid the need for using any form of motor transport—even motor-cycles—to get from the helipad to the Tower entrance in Maple Street, thus avoiding the tangle of one way streets that isolate the Tower from normal traffic flows.

Delighted at finding the whole area to the north and west of the Tower being subjected to a massive rebuilding programme the RAF cast envious eyes towards one of these construction sites. Only the width of the road separated it from the base of the Post Office Tower and it wasn't more than a couple of minutes away from the check-in station, even calculating the elevator being down to half speed.

The construction firm, William Moss Ltd, far from being reluctant to let the RAF have use of a corner of the site on which work, apart from excavation, had not been started, were incredibly enthusiastic. They even arranged for their giant construction cranes to be lined up in such a way as to give an unmistakable lead to approaching helicopter pilots as they touched down less than 25 yards from the Post Office Tower.

The first any observant outsider might have noticed of the RAF plans was when workmen began to assemble a scaffolding framework on the excavated site just opposite the Tower. When the scaffolding reached ground level it was topped with board and a catwalk was run off from it to the public highway. But the full impact of what was happening on the Moss site was not revealed until the week before the actual Race when the wooden hoardings surrounding the site were peeled back from the corner and replaced by open wire fencing to allow spectators and the press a full view of the new helipad. Until then it was to stay a closely-guarded secret in case any mischievous Member of Parliament or anti-noise enthusiast tried to have the plan scrapped, or attempted to muster up public opinion against Service participation in the Race.

Chapter Seven

FALLING INTO PLACE

'Men ought to know that in the theatre of human life it is only for Gods and Angels to be spectators.'

Francis Bacon

CONCERN OVER POSSIBLE public reaction was exciting the interest of the Post Office as well as the Services, only in the case of the Post Office it was not noise but what kind of an outcry there would be if they agreed to hand over the public viewing platform at the Post Office Tower for use as the London check-in station.

In the middle of January the proposition had been put up to them and I was summoned to a decidedly chilly meeting at their St Martins-le-Grand headquarters in the heart of the City of London. Our case was not helped by the publication, in the 20th January issue of the *Daily Mail*, of a letter of complaint about the curtailment of public facilities—on the very same 33rd floor—during an annual university student race up the 798 steps, in an attempt to beat the $4\frac{1}{2}$ minutes record.

There would never have been any need to ask for the use of the public gallery had it been possible to glaze the open observation platform that runs on the outside of Butlin's 35th-floor Top of the Tower cocktail bar. But that had proven too costly and was in many ways impracticable because of the nature of the grilled structure on the outside. The Post Office, without hesitation, had offered a partially covered-in public gallery on the 32nd floor. But it was not big enough for Race purposes, even though the bulk of the administration was to be done at a ground-floor control centre.

Our only lever was to point out the tremendous publicity the Tower would get, not only in Britain and America but throughout the world. To prove this sweeping statement was difficult, but the point was not altogether lost.

What troubled the Post Office was not only the public reaction to being denied access to the main viewing gallery, with its weatherproofed, panoramic view of London, but also the loss of revenue which curtailment would bring. For the public sections of the Post Office Tower operate on strictly commercial lines under the careful scrutiny of Fred Joyce, the Tower Manager, who caters for a million visitors a year. It is an operation about as far removed from the usual stifling Civil Service attitudes as it is possible to get. During May 5,000 people a day would normally visit the public viewing galleries.

Up to that point, the Post Office had co-operated magnificently —even before they had learned that the Postmaster-General, and former Aviation Minister, John Stonehouse was to be the official starter for the Race at 8 a.m. on 4th May. The negotiations which were held throughout the pre-Race period, chaired by Tom Gibson, were remarkable for their efficiency and lack of bureaucratic bumbling.

But when it came to directly interfering with the public they were stubborn. A principle was at stake. In the end they compromised and turned over half the 33rd floor and launched a campaign to alert the public to the limitations on their facilities. Things turned out just fine. The public could get close enough to see what was going on and apart from a few peak times there was enough room for all the officials, the press, radio and TV and competitors during the eight-day period.

Matters were helped by the decision, taken in the very early days, to erect a temporary control centre under the overhang of the west side of the Tower, to which all competitors had to report prior to starting the race. That decision had an unexpected beneficial side effect. For when the British Broadcasting Corporation entered into negotiations for live coverage of the event several months after the commercial television company, Independent Television News, led by John McMillan and John Cotter, had secured the exclusive rights to film live from the top of the Tower

1 Naval helicopter waiting to rush a competitor from the Post Office Tower. During the ace it was repeatedly proved that helicopters could operate safely in the heart of London.

Captain Alcock (righ[t]
and Lieutenant Whit[e]
Brown before the flight t[hat]
made history. Abov[e]
They take off from [St.]
John's in their Vick[ers]
Vimy.

Above: 'The plane now taking off from platform seven is the 10.32 Harrier for New York.' Left: The revolutionary jump jet settling down in the heart of Manhattan after its trip from London in 6 hours 11 minutes.

The Phantom is refuelled over the Atlantic by a Victor tanker. Below: After its record-breaking flight the Royal Navy's competitor Lieutenant Paul Waterhouse scrambles from the cockpit to board a waiting helicopter at Wisley.

Left: *First competitor to arrive from New York, Lieutenant Waterhouse jumps from his naval helicopter for the last 100-yard dash to the Post Office Tower, for a time of 5 hours 30 minutes 24 seconds.* Below: *Lieutenant Hugh Drake, after another supersonic flight over the Atlantic by a Royal Navy Phantom, sprints to the Post Office Tower from the temporary helipad to achieve a time of 5 hours 19 minutes 16 seconds. But neither of these was the winning time.*

After all, a thumb print is a valid signature in English law.

Clement Freud and ten-year-old Dominic Faulder had just *11* minutes and *15* seconds to get from the river to Heathrow Airport if they were to meet the Aer Lingus-Irish deadline.

An instant turn-round for flying grandfather Max Conrad.

Britain's bowler hat brigade under the generalship of Edward Drewery, in the light overcoat (front centre), prepare to board their jet with their sights set on getting Air Race and export order prizes.

There were no paper arrows to help Harlem ghetto worker Marvin Gathers to get to London Airport.

'So what if my daddy did fly the plane?' called out Susi Scribner.

check-in station, Brian Harpur deftly sold the BBC the idea of tying up for exclusive live coverage from the ground-floor control centre. The deal was agreed over a dinner at the impressive enclave of the show business world, the Garrick Club, and by the end of the meal even I was enthusiastic about the proposition Brian had put forward to Alan Chivers, the head of the Corporation's Outside Broadcasts.

But to turn the, as then, unplanned control centre into an outside broadcast television studio, from which thirteen programmes totalling 2 hours 40 minutes viewing time were mounted, as well as making it into the Race nerve centre and press room, took hours of painstaking effort on the part of the BBC 'Wheelbase' producers, Brian Robbins and John Mills, and *Mail* man Norman Heath, who joined the Air Race team at the end of January 1969 and on whose shoulders the main administrative burden fell in mid-March, when Promotions Manager Bob Simpson went into hospital.

New York didn't have the same problems over space, but they too decided for administrative convenience to follow the London example and divide the operation into two sections. The check-in station was to be located at the 86th floor of the 1,742-foot-high building, but the documentation and communications centre was to be established at the 81st floor.

Gradually, the operation of the Race began to take shape. Because it had a built-in flexibility, the organization was able to take advantage of every opportunity. That is why, when public relations man Colin Hodgkinson made a tentative approach in January to see if his clients, Brooke Bond Tea Ltd, could join the list of sponsors, he didn't get an immediate turn down as had several would-be sponsors some months before. For some time it had been apparent that a lot of people who didn't stand a chance of taking one of the 'speed' prizes also fell outside the scope of either the Butlin's or the Ziff-Davis categories for the most meritorious non-winning entries. They were such people as Neil Stevens with the Tiger Moth, Patrick Watson with the Stranraer flying-boat, a man called Pope from Fiji, a West Indian living in London and a couple of Australians who wanted to make the slowest time, going via Europe, Africa and Mexico. The existing 'most meritorious'

E

prizes would also be outside the scope of Air India and Air Canada, who both had ideas of capitalizing on the Race, and might put up a more eye-catching proposition if they had a secondary prize to aim for.

After two days of thinking the proposition over, Brian Harpur reached his decision at an unexpected moment as we were walking along Tudor Street, past the front of the *Daily Mail* printing plant, which at that time of day was spewing out copies of the *Evening News*. We stopped at the corner of the block. We had been talking about the prospects of the Tiger Moth entering the Race, which provided an ideal opening for suggesting that Brooke Bond put up a 'most meritorious—Commonwealth' prize. Brian, who has a knack in creative moments of thinking in newspaper headlines, looked at me with one of his mischievous twinkles playing around his eyes '£60,000! $144,000! a nice round sum—good!' He watched for signs of any reaction.

I gave none.

A moment's pause. 'It would look great in print!' he exclaimed quietly, confidently.

'Definitely! Then the Canadian Government would have no excuse for staying out!' I countered.

With authoritative quietness, he announced his verdict. 'All right! As long as it doesn't take away any competitors from the Butlin's category. We must do everything to protect the sponsors who have been with us since the tough days in the beginning.'

A pregnant pause. As he was about to turn and to walk across to Harmsworth House he added, 'Go ahead and see what you can do.'

Getting Brooke Bond to put up £4,000 was easier than I expected. This was mainly due to the enthusiastic support of Colin Hodgkinson, a giant of a man who gamely struggles about on tin legs with the same defiance with which he flew Spitfires during the Battle of Britain, ignoring his disability.

Unlike many other companies who, to their later anguish, were too slow to appreciate the product promoting potentialities of the Air Race, Brooke Bond Tea's Marketing Director, Sidney Hoare, grasped its significance immediately. He saw the proposed

Commonwealth category fitting snugly in Brooke Bond's over-seas publicity schemes at a time when they were bidding for a larger share of the North American market. After Colin and I hammered out the details—they did not like the use of the phrase 'non-winning', but acceded under pressure—Sidney Hoare not only agreed to put up two £2,000 prizes for the category, one in each direction, but he set in motion a full scale campaign to see that Brooke Bond were able to capitalize completely on their investment and add to the Race success. This included establishing a free refreshment bar next to the Control Centre and entering Tina, the chimpanzee, as a competitor; though it was some time before I dared to break the news to the *Mail* that Tina would be competing. It was too early for them to be made aware that such 'touches of light relief' needed to be encouraged if the event was to have a universal appeal. At that point the *Mail*, sensitive to any suggestion that the event was simply a circulation-building gim-mick, were anxious that nothing should undermine the high standards they had set for the Race.

In a blaze of publicity Brooke Bond's entry into the Air Race was announced, and the magic prize-money figure of £60,000 ($144,000) duly hit the headlines. So much so, in fact, that one man in Michigan, who heard about the Race on his car radio, immediately pulled in at a phone box and called Jeffrey Blyth in New York. The man, a light-plane owner, wanted entry forms. Another American radio station got the story somewhat mixed up —they said entrants had to *land on* or *take off* from the top of the Empire State Building and the Post Office Tower! 'How do I do that?' came an immediate query from a baffled Piper owner, who had been tuned into the programme as he sat in his golf club-house.

Envious glances from rival newspapers around Fleet Street accompanied the announcement of the revised total prize money that had been amassed for the *Daily Mail* Air Race. The £60,000, divided up into twenty different prizes, dramatically overshadow-ed the £20,000 ($48,000) raised by the *Daily Express*—the *Mail's* chief circulation rival—and the *Evening Standard*, Australia's *Sydney Telegraph* and the Carreras–Guards Tobacco Co. for the 10,000-mile November 1968 London-to-Sydney Car Marathon.

Undoubtedly, the *Mail* Race prizes were higher than for any other single British newspaper promotion, and probably the largest sum offered in prizes by any periodical anywhere in the world.

There was never any intention of letting the prize money go any higher, although undoubtedly, by agreeing to requests to dilute some of the existing categories, the figure could have been pushed close up to the £100,000 ($240,000) mark. But in the middle of a sponsors' working session the phone in the directors' dining-room began to ring, which was unusual, for the operators had been given strict instructions not to put through any calls.

Reaching the phone, intent on blasting off at the switchboard in disgust at being disturbed, I was stopped short as the familiar hollow crackling within the receiver alerted me to the fact that it was an overseas call. Seconds later, Jeffrey Blyth was speaking from New York to recount, in a burst of great enthusiasm, that Dan Howe, the Public Relations Director of the Empire State Building, had called that morning and offered to put up a £1,000 ($2,400) 'supplementary' prize for the Race. Without a moment's hesitation Brian Harpur counted them in. From the outset the Empire State Building had been enthusiastic supporters of the Race even in the days when many American newspapers and magazines, radio and television stations were inclined to scoff at the idea.

Moving towards the 18th April deadline for entries, the pace of the whole operation began to mount with growing intensity. Amid it all Ken Corney, Geoffrey Golden and Henry Clapp were briefed for their staggered departures for America to lift some of the burden off Jeffrey Blyth who, like me in Britain, had the responsibility for handling all the press and public relations effort, in addition to the major share of the day-to-day organization.

Frantically he had been negotiating with the government agencies in America who had interlocking interests in varying aspects of the Air Race. After one of a series of long negotiations he was able to report,

> Things at the airport went well. Everyone very enthusiastic and helpful. However, there is no chance of any competitors being allowed to land a helicopter on the tarmac

near a plane. This has had to be ruled out because of all the construction work going on at the moment at JFK.

There are only two places helicopters will be able to land or take off and these are at the General Services Building and alongside American Airlines Terminal. The latter is only for New York Airways helicopters. Also contestants will have to use the public roads from the arrival and departure building to the 'copter pads.

The meeting was a follow-up to a policy letter sent earlier to all airlines by Morris Sloane, General Manager of Kennedy International Airport. In it he laid down the guidelines for treating competitors. He wrote:

> The Port Authority, as the public agency operating the airports in the New York Area which all contestants will probably use, must, of course, maintain a position of strict neutrality. It is obvious therefore that, in order to do so, the Port Authority cannot provide transportation for contestants, cannot allow transportation by private vehicles on other than the public highway system on the airport, cannot provide police or operations vehicles as escorts, nor can it extend permission for any special arrangements.

What a missed chance for experimentation with alternative ways of beating the ground traffic snarls that have throttled Kennedy Airport for the last three or four years! Where was the American flair for exploiting any given situation? Couldn't they have come up with an idea to equal Aer Lingus–Irish International's Heathrow pavement rendezvous system for departing passengers at Kennedy Airport? It seemed not; on the contrary, they were even refusing to grant 'permission for any special arrangements' which meant they were in fact being far more restrictive and inflexible than normal.

However, Sloane did add, in his letter to the airlines: 'Contestants are, of course, free to make special arrangements in co-operation with any airline or any other airport tenant, as long as these arrangements do not violate Port Authority Rules and Regulations or require the Port Authority's permission or concurrence.' After that mouthful of apparent contradictions he ended: 'May the best man (or woman) win!'

It would be wrong to be overcritical of a letter that was obviously intended to protect the Airport Authority from any repercussions that might follow the Race. When put to the test, of course, with few exceptions the airport officials were marvellous. But such a negative approach prevented the systematic study of passenger reactions to airport problems when they could have been given a large degree of freedom to find their own solutions, uninhibited by doctrinaire rules imposed for the benefit of officialdom rather than for the customer.

Even if Kennedy Airport Authority were not prepared to use the Air Race to provide pointers for the future, Philadelphia Airport's managers certainly were. Specifically intent on proving that the shortest distance between Europe and the United States is 'not necessarily via New York City', Thacher Longstreth, executive vice-president of the Greater Philadelphia Chamber of Commerce and councilman-at-large, and Robert H. Wilson, vice-president of the Girard Trust Bank, entered the Air Race.

Interviewed over a car-to-helicopter radio during the actual race as he sped the 120 miles from New York to Philadelphia, Longstreth said he was more interested in proving that Philadelphia offers the most convenient if not the fastest route between New York and London, adding, 'Our competition will highlight the Philadelphia Airport as the international gateway to this part of the United States'.

The helicopter touched down about 30 yards from a Pan American Boeing 707. Longstreth and Wilson were inside the plane within seconds,* underscoring the tremendous co-operation of airport officials and customs and immigration authorities.

Flexibility in complex situations is always possible, as was clearly proven by the reaction of the Canadian Government to the request that they amend slightly their extremely stiff rules with regard to procedures for light aircraft flying the Atlantic. The Canadians readily agreed to adjust their inspection routine, where

---

* Ironically, because thunderstorms created chaos with air traffic, there was a nine-plane stack-up on the runway and the jet was delayed 25 minutes on the ground. Longstreth still did a commendable race time of 8 hours 28 minutes and 41 seconds.

a pre-Race examination of competitors and their planes had been conducted by acceptable persons such as qualified members of the Royal Aero Club, or the Board of Trade, or the National Aeronautical Association of America, or the FAA. As several light-aircraft entrants intended making a 'pilgrimage' to St John's, Newfoundland, before setting off across the Atlantic, the Canadian Department of Transport, in recognition of the fact that St John's had been Alcock and Brown's departure point, agreed to allow aircraft inspections to be carried out at St John's instead of at Moncton, New Brunswick.

It was a refreshing approach which augured well for the actual event.

Chapter Eight

HIGH FLYING IDEAS

'In many subtle ways, the rise of pseudo-events has mixed up our roles as actors and as audience.'

Daniel J. Boorstin

BEATING THE BRITISH at their own game had for months been the preoccupation of American Bob Ottum, Senior Editor of *Sports Illustrated*. He saw the Air Race in terms of an irresistible challenge where the 'inborn' American skill in organization could destroy the 'sham innocence' of the British and result in a walkaway victory to take a string of major prizes which, on Bob's quick calculation, would top $21,000 or more.

Swinging the resources of the magazine and its parent company, Time–Life, behind him, Bob, with photographer Jerry Cooke as co-contestant, held a series of detailed plotting sessions which fed on information gleaned from on-the-spot inspections of the New York route and cabled advice from Gwil Brown and Lavinia Scott-Elliot in the London office. They had already decided that it was 'part air race, part track meet and part broken-field run'.

But not until they linked up with fresh-faced 17-year-old Susi Scribner were the ingredients distilled into something like a victory brew. For Susi's great asset, apart from her bubbling charm, was that her father happened to be a Senior Pan American Airways captain, flying 707s in to London. That fact sent the trio into a series of pre-Race huddles which the self-styled 'Sixth Avenue Racing Team' believed would produce 'a sure winner' in a race which Bob described as 'diabolical and fiendish in its scope'.

From the outset they realized that to do their devilish best for America they needed to be backed with hard cash. Lots of it. For as Bob told the editor: 'You do not just go off and win an international air race on nickels and dimes. People have to be hired.'

Anyway, why worry about cost? It would all come out of the prize money the trio were convinced they were going to win. So the London office was ordered to spare no expense to smooth the route at the other end.

A conspiratorial huddle in a plush restaurant at Seventh Avenue and 51st Street between the Team and Captain Kimball J. Scribner really got their temperatures soaring with sheer anticipatory delight. Their winning ploy would be to board the Boeing 707, when it was already lined up on the runway with its engines running ready for take-off, through a secret hatch in the belly of the plane. So as not to alarm the other passengers, the trio would be slipped through a false door in a rest room and troop out through the normal rest room entrance moments before the giant jet surged down the runway for take-off. Kimball assured them that the PAN AM computer would already have picked out a winning air current that would slice minutes off their air time by pushing them along from behind.

Getting into that hatch would be no simple matter, with blasting jet engines sucking in and blowing out millions of cubic feet of air every minute only feet away. So—in keeping with the 'American Dream' of super efficiency—a try-out was arranged. Small! That hatch was so minute that it didn't seem big enough for a cat, let alone a panting, nervous human being. They reached it by doubling up around the nose wheel and under the belly. A push by unseen hands from the inside, and the foot-square hatch fell open to reveal a crawlway into the heart of the jet. With a bit of a tussle they made the ascent. For the try-out, the Boeing 707 stayed firmly on the ground.

Triumphant, and with Susi leading the way, her smiling face half concealed by mod sun-glasses, the Team headed back to the Pan Am terminal smugly satisfied—at least as far as the flight was concerned, the plans were in good shape. Back in Manhattan, Bob and Jerry set to work teeing up the transport for the dash from the Empire State Building to the helicopter pad. The essential

thing was to make sure all three arrived at the helipad together; this automatically ruled out motor-cycles, for these could
be separated as they rocketed their way through Manhattan streets,
while cars could easily be fouled up by traffic and red lights.
Something to cancel out such hazards was called for, and Jerry had
got just the answer: a siren-blasting, light-flashing ambulance!

'Get it,' said Bob. 'Don't worry about the cost.'

He just couldn't wait for the big day. He was going to teach
those Englishmen a trick or two! 'Just imagine their faces,' he
thought to himself, 'when they have to present Susi with the prize
for the unsponsored contestant flying on a regular scheduled airliner, one to Jerry—the prize for the fastest subsonic time—and
most important, my own for the fastest passenger flight! What
will that make? Let's see, $6,000, $12,000 and $9,000—that's all
of. . .!' His mind raced on, totalling up the prizes, convinced that
the Sixth Avenue Racing Team were going to win.

But those Englishmen were not such easy game. Londoner
Peter Hammond had also put flight times through a computer.
What's more, three different teams of BOAC employees knew all
the tricks of the airline game. Detailed research was also being
carried out by two brothers, partners in James Vance Travel of
Fulham.

It was early April when the Freudmanns burst in on the Air
Race Bureau in London. Edmond, 28, and his 23-year-old brother
Joey brought into the Race a special blend of determination and
precision planning. Edmond, a Maccabi footballer and accom-
plished sportsman, decided they should make at least five attempts,
though each would undertake separate runs. With a quarter of a
million miles of business travel behind him, Eddy—as he prefers to
be called—summed it up: 'If you are not using your own, or a
firm's, private aircraft, the Race really comes down to how fast
you can get from the airport to the top of the Post Office Tower,
or the Empire State Building. A traffic hold-up of only a minute
or two could be enough to rob you of your chance and make the
rest of the three-thousand-odd miles a waste of time.' He looked
across my desk as though in search of reassurance.

Having identified the problem, the brothers set about an exhaustive series of practice runs between the Tower and Heathrow

Airport. They were thinking in terms of seconds. With remarkable dedication they were to be seen hurtling to and from the
Tower on motor-cycles, experimenting with helicopter boarding
techniques, trying out speedboats and even checking on the right
gear to wear for the event. In one try-out Joey did a 15-mile trial
run from the Post Office Tower to Heathrow in 18 minutes 45
seconds. Immediately they decided that in the actual race they
should use the same combination of motor-cycle, speedboat and
helicopter to link up with their Aer Lingus flight. With such precision timing, it became obvious at once that Clement Freud
would face tough competition from the Freudmann brothers. So
too would the other 40-odd people expected to enter for the
westbound *Daily Sketch* and Aer Lingus prizes.

Try-outs were the keynote for competitors in another westbound category; the Rothmans £4,000 ($9,600) prize for the
fastest time flying direct from London to New York, using a subsonic aircraft. Former world-renowned racing motorist Stirling
Moss had been tempted to use the opportunity to make a spectacular return to international competitions. But on this occasion
his bid for the winner's accolade was to be made by motor-cycles,
speedboats, helicopters and a VC 10 specially chartered for the
Race by Crosse & Blackwell. Travelling with Stirling—but not
actually entered in the race—were to be a hundred of Britain's top
provision merchants, who would spend the three days in New York
studying American grocery sales trends and marketing methods
at specially organized seminars. Canned goods manufacturers
Crosse & Blackwell were one of the many British companies who
linked sales incentive schemes or marketing projects to the *Daily
Mail* event.

Stirling Moss made a trial run in a blaze of press, radio and TV
publicity, with disturbing results. As Stirling ruefully put it:
'We were the first to test the helicopter pick-up in mid-river.
Now some of our rivals have pinched the idea.'

Pre-Race reticence didn't stop Olympic star Mary Rand from
disclosing her plan of campaign. Geared out more for the race-
track than for Atlantic-hopping, Mary ran out from the Post
Office Tower during a trial run, sprinted to the near-by Warren
Street Underground station, took a Victoria Line tube train to

Seven Sisters Station in north London, before switching to a car for the remainder of the journey to Stansted Airport. Her total try-out time was 1 hour 5 minutes—hardly enough to give rival Stirling Moss any loss of sleep before the big day.

Heading in the opposite direction for the first of three attempts would be Miss Ruth Knight, who was the first woman Air Traffic Controller to work in the operations centre at Kennedy Airport in 1941. Currently an Eastern Airlines employee, Ruth Knight worked out a schedule for three trips in three days using QANTAS, BOAC and TWA. As she prepared for the Race she said: 'When I was a child, I used to dream there was a bridge over the Atlantic. Now there is. It is made up of constant air traffic.'

Crossing that 'bridge' in the fastest possible time was uppermost in the mind of Helen Lysaght as she headed to New York City Hall in search of help for her attempt. She was trying to drum up support for the Race which, in her view, up to that moment had not had enough publicity in New York. She wanted to do something about it, for she saw the *Mail* enterprise as a way to bring the two cities—and indeed countries—closer together. The response to her pleas for help amazed her. 'Everyone in New York was so co-operative you could hardly believe it,' she said.

But on one essential point she was over-cautious. Being advised that to speed through New York in an ambulance was illegal, she dropped the idea and it probably cost her a prize, for an ambulance might well have helped her to narrow the two-and-a-half-minute gap between her time and that of the *Sketch* prize-winner for the New York to London leg.

In fact, several contestants, including prize-winners, took to ambulances as a means of clipping minutes off their ground times. Some had sirens blaring and lights flashing, but as the police raised no official objections, the organizers ignored the incidents. It had been decided very early on that the guiding principle on rule breaking would be that where a prosecution for an offence would normally be instigated by the police, the organizers would ignore any infringement if the police chose to let it go. The use of ambulances was a case in point; breaking traffic speed limits—which 90 per cent of the contestants did—was another.

One man who could have used an ambulance with impunity but didn't was Captain Alan Clark. Crippled limbs never for a moment prevented him from turning his thoughts to getting into the Race on equal terms with everyone else. Struck down by poliomyelitis in 1944 and confined to a wheel chair ever since, the ex-Grenadier Guardsman was among the first to send in his entry. He scorned the sympathetic approach, the slow pathetic wheel-chair amble to a waiting ambulance. Captain Clark wasn't looking for sympathy. He was out for adventure and a prize.

'Going in for a race of this nature is like entering for a race in the Olympics; it's for the fun of taking part, taking part in a tiny bit of history. All this, and all the more so, as I can't walk and will have to make use of a wheel-chair and a body of volunteers who will, as a team, get me from A to B,' he declared.

What a formidable team the affable London stockbroker assembled! In Britain, members of the Guards Independent Parachute Company turned out, in their camouflage battledress and red berets, to help him race from the Post Office Tower to his BOAC VC 10 at Heathrow Airport. With the Atlantic flight over, the problem of getting the gallant Captain out of the aircraft was neatly solved by members of the Guards Comrades Association in America. With meticulous planning he returned a fast time of 8 hours 18 minutes and 30 seconds on the first day. Glowing triumphantly at the end of his adventure, he called out, 'It took us 14 minutes on the final stage, from the heliport to the Empire State Building—not bad for an old Guardsman in a wheel-chair.'

Such exploits earned him the title of the 'pluckiest man' in the race.

Others showed similar courage, including Rosslyn Murcott, who overcame adversity for the 'adventure of a lifetime'. A 34-year-old Shropshire accountant who can only get about on crutches and with the aid of callipers, he sent in his entry form without fuss. The first anyone was to know of his disability was when he turned up at the Post Office Tower on his crutches and backed by enthusiastic family supporters. From the moment they left him at London Airport he was on his own. Murcott decided to take 'pot luck' when he arrived in New York and make the best arrangements possible to reach the New York check-in station. His effort of 8 hours 43 minutes 13 seconds beat dozens of competitors who had the full use of their limbs.

Both Clark and Murcott had the advantage—if it can be termed one—of having learned to live with their handicaps and to surmount them. The same could not be said for Clement Freud who, in a minor panic before the 18th April deadline for entries was reached, phoned to explain sorrowfully: 'I may have to change my plans. I have broken my leg.'

Taken aback by my burst of laughter he responded, 'It's true. I broke it learning to ski in Switzerland.'

He accepted my condolences with a grunt.

'They wouldn't believe me when I told them. They made me walk. Typical of the Swiss, don't you think?'

There was another studied pause.

'Now I am dragging the leg around in plaster. Not at all good for jumping in and out of helicopters.'

I agreed.

But he was not after sympathy. Freud simply wanted reassurance that he could use the same entry form to try for the Butlin's most meritorious prize entry as for the Aer Lingus prize. He would, he reassured me before he put the telephone down, prepare yet another plan of campaign in case the plaster didn't get taken off the leg in time for him to stick to his original plan.

Problems were not confined to the British side of the Atlantic. Fred Clauser of Pennsylvania, the first American to enter the lightplane class, was having big troubles. He couldn't get insurance cover beyond Newfoundland. Lloyds of London said they would give him special cover only if he had a co-pilot—which was a bit 'stupid' as they were aware his plane was not big enough for two. But Clauser was not easily put off. For as Leonard Kucinski, of the Allentown, Pennsylvania, *Call-Chronicle*, said in a letter: 'Clauser comes close to being the ideal contestant. He is really sincere and exemplifies a pioneering spirit that has long been on the decline. He is paying his own way, and believe me, it is going to take his last dollar.'

Clauser, 33-year-old assistant treasurer of an engineering manufacture and import firm, decided to enter in a single-engined 180 horsepower Mooney Mark 21. Immediately on entering the Race he said:

It may not be the fastest or the most powerful plane in its class, but it has some features I think will make it a winner. I just want to point out that this is no stunt. I have a wife and three kids and I wouldn't do it if I thought it would be dangerous.

Lots of pilots have made a transatlantic flight. Some of them in smaller craft than my Mooney. But what I believe is going to win this race is planning. And I have been working on my plans since July 1968.

This isn't going to be some daredevil dash across the Atlantic. The further I go into preparations, the more confident I get. Plenty of people have made the crossing before. It's not like in the days of Lindbergh or 'Wrong-Way' Corrigan. The equipment today is pretty sophisticated and most of the chance has been removed.

How wrong a prophecy that was to turn out to be! But when he was still hunting for insurance cover, disaster was not a word that loomed high in his thinking. Nor should it have been, for he had been flying since 1964 and held a commercial licence.

In fact, a fellow Pennsylvania resident, 42-year-old one-legged pilot and Korean war veteran Bill Guinther from Kutztown, went in for the Race, his second solo flight across the Atlantic, specifically 'to show there are no adventures if you are properly prepared'.

Getting properly prepared wasn't easy; at least not for 48-year-old Robert Speers from Lansdowne, Pa. With two days to go before the start of the Race, he was to be seen peering gloomily at his hired Cherokee on the tiny air-strip of Cross Keys, New Jersey. Pulling himself away from the aircraft for a brief moment he stated the obvious: 'There's still a million things to do. Looking at the plane we seem to be in a no-go condition.' And that, after Speers and a party of friends had welded an extra fuel tank into the space normally filled by the rear seat.

The big snag was the radio due to be delivered from the manufacturers.

'That radio is holding us up. If it doesn't come, it will be all washed out. If only I could get off the ground. Flying doesn't present many problems—it's just getting the plane ready that's giving us a headache.'

It was an understatement. For as he admitted: 'If anything goes wrong I will have to pay out 5,000 dollars [£2,083] on the lease for the Cherokee. And that, for an oil refinery worker, is a lot of money.'

A 2,000-mile pre-Race dash to Texas for a new fuel tank for their Cessna 310 was necessary for wealthy Quakertown, Pennsylvania, contractor Kerwin Kelly and his wife Nancy before they were ready for take-off.

It was like that on both sides of the Atlantic. Light-aircraft enthusiasts were making ready, with gusto, enthusiasm and in some cases minor panics, for what is still a hazardous journey, taxing the skill of the most experienced pilot, even when assisted by the latest navigational aids and in flying machines with built-in reserves of power and fuel.

But up in East Brunswick 32-year-old Ben Garcia, co-founder of Fifth Avenue Opera Company, owner of a trucking business and a pilot with two years' experience of flying very light aircraft, didn't see it quite that way.

When it was pointed out to him that by fitting a small auxiliary tank he would have sufficient fuel to make the longest crossing between Iceland and Shannon without having to glide for ninety-nine miles, he replied:

'That's too easy. Anybody could fly across the Atlantic with enough fuel. What is called for in this race is the pioneering spirit. This is one of the last chances man is going to have to delve into his consciousness and find a *unique* way of getting across the Atlantic.'

Which was why he shrugged off criticism of his inadequately equipped Piper Colt. With only a fabric body to protect him from the sub-zero temperatures of an Atlantic crossing, Garcia announced his route as being via Canada, Baffin Island, Greenland, Iceland and Shannon, done, he assured everyone, 'strictly by compass navigation'. Which was just as well, as his radio was more suitable for a hop across the Thames than a near 4,000-mile, nerve-tingling trip from America to Britain, in a plane a quarter of the horse power of Lindbergh's *Spirit of St. Louis*.

The Garcia problem had only just dropped into my lap when news came in of an even more alarming attempt proposed by Stephen Lowell Smith from Missoula, Montana. He wanted to scoop the £5,000 ($12,000) Ziff-Davis Prize for the most meritorious American non-winning entry—the same prize Garcia was aiming for. But not in an aircraft. In a balloon!

Certainly Smith hadn't a hope of winning any prize calculated on speed. He accepted that even a week might not be time enough for his hot-air balloon. He aimed to lift off from White Plains, New York, and drift his way across to London via Halifax, Goose Bay, Greenland, Iceland and Ireland. It was the neat listing of interim stops which alarmed me—and certainly the Royal Aero Club and the National Aeronautic Association—for no balloonist of international standing would have tried to predict such an accurate course for a balloon, which would be at the mercy of every subtle shift in the direction of air currents.

Steve, a graduate student at the University of Montana, wasn't in the least perturbed. He believed he could do the journey and arrive intact within a week to win the Ziff-Davis award. For months he had kept the Montana campus agog with speculation about his novel form of transport. There was even speculation that he would try out 'man-made' wings. More serious informants believed he was working on a scheme to lift off from the top of the Empire State Building with his balloon. He was, until he had to switch to White Plains because contestants were banned from getting outside the top of the Empire State Building.

Freddy Perryment of the Cinerama International Releasing Organization was having balloon trouble of a different kind. He wanted one, but couldn't immediately track one down. The British Balloon and Airship Club said, 'Sorry—we don't own any' but after a lead from them he finally located 20-year-old Christine Turnbull, Britain's only licensed woman balloon pilot, at her Farnborough home.

She agreed to enter the air race in a balloon, carrying a publicity blurb for the film *Krakatoa: East of Java* and wearing an 1883 period costume used in it. But the red-headed balloonist was too

F

old a hand at the game to predict her route. 'It will depend entirely on the wind,' she said disarmingly. 'All we can be certain of is that we will take off in the Farnborough area.' Yet she was intent only on making a nominal flight before boarding a regular jet service to America.

By this time it seemed that we were being hit by balloon fever. In the same week that Christine sent in her entry form, Jeffrey Blyth was telexing news of another balloonist, Baltimore travel agent Cooper Walker, who had already grown a choice set of mutton-chop side whiskers for the occasion to fit in with his 1919 costume. Cooper Walker planned a mini 'Round the World in Eighty Days' escapade, including pilgrimages to the starting and finishing points of Alcock and Brown's flight, St John's, New-foundland and Clifden 'bogsite' in Ireland. Cooper Walker announced that he would carry greetings from the Mayor of St John's to the Mayor of Clifden.

Not for a moment did the 54-year-old former World War II pilot, who along with Barry Goldwater was one of the ten pilots to fly the first squadron of single-engined Republican P-47 pursuit aircraft across the Atlantic, think in terms of ballooning all the way. He had a much more imaginative scheme thought out, as befits an ex-commercial pilot who holds the 'questionable' distinction of flying the first cows across the Atlantic—for the American 'Give-an-Animal-to-Greece Program'.

Getting rigged out in uniforms identical to those worn by Alcock and Brown was the plan of BKS airline station superintendent, 31-year-old Brian Lathey, and BKS flight despatcher 24-year-old Derick Williams. Their aim was to use a 1919 vintage motor-cycle to connect with an Aer Lingus flight, which, in addition to fitting into the historical context of their pilgrimage, also satisfied a personal whim of Derick Williams, who declared: 'I want to marry an Irish girl, and I will see some lovely examples during the flight and at Shannon Airport.'

Across the Atlantic, in the small town of Sault Ste Marie, in Ontario, Canada, Captain Alcock's namesake Charlie, a 43-year-old department store worker, was busily firing off scores of letters, trying to raise sponsorship and tracking down his family tree.

'I believe my grandfather's father's brother was the father of

John Alcock,' Charlie Alcock told Barry Conn Hughes of the Canadian magazine *Star Weekly*. 'The fascinating thing is that though there are so few Alcocks, my best friend of twenty-five years is called Brown.'* Together, Charlie and Fred Brown, manager of a grocery store in Toronto, were desperately raising funds as the deadline for entries drew close.

Also searching for sponsorship was Anthony Russell, whose Vintage Aircraft Flying Company of Weybridge had been hectically at work preparing an exact replica of the original Vickers Vimy to take part in the Race. But they had hit snags. One was technical, which resulted in production schedule delays and which, in the end, caused them to miss the Race. The other major snag was the cost. Originally, work on the replica was carried out by the apprentices of the British Aircraft Corporation, but when it became too costly to finish, Vintage Aircraft Flying took over, only to find themselves handed a £25,000 bill from BAC. Had it not been for the stunning blow, almost everyone connected with the project was certain it would have been flying in time to take part in the Race.†

The disappointment about the Vimy was compounded by the news that Heirloom Airlines of Toronto, Canada, were pulling out because they couldn't raise the funds to finance the Stranraer entry.

But there was good news about the Spitfire and Hurricane. Company director Anthony Samuelson of Totteridge, London, announced his entry using the two vintage warplanes, two helicopters and a modern Piper Comanche twin-engined light aircraft to get him to New York. His plan was to go by motor-cycle from the Tower to a Thames-side barge, switch to a Bell helicopter as far as Elstree, where his Hurricane would be ticking over, ready for him to fly it to Rhoose, near Cardiff. There, he would switch to a Spitfire which would take him, and a co-pilot, across the Irish Sea to Shannon where they would scramble into the Piper Twin for the flight to Flushing Airfield in New York. The Spitfire, which

* Captain John Alcock was intrigued by the idea of locating an unknown relative, and set about tracing the connection. The only possibility was that they were related to his 'black sheep' Uncle Tom, who disappeared after going to America in 1909–10.

† With Dizzy Addicott at the controls, the replica made its maiden flight early in June, in time for Alcock and Brown anniversary ceremonies at Manchester Airport.

saw action on D-Day and has two 'kills' to its credit, was picked up in pieces by Samuelson at a sale in Ostend. It took three years to rebuild. Almost as soon as it was ready he turned it over for use in the Battle of Britain film.

Announcing his participation Samuelson, father of three young sons, declared he had no qualms about the trips in the warplanes, or the light aircraft. 'I honestly believe that the men who control pedestrian crossings take more risks than I do when I climb into the aircraft.'

But he quickly added: 'I need a co-pilot over the Ocean. I can't navigate for toffee.'

An unusual method of crossing the ocean had been worked out by John Webb, 38-year-old Managing Director of four British racing circuits, including Brands Hatch. He was determined to cross the Atlantic sitting in a car. His scheme—worked out in great pre-Race secrecy—was to jump into a factory-fresh export Ford Cortina at the foot of the Post Office Tower, drive it to the Airport and directly to a BOAC Boeing 707 jet. With co-driver Geoffrey Clarke, Webb planned to stay inside the car all the way over the Atlantic. On touch-down he expected to drive it out through customs and deliver it at a special sales counter set up by Fords outside the Empire State Building. Webb believed that the Cortina, bought by John Hearst, grandson of the late American newspaper tycoon Randolph Hearst, would have the 'Quickest delivery time for a British export car to an American customer'.

Not everyone was as tuned up to the export selling potentialities of the Air Race. Certainly not most of the British plane-makers. At the end of March a letter arrived from Handley Page Ltd finally turning down the idea of entering a Jetstream in the Race. The excuse given was 'the increasing pressure on our programme of work means that it is now virtually impossible for us to make an aircraft available'. Behind that formal note was a tale of slipped production schedules and a fear that even with a handicap bonus of 408 minutes on the London–New York leg and 321 minutes the other way round, the turbo-prop-engined Jetstream would not show up very well when compared with other executive jet aircraft.

It was bitter news. Ironically, as already recounted, it had been because of pressure from contacts within Handley Page that the handicap system had been worked out at all. It was also with an understandable desire to help boost British aircraft exports that Winston Churchill Jnr. had offered to co-pilot the Jetstream, or any other British manufactured aircraft, in the Race. To give punch to the point, the organizers agreed that he should be one of the very earliest competitors away on the first day. Handley Page's attitude was not surprising, but it did underline the lack of aggressive salesmanship on the part of Britain's plane-makers.

The proposition was too good to throw away, so I made a quick check among other manufacturers. The response was pathetic. Shorts in Belfast, manufacturers of the plodding turbo-prop Skyvans, were against entering in spite of the enthusiasm of Rod Rodwell, their publicity man. Nor could I interest Britten Norman, who regularly ferry twin-engined Islanders over to America, and Hawker Siddeley's executive jet division had already given the thumbs down to the participation of one of their HS 125s. Just as things looked their blackest, it seemed as though the British Aircraft Corporation were going to be able to enter an executive version of the medium-sized One-Eleven jet. The proposition collapsed, leaving Beagle, the part government-owned light-aircraft manufacturer, as the last remaining hope. Encouragingly, a quick check turned up the fact that they were delivering a Beagle 206 twin-engined light aircraft to America around the Race time. But Beagle chairman Peter Masefield, after making inquiries, said it was impossible to get the American company who had purchased the Beagle to allow it to be entered in the Race. With that, young Churchill dropped out.

Somewhere, Peter Masefield, who is also chairman of the British Airports Authority, got his wires crossed. For that Beagle was later entered in the Air Race by the Miami Aviation Corporation—the American distributor of Beagle's wares—and it won a prize.

It almost seemed as though the aircraft manufacturers had entered into a conspiracy not to show up one another's weaknesses by pitting products against one another in the full glare of the publicity attendant upon the Air Race. For though individuals readily entered their light aircraft, not one of the British or American manufacturers did.

So much for the spirit of Alcock and Brown! In the end, the fact that no light aircraft were entered by manufacturers probably made the Air Race far more exciting. It became overwhelmingly an individualistic affair. And individuals breed variety, contrast and excitement. Exercising initiative is a great spur to original thinking, as was humorously illustrated by 25-year-old Kenneth Crutchlow from Edmonton, London, when flying across America towards New York on an internal flight. Suddenly he decided he wanted to enter for the Race. But lacking the necessary currency for the entry fee, he turned to a fellow passenger and pawned his bowler hat for the required twenty-four dollars. Within minutes of landing he had handed the money over to the New York office to secure his place in what the Mexican magazine *Hablemos* was already calling 'The Race of the Century'.

Chapter Nine

DEADLINE APPROACHES

*'In New York we are all pleased at the prospect of
being linked [with London] in such a spectacular
fashion by the Transatlantic Air Race.'*

Mayor John Lindsay of New York.
1st May 1969

OF ALL THE mysteries surrounding the build-up to the Air Race
none was more intriguing, or the subject of more speculation,
than that of the requests for entry forms from the office of Laurance Rockefeller. At first it was optimistically assumed that it was
Larry Rockefeller, Laurance's son, who was going to enter the
Race. Rumour had it that he was to use a Lear Jet. When five more
entry forms were requested it gave strength to that line of thinking. But when this was checked with everyone, including air
traffic control, immigration and customs, it didn't quite stand up.
Still, several aviation people in London confidently persisted in
telling us to expect Larry in an executive jet.

When the entry finally arrived, it turned out that neither Larry
nor Laurance was taking part. What had happened was that Larry
had been working on a project to enter a young East Harlem
Negro slum worker in the Race. He was 26-year-old Marvin L.
Gathers, whose entry was officially sponsored by one of Larry's
pet projects, the East 121st Street Neighborhood Association.
Marvin, who comes from the Bronx, works for an organization
called Street Academy, which has the task of looking after High
School drop-outs.

Business backing for worthwhile causes was also a keynote of
several British entries, but none was more spectacular, or colourful,

than the team of ten London University students who went into the Race on behalf of the MacIntyre Schools for the Mentally Handicapped. The attempts wouldn't cost the charity anything since all the students' flight expenses were met by individual business firms sponsoring their attempt to win the £5,000 ($12,000) Butlin's prize for the most meritorious non-winning effort. Any money they won or raised during the Race period would go towards the cost of opening a village for the education and life-time care of the mentally handicapped, on a 40-acre site at Westoning, near Bedford.

Four of the students, sponsored by the Carnaby Street firm, 'Just Men of Chelsea' and led by 20-year-old Christopher Foley of Moston, Cheshire, were kitting themselves out in the style of the 1770s to 'reclaim America as a British colony'. In marked contrast, 19-year-old Janice Thorpe, of Little Shelford, Cambridgeshire, was dolled up in an eye-catching mini skirt as she hurried off in a vintage car during a rehearsal. Her trip was sponsored by Pussy Galore of the Henry Moss Group of companies. Other members of the group had lined up stage coaches and vintage and modern cars for the first leg of the trip to Heathrow, before starting on the roundabout air route to New York, where they would link up in a procession of vintage cars for the drive to the Empire State Building. They were taking with them Kenneth Newton-Wright, founder-secretary of the MacIntyre Schools, who was returning to America for the first time in twenty-five years. On the last occasion he had stayed at the White House as one of Sir Winston Churchill's personal couriers; at that time he was a Royal Marine.

News leaked out that the Queen's cousin, Prince Michael of Kent, was entering the Race when he was photographed trying out a speed boat on the Thames. He was part of two-man team, entering for the 11th Hussars, using the same RAF VC 10 as the paratroopers. Until the cameraman's shutter clicked early one evening just before the final deadline for entries was reached, all the transactions had been carried out in the name of the Prince's race partner, Capt. Eric Westropp of Wareham, Dorset. It had been the Prince's own idea to enter and his inquiry was received with the first batch of applications for information which arrived after the announcement of the intention to hold the Race had been made.

One closely guarded secret was not revealed until the 18th April deadline was reached—not even to the organizers. From an exchange of letters to an address in France we had learnt that a Lieutenant-Colonel Hunt was intent on taking part in the Race and that he was leaving very little to chance. In fact, thanks to several points he raised about the definitions of 'sponsorship' we were well armed with legal opinion to sort out queries on this score raised against the actual prize-winners. But not until his entry form arrived did we discover which category the retired Colonel was aiming for. It turned out to be the Aer Lingus-*Daily Sketch* prize he was after on the London–New York leg, and the BOAC prize on the return. His original scheme was to make his attempt on 7th May, using motor-cycles for the ground legs. Then, on reaching New York, he was to phone his 17-year-old daughter Elizabeth a military-style briefing in preparation for her attempt the following day.

Though Colonel Hunt's plans became clear immediately entries closed, there was little on the entry forms submitted by Peter Hammond of the Green Diamond Club to indicate the detailed research that had gone into the preparation of his attack on the BOAC £5,000 ($12,000) New York to London prize. It was designed as a complete club effort by members whose main object is 'to promote International Friendship leading to perpetual World Peace', but at the same time to prove that they are not 'a namby pamby bunch of people'. There was nothing weak or 'cissified' about the Green Diamonds, who turn over 25 per cent of their annual financial surplus to international charities.

From the outset they aimed to prove that they know what they are talking about when it comes to organizing foreign travel, and so, although 'completely unfamiliar with New York', they set about planning their Race-winning strategy.

Choosing the day and time was one of the most critical pre-Race exercises. They put all the take-off times from Kennedy through a Port of London Authority computer to see which flight had the best record for the shortest Air Traffic Control delays. It came out as a BOAC VC 10 flight leaving Kennedy Airport

8 p.m. on Sunday. So Peter Hammond settled on 4th May for his first attempt. His next step was to endeavour to get the maximum co-operation from the airline. That presented snag number one.

Initial approaches to BOAC for special help produced an uncompromising refusal. BOAC said that, as sponsors, they could not give preferential treatment to any competitor. Nevertheless, an official refusal didn't deter them and they quickly established direct contact with the BOAC VC 10 Fleet. Without hesitation it was agreed that a pilot and a navigator, who were ex-Green Diamond Club members, should be crew-members on the day Hammond made his attempt. For although the official BOAC attitude was geared to ensuring that they could not be accused by other airlines of cutting corners and breaking rules to make sure their prize went to a competitor flying on a BOAC jet, the actual down-the-line staff were, in general, all out to make sure that a BOAC passenger won. For that reason Hammond, and many other competitors, got a helping hand from the airline staff.

The next major task that the Green Diamonds applied themselves to was the trip in from London Airport to the Post Office Tower. An examination of helicopter sites followed and, quickly ruling out Battersea Helipad as being too far away, they settled on the Thames. That is where their jobs helped, for most of them are connected with the Port of London Authority. They spent hours studying the river flow, winds, tides and traffic movement to earmark the exact spot to moor the barge which would be used as a temporary helipad. Satisfied, they sent in their entry form. But it contained only the barest details and gave no clue to the unexpected gimmicks they had worked out. They were not prepared for anyone to cash in on their exhaustive research.

Similarly the Automobile Association were being inundated with requests for 'secret' routes. On the eve of the Air Race a spokesman said: 'Entrants have come to us for really detailed road routes from the Post Office Tower and their take-off point—or vice versa. Others have had us checking out routes they have worked out themselves. Some of them are quite unbelievable. I've known London for twenty-five years but four or five of the competitors have come up with traffic-beating routes which I didn't appreciate existed. I shall certainly follow some of them myself when the Race is all over.'

Some competitors even got the A.A. to check on the timing of traffic signals and working out the time intervals necessary for cars to be positioned on activator studs to get the lights all to show green to allow a motor-cycle to burst through at top speed without fear of the light turning against it.

After surveying the routes most competitors had decided that the best road transport to use was the motor-cycle. For once, the much spurned vehicle was going to hold its own against all comers, either dashing to helicopter pads or directly between the check-in stations and the airports. For world speed record holders Martin Hoder and Charlie Rous from Kettering, Northamptonshire, it meant a busy week. Hodder, who broke six-hour, 1,000 kilometre and twelve-hour records at Monza, Italy, in July 1968, had as his first assignment to rush Jersey businessman Terry Connolly to the Airport. Rous, holder of the 750 cc. standing-start kilometre world record, was lined up to speed Stephan Wilkinson, of *Flying* magazine, to Gatwick Airport to pick up his Beagle.

Also running a shuttle service for competitors was motor-cycle enthusiast Allan Robinson from Ripley, Surrey, looking after the BSA Triumph operation in London. Over in New York, off-duty 'speed cop' Andrew Davey was about to start a 500-mile marathon running contestants on the back of his 120-mph machine.

In addition to such 'elder statesmen' of the motor-cycle art there were dozens of youngsters turning out to help. For once the sight of leather jackets, glinting metal studs, and highly polished individualistic machines didn't cause anyone to recoil in horror. In fact, around the Post Office Tower they were a welcome sight, ready at an instant to fill some gap in a contestant's carefully laid plan. Together with the military motor-cyclists, the men with the two-wheeled machines proved just how much time is lost around town once you step into the four-wheeled car—even when the speed limit is observed. Prior to and during the Air Race week, the concourse around the Control Centre at the Post Office Tower looked like the parking ground for a motor-cyclists' convention, and a well-behaved crowd they were; even the police and traffic wardens were lavish in their praise for their efforts.

They were quite a contrast to the two rickshaws that were destined to turn up at the Post Office Tower. The first was essential equipment for kimono-clad 22-year-old Miss Setsuko Kusaka, a ground hostess with Japan Airlines, and one of the three official entrants for the Airline. Prior to the Race she caused quite a stir when she handed over the entrance fee for herself, Martin Sillwood and Brian Dumbelton to the Royal Aero Club's John Blake, for instead of a pocket-book sized cheque for £30 ($72) she handed over a giant scroll with the entry fee written on a traditional print of Mount Fiji. It gained an immediate place of honour in the organizers' headquarters and at one stage threw all the financial calculations out because on cashing up at the end of the day we were £30 short of the amount listed. Just as we were about to go through hundreds of entries, marking off cheques and cash against receipts, the scroll cheque was remembered and everyone breathed a vast sigh of relief—after all, counting money at five in the morning after a non-stop thirty-two-hour stint is not the easiest of tasks.

The second rickshaw arrived in England from Singapore secretly in a submarine, having been carried in the torpedo compartment. The rickshaw was the idea of Captain Ray Lygo, who thought it would add a touch of Far Eastern nostalgia for one of the two seamen from H.M.S. *Nubian* to use the rickshaw as part of his transport to link up with the Aer Lingus flight to New York. Completing the 'Jolly Jack Tar' image, he was to carry a kit-bag and a parrot in a cage, though for U.S. health regulation reasons the parrot wouldn't go all the way and the seaman would pick up a second parrot at Kennedy Airport.

News of the unconventional performance came after Captain Lygo finally made the momentous announcement of the Naval entry on 10th April. The Fleet Air Arm were entering three supersonic Rolls-Royce-powered Phantom jets. His quiet deliberations had paid off, for it had been as much a victory for steering the project through the unpredictable government political machine —especially the financial departments—as it had been ensuring that the back-up for the attempt could be mounted.

On handing over the entry forms to the Editor of the *Daily Mail*, Arthur Brittenden, Captain Lygo said:

We all enjoy a race, especially if, as in the case of this one, it is a race between highly skilled teams. It is no 'gimmick' and by no accident that the Royal Navy's is to be the only British supersonic entry.

It results from the steady development of our Naval air-weapon system which has gone on for over fifty years. Naval aviation started before Alcock and Brown's achievement and it reaches its peak with the Phantom. Fifty years of training and breeding produced this entry and it is a moment for pride to be the first in the field with this aircraft. [By inference he was referring to the fact that the Royal Navy had got Phantoms operational before the RAF.]

Like everything else in the complex world of defence, however, it rests for its success on the co-operation of others.

We have planned and worked in harmony with the Royal Air Force, on whose tankers our success rests, and we depend on H.M.S. *Nubian* to effect the last vital rendezvous between tanker and fighter, approaching each other at nearly twice the speed of sound. Helicopters will be essential in the terminal phases and our world-wide experience in this field —another Naval first—will be used to advantage.

If he sounded confident, Ray Lygo had every reason to be so. With the collapse of the U.S. Navy opposition, a Navy Phantom win was a foregone conclusion. It was simply a question of by how much they would beat the Harrier and the RAF V bombers, and to what extent they could manage to snatch the publicity away from the Royal Air Force's revolutionary jump-jet.

News of the Navy entries, particularly the decision to send two ratings—Leading Seaman Stewart Dow from Leyland, Lancashire, and Leading Mechanician Howard Evans of Neath, Glamorgan— on a commercial airline was received with mixed feelings in Whitehall. So much so that no less a person than the Chancellor, Roy Jenkins, Britain's exponent of the economic squeeze, was prompted to write a 'scolding' note to the Navy, questioning the use of public money to enable the men to enter the Race. In fact, he was misinformed, as the fares were paid for by non-public funds. That they should ever be questioned at all gave some indication of the low value the Treasury places upon Service morale.

In the final week before the entries closed, would-be competitors began flocking to the Air Race Bureau in Temple Avenue, between Fleet Street and the Thames Embankment, and into Jeffrey Blyth's office in New York. For some it was a visit merely to hand over cash and entry forms. For others it was to clarify a final point. Dozens dropped in just to see where we were, while many more appeared urgently seeking advice.

Among the latter were William Neil Finlayson and Clive Easton, both newly qualified commercial pilots who had just passed out from the London School of Flying at Elstree. They were looking for a sponsor to pay for the cost of their hiring a light aircraft. With 440 flying hours between them they hoped to win the £5,000 ($12,000) Butlin prize. They both said they needed the money to help offset the costs of learning to fly. It was the first of many trips they made, each time leaving with a handful of names of potential sponsors, each time returning more dejected than ever, having found, as John Wilsey had before them, that there was precious little money about in London in April.

One of the arrivals in the London office during the final countdown to the close of entries was 27-year-old BEA steward Peter Palmer. He had decided to enter by taking advantage of the concession tickets available to BEA staff on BOAC flights. But there is one draw-back to such arrangements: Passengers paying full fare always take priority. That is why Peter asked passengers flying BOAC to New York on Monday 5th May a favour: 'Please don't all travel on BA 501'—the flight he had chosen for his trip. Before the Race week he said: 'BOAC have given me a lot of good advice and I am optimistic that I will get on the flight. I'm dashing to the airport on the back of a ton-up motor-bike, with only seconds to spare before take-off, so I hope that no last-minute passenger has turned up to take my seat.' None did, and he achieved a time of 8 hours 30 minutes and 23 seconds for the London–New York leg.

The BEA steward decided to take part in the race entirely unsponsored, simply because he wanted to have 'a bash'. Similar thoughts crossed the mind of Captain William A. Guenon of the U.S. 7 Special Operations Squadron, and he filed off his entry form. He returned a commendable time of 7 hours 28 minutes and 30 seconds.

One late entry was one of the most anxiously awaited in the light-aircraft class. It was from world record holder Sheila Scott, who decided not only to compete in the *Daily Mail* enterprise, but also to try, at the same time, to break her own North Atlantic record using the same single Lycoming-engined aircraft, a Piper Comanche, which she flew round the world to break sixty-seven world-class records. Though cramped for space, because of extra fuel tanks, oxygen and survival kit, Sheila had promised to find room for a horseshoe from a shire horse at the Whitbread Brewery, owned by Colonel Whitbread, who was one of her sponsors.

For the executive jet category a handicap system was introduced. At one end of the scale this gave a bonus time of 185 minutes to a Hawker Siddeley 125 jet, and a 5-minute bonus time to an executive jet version of the Douglas DC 9. The Jet Star could collect 122 minutes and the Gumman Gulf Stream I, 292 minutes.

With only a week to go before the entries closed, only 69-year-old Sir William Butlin had entered an executive jet, a Hawker Siddeley 125 which he had leased from Greagory Air Services. The holiday camp millionaire was determined to have a go and repeat his success of ten years before, when, during the London to Paris Air Race, he had been placed fourth.

This single entry, with the deadline only a week away, was a bad omen for the executive jet class.

Chapter Ten

THREE DAYS OF HELL

'No man who is in a hurry is quite civilized.'

Will Durant

THE MOMENT ARRIVES when the kidding has to stop and facts have to take the place of conjecture. That moment arrived for the Air Race on Monday 14th April one hundred and eleven hours before the midnight deadline on 18th April. For months it had been necessary to resort to devious ploys to prevent the chilling truth about the actual number of entrants being made public, either within our own organization, or to sponsors or the press. The blunt truth would only have got them panicky, for they could hardly be expected to appreciate that one of the natural hazards of running such a promotion as the Air Race was that would-be competitors held out to the last moment before finally committing themselves to taking part.

Long ago, I had developed a quick-fire morale-rousing technique of glibly explaining, under questioning about numbers, that there would definitely be between 300 and 500 competitors. Every indication pointed that way. A survey of people from Britain who had written for information gave the figures credibility. But there is a vast difference between a forecast and a fact.

That is why my stock phrase froze on the tip of my rolled-up tongue when I was confronted by Reg Watson, head of the Group's Buying Department that Monday morning.

'Will two hundred and fifty commemorative medals be enough?' he asked, his brown eyes searching my face intently. 'Or shall I get them to strike some more?' He was committing me irrevocably to telling the truth. His unexpected bombshell left me groping for words. For a few moments I said nothing. He let me sweat.

On another occasion I might have turned round and suggested he double it. What tugged at my conscience at that moment was that barely half an hour before, I had been dejectedly adding up the response with the Royal Aero Club's Competitions Manager, John Blake. Dejectedly was the right word. At the end of the count there were only 40 fully paid up entries. And the deadline was less than four days away.

The gap between 40 and 250 seemed ominously large as I stood there in front of Watson's desk. Even when you earmarked a handful for key officials, there were enough medals for over two hundred competitors. For once, my bounding optimism began to ebb. Not until that moment had I doubted my own calculations. But, charged with the responsibility of having a new batch of costly commemorative medals struck, I hesitated.

Watson detected my nervousness. With unusual impatience he pressed me: 'How many? A hundred and fifty? Two hundred?'

Norman Heath, who had burst into Watson's office with me on a totally different mission, hadn't said a word. I looked at him but, like Watson, his eyes were following my reactions as though waiting to see if I had the courage of my earlier convictions. To mislead them when they were about to place a costly order would be unforgivable. Even though ninety per cent of the 186 entries for the London to Paris Air Race had turned up during the last three days, it would be an enormous gamble to expect a repeat ten years later.

The time for bluffing was over. Watson needed as exact an estimate as possible.

In fact, the 40 entries received included only a handful of the 20 competitors from whom Doug Kelley had received firm seat bookings for the Aer Lingus-Irish flights on 7th or 8th May. The figure didn't take into account the 60 or so people who had confirmed their 'definite intention' to enter following an interim check of 2,500 people who had applied for details of the Race from the London Bureau. Another 30 or more people who would be entered by Capitol International Airways, if our talks came to a successful conclusion later that week, could be added in. Even so,

G

that was still way below the 250 mark, however you added it up. My courage faltered.

'All right, let's stick at 250,' I said. 'We can always re-order.'

Watson relaxed, tension evaporated from everyone's face.

'That's exactly what I would have done in your place,' declared Watson, already his normal affable self.

We all laughed, and Norman and I left without concluding the business for which we had gone there. For the first time, I had an uneasy feeling that the target figure of 300 was going to be almost impossible to attain. Not that failure to do so would have wrecked the promotion. For, provided the Race created more interest than the London to Paris event, the *Mail* would have benefited. But to get fewer than 200 competitors would seriously restrict its chances of becoming a great event. This was important, because the public likes to be associated with success. That is the point at which they begin to turn to a newspaper, and are proud to be counted among its readers. That was the kind of breakthrough we were aiming at.

Tuesday morning's post should have brought in about 30 or 40 fresh entry forms. It didn't. There were only 4 and none of them was accompanied by money, so officially they did not count.

After that shock, the telephones began ringing, keeping the three secretaries and me so busy that there was no time to worry about the missing competitors. Under journalistic pressure, I began to stall. For the first time during the build-up, I deliberately glossed over the number of 'paid-up' entries and began giving out addresses of dozens of people who had not actually sent in forms, but who I was positive were about to do so.* At that point, with three days to go, the outlook was decidedly bleak.

Fortunately, regional press, radio and television coverage had begun to build up, largely feeding off information sent months before which identified potential competitors. Enthusiastic producers had done the rest, lining up dozens of prospective entrants. Gradually, interest in the Race began to snowball, urged on by a burst of publicity in the Group's own newspapers. But this was not translated into tangible results—entry forms.

* Only three or four of the people whose names were handed out did not in fact officially enter.

Wednesday morning's post was again bad. But it was a freak delivery. In the afternoon, the Royal Aero Club received 14 entries, and 6 came straight to the Bureau.

Just before I hurried off to an evening round-up conference with Brian Harpur, Jeffrey Blyth phoned from New York. He reported that they were being crowded out of their office by Americans demanding entry forms. As a result they had run out of forms, and even with a photocopying machine turning out emergency supplies, they were not able to cope. Even as I spoke to him his secretaries were holding on to calls from Los Angeles, Florida and Arizona. As soon as we promised to air-freight him new supplies he was off to sort out the problems of a couple who had flown in from Washington to sign up for the event.

Excitement was beginning to build up on both sides of the Atlantic. By Thursday morning, a line-up of people brandishing money and entry forms was waiting in my office. There were a cable from Tasmania and one from New Brunswick demanding immediate information. The three secretaries were fighting a losing battle with the telephones, and suddenly the 100 mark was reached, even without the Capitol Airways party.

A lunch-time meeting had been called by the Managing Director, M. J. Hussey, to enable Brian Harpur to make a full-scale presentation to key executives from the editorial, advertising, circulation and business sides of the *Mail, Sketch* and *Evening News*. It was to be a pep talk to convince everyone that the Race promotion was a winner and to get them personally involved in supporting the enterprise. Surprisingly enough, one of the hardest problems any promotions man in the British newspaper industry has to face is convincing his own paper's editorial staff that a project is worthwhile.

With a superb sense of showmanship, Harpur had arranged for the walls of the Directors' dining-room on the sixth floor of Harmsworth House to be covered from ceiling to floor with newspapers and magazine cuttings about the Race which had appeared in papers throughout the world. There were pieces from papers published in France, Germany, Italy, Spain, Japan, Australia and even the Iron Curtain countries, as well as Britain, America and Canada. Vivid red headlines of a Swiss article vied for attention with the delicate colour photographs in a Mexican magazine, snappy headlines from the North American continent contrasted sharply with the parochial headings of some of the British provincial papers. It all added up to an international stamp of approval.

As a scene setter, the cuttings were superb. Harpur skilfully used them as a back-drop as he unveiled the full details of the operation and, pointed out the uses for all the signs and placards that had been especially assembled. He seemed to be promising each newspaper the most newsworthy event of the years. His enthusiasm was catching. By the end of the session, even the critics from the early days were won over. Their conversion was genuine.

The scene was set. All it needed was the players.

And how they came in! Pandemonium broke out at 8 a.m. on Friday, 18th April. Apple-cheeked Joan Farthing's desk looked like a corner of the Bank of England, with British, American and Swiss cheques piled high, dollar bills and pound notes clipped to entry forms which were arriving too quickly to allow the normal cash clearance to be carried out.

By mid-morning competitors were overflowing into the corridors from the three Air Race Bureau offices in Temple House. A taxi shuttle service had to be arranged to keep pace with the forms sent direct to the Royal Aero Club and which had to be retrieved for processing. Air-freight messengers arrived with packages from the New York office. There was a constant buzz of telephone inquiries as competitors made last minute checks before setting off on foot, by car, taxi, bus or underground to bring their entry forms in personally and be sure not to miss the midnight deadline.

No one had lunch. The pressure was too great. At 5 p.m., at which time it had originally been decided to switch the operation over to the second floor of Harmsworth House, people were still arriving. Yet it was essential the move be made, for the new location was to be in the room next to the machine needed to copy every entry twenty times. John Brewer battled with the task of making the switch piecemeal as the rest of us tried to keep on top of the surging tide of applications. The timing of the move was important because a vetting committee of Royal Aero Club members was due to arrive and begin checking the validity of entries. Somehow, by 6 p.m. the transfer was almost complete and the Bureau, swollen with help from the Buying department, were working from their new desks to process the duplicates being spewed out by the copying machine.

It had been decided that entries should be successively scrutinized by Beverley Snook, Maurice Imray and John Blake, on behalf of the Royal Aero Club. Their task was to see that the forms had been filled out according to the Race rules and to check that aircraft and methods of transport being used were capable of participating in the Race.

Before the original yellow forms were handed to the Royal Aero Club trio, they had to be copied and arranged for rapid distribution, as soon as the processing was completed. They were destined to go to the Group's newspapers, BBC radio and TV, Independent Television News, all the co-sponsors, as well as key government bodies including the Board of Trade and Customs and Immigration authorities. Yet another copy was used by two of the secretaries to prepare a master list of competitors and a label for each entry received.

The Royal Aero Club found problems arising in two main areas: ambiguity in filling in the details of the flight across the Atlantic, or vague or missing information; and a small number of light-aircraft entries where further information was required on the validity of the entry from a safety point of view. Stephen Lowell Smith's balloon entry was the first to be thrown on to the query file.

But to aid the administrative process, and in view of the fact that the event was to start within sixteen days, all forms against which queries had been raised were provisionally accepted, the one exception being Smith's balloon. That was immediately referred to General Brooke Allen and the National Aeronautic Association of America, with a note saying that the Royal Aero Club would accept it only if the NAA specifically requested them so to do. A half dozen light-aircraft entries who looked doubtful starters were also passed to the NAA for close scrutiny.

As London became the initial sifting centre for all the entries, American as well as British, it was arranged for Ken Corney, the Mail Group's Exhibitions Manager, who was to be in charge in New York, to collect all entries originating in America and take them there on Saturday for scrutiny by General Brooke Allen.

Neat and tidy in theory: in practice it was chaotic. As a direct consequence of the glut of last-day entries, instead of our being able to spread the work over a two week period everything had to be done in a matter of hours.

Ambiguous wording in the rules added to the congestion, because it caused many forms to be filled in incorrectly. In particular, mistakes were made when competitors assumed that one entry form covered them for competing in both directions. It didn't. Another weakness was that the forms did not stipulate how exact the information about ground transportation should be; a slip which was to cause untold headaches over the following weeks.

Processing such queries took time. As we broke for a buffet supper at 9 p.m., only a quarter of the entries had been dealt with. It was like stepping into a paper warehouse disturbed by a whirlwind when we returned to the fray. Forms lay on a dozen different desks in various states of processing. Teetering above the rims of twenty trays were huge mounds of copied entry forms; stacked on trestle tables could be seen piles of envelopes, already stuffed with competitors' lapel tags, car stickers, Race instructions, specimens of the vital time card and a background note. They were ready to be united with the key Race acceptance document quoting their official race number.

To maintain an orderly numbering of competitors to coincide with their time and date of start, it was necessary to have each form processed by the Royal Aero Club. That was taking time, and finally Norman Heath and I took over the bulk of the remainder of the verification, except where light aircraft were involved; this enabled the Royal Aero Club team to leave before midnight.

After they left, several competitors turned up with their entry forms. One group were backing Jeffrey Dearden from Epping; another competitor, Frederick Robinson, arrived from the Wirral, Cheshire, to put in his light-aircraft entry. Originally he was to have flown on a scheduled air service but he decided to charter a light aircraft, even though it would take most of his savings. He believed it was worth it, because, as he said, 'It will be the only chance in my life-time to take part in something as dramatic and historic as the Air Race.'

Clement Freud was one of the last to arrive. We had been expecting him in a fire engine or an ambulance; instead, he quietly pushed through the swing door unheralded, bringing with him three entry forms: one for himself and one each for his son Dominic and his son's school chum Dominic Faulder, both of them only 10 years old. Clement, an assiduous student of the rules, insisted on handing over ten pounds in cash for his son's entry fee so that no one could say that he had been sponsored by his father. To have been so classified would have ruled him out for the *Daily Sketch* prize, and Freud was determined his son would win that, while he took the higher prize money in the Aer Lingus category. He was leaving nothing to chance. It was an unnecessary precaution, but typical of his approach to the Race.

Even under ideal conditions, relieved of all interruptions, and with treble the staff, the work load would have been gigantic. For our small team, constantly dealing with a flow of queries, it was crippling. When midnight arrived, with dozens of entries stacked in arrival baskets awaiting processing, telex messages from Jeffrey Blyth alerted us to the fact that more were on their way from his office. He also gave a long list of Americans who had phoned to check that their entries—posted direct to London—had in fact arrived. A quarter of them had not, but it was agreed to count them as legitimate entries when they subsequently turned up. Shortly after midnight John Drysdale, who had been in charge of making nearly ten thousand copies of the original entry forms, had to leave to take home the two secretaries on loan from the Buying department.

The early morning vigil continued, led by Brian Harpur until he was persuaded to break off at 3 a.m. By that time we were beginning to bring order out of chaos. While I took over the Royal Aero Club vetting task, Norman and Joan Farthing began grouping entries in time and date order ready for the allocation of a Race number. Once an entry form had been allocated a race number and marked up with any queries, six master copies had to be made before the acceptance slip was made out. It was then added to the contents of the envelopes ready for posting.

Time was without meaning. Hours before, we had stopped being a curiosity for the night watchmen. But when we heard the growing noises of early morning traffic, everyone realized that it was the bustle of Saturday morning business traffic. Smartly, Graham Beverley, the office boy, and Joan Farthing were sent off home. Armed with coffee and sandwiches, the rest kept going.

When Ken Corney arrived at noon, he was shattered to see us still there. Even at that point we had not been able to process every application, but he was able to take to America over 140 entries of people starting from New York. His first task would be to discuss them with General Brooke Allen, and cable us with any queries. Twenty-four hours later the first of his queries arrived. At 3 p.m. it was decided to break off for the day. We had worked non-stop for over thirty-one hours.

With 300 confirmed entries and more forms still to be vetted, there was at last something to shout about in a press release. Even though each entry form had not been double checked, and many were en route from America, the fact that some competitors were racing in both directions put the total number of entry forms received to over 375.

What a collection! A quick check showed that over 200 helicopters, 500 motor-cycles, a dozen power boats, taxis by the score, buses, trains, stage coaches and even a rowing boat had been hired, begged or borrowed, to help competitors to win. Among the entries were competitors using 28 light aircraft to make 40 Atlantic crossings, including famed American aviators Max Conrad and E. D. Weiner, four times winner of the American intercontinental races, who entered a Mustang. From Britain three women entered in light aircraft, including Sheila Scott. Four competitors aimed at using balloons for part or, in the case of Stephen Lowell Smith, all the way. Anne Alcock, the 18-year-old niece of Sir John, was one of the 54 entries received from Capitol International Airways, and she was destined to be the first competitor away.

Her entry was predictable. But that could hardly be said for the one received from the Royal Canadian Air Force Number

Ten Experimental Squadron based at Shearwater, Nova Scotia. They had decided to commemorate the Alcock and Brown flight by flying across the Atlantic in a CH SS-2 helicopter. It was to be refuelled at sea from two helicopter-carrying destroyers between Goose Bay, Labrador and Lossiemouth, Scotland. First hint that there had been that something was afoot came with a cable message in April from Dartmouth, Nova Scotia, from a Lieutenant-Commander Cook, requesting Air Race details. They were duly despatched. Nothing more was heard until an envelope was opened just before the Friday midnight deadline. Out dropped a completed form, a cheque for $24 (£10) and a letter from the Commanding Officer of the unit. Lt-Cmdr Cook was to be the entrant.

The letter said:

> In the event that our transatlantic effort be judged worthy of financial award it is our intent to donate the proceeds to a suitable medical research organization located in the United Kingdom which specializes in children's disease.
>
> You are to be congratulated on organizing such an imaginative event, which undoubtedly has stirred the aviation pioneering spirit in many people. It is with this spirit that we hopefully will join in this historically significant and worthy undertaking.

But the Number Ten Experimental Squadron of the Royal Canadian Air Force were destined never to join in the 'historically significant' undertaking. Though it had been indicated in the letter accompanying the entry form that official approval from the Canadian Forces authorities had not been received, the writer said the indications were that the approval would be given.

It wasn't. All hell broke out in Ottawa when news of the bid to enter the Race reached the politicians and other Service Chiefs. The row went on for a couple of days. The rest of the Royal Canadian Air Force were angry because permission for them to take part had already been turned down, and they did not want to see a specialized unit grab all the honours; while many others believed that to have no official Canadian representation in the Race was a major snub to the memory of the two great aviators who had pioneered the way across the Atlantic, using Canada as a springboard.

In the end the politicians had the final say. It was a definite NO! They were having nothing to do with the Great Air Race.

The official reason for the turn-down was that 'administrative reasons' did not allow them to make available the two helicopter destroyers which were essential if the CH SS-2 helicopter was to fly the Atlantic. That was about as lame an excuse as has ever been given. The two destroyers were earmarked and all ready to go when the official cancellation order arrived.

From a military point of view, participation in the Air Race would have been of great training value, and absolutely within the terms of reference of the Experimental Squadron. But at the time of the release of the information on 20th April, nothing of the row boiling up in Canada was known.

Saturday had been productive. Sharp at 8.30 on Sunday morning the small Air Race Bureau team were back at work wrestling with the remaining problems and drawing up query lists for telephone checking the following day. There was no diabolic driving force pushing us on. It was simply that everyone realized that with only fourteen days to go before the start of the Race it was necessary to sort out all the queries before the normal working week began on Monday. Only in that way would it be possible to contact people and get back answers, readjust the starting schedules and prepare the information boards and published lists which were an essential part of the operation. Precise timings were needed because a missed elevator could mean a wait of more than two minutes, which could wreck a competitor's detailed planning and lead to his missing his connection at the airport. For the Air Race to be successful, the public and the press had to be able to follow what was going on, and that meant scheming everything into an orderly pattern.

That day, our only break was at the Sterling Area Club—whose owner, Alex Sterling, had wanted to enter an ostrich as a means of beating the one-way traffic snarl-up around London's Post Office Tower but could not get one from South Africa in time.

Working with nervous rapidity to overcome exhaustion's soporific power, we tackled the assembled yellow entry forms:

filled in Race numbers—in red ink—checked off the entry fee—in green—made query notes along the margins, transferred the 'action' comments on to the acceptance forms and by two o'clock on Monday morning had them all completed, enveloped and ready to post. Bulging from the boot of Norman Heath's car, the packages were taken directly to the main British postal sorting office at Mount Pleasant.

After a minimum of sleep, we all reappeared in the office less than six hours later, swinging into action to prepare a mass of schedules from the tentative list of entrants. Quickly, other departments were set to work telephoning queries through to competitors, confirming starting times, pointing out errors, checking insurance cover, asking for money from those who had forgotten to send it, or ensuring that people who had filled out an eastbound and a westbound attempt on a single form realized that they needed to have a separate one for each direction.

By midnight Monday, after three days of hell, it was possible to announce the receipt of 390 entries from 365 individual competitors—the difference being made up of those who were making attempts in both directions. Our problems were far from solved; about 60 per cent in the next thirteen days discovered some reason for changing their time of start, method of ground transport or category. From Monday onwards the telephones never stopped ringing. Rather like some over-life-sized-tycoon figure from a Hollywood movie, I was compelled to place a swivel chair in the centre of the office to keep pace with the jangling of six telephones. Only then was it possible effectively to keep abreast of the ceaseless torrent of press calls, competitors' queries and sponsors' pleadings that babbled from the battery of telephones and were unanswerable by my three secretaries. Next door Norman was under similar pressure, and we still had thousands of administrative points to clarify and set in motion. As it became more difficult to reach us when we were tied up on other extensions, the telephone bells would go on interminably. The *Mail* and *Sketch* switchboards became jammed with waiting Air Race calls. At one point, having escaped from the office for a quick sandwich meal, I tried to phone the office. The first extension number I asked for was engaged, so was the second, and the third ... at that point the Fleet Street 6000 switchboard operator said every extension was engaged.

'I have six people waiting for extension 344, another five on 40 and eight on 41—the Air Race has gone mad,' was his voice-weary explanation. When I said it was my own office I was trying to reach, he replied. 'Now you know what it's like on the outside trying to raise you,' he said, agreeing to put me through immediately a line became free. Seven minutes passed before that was possible.

Similar pressure was being experienced in the New York Bureau and Jeffrey Blyth cabled, 'One requires six arms and two heads to deal with all that's happening here. Phone never stops for a second. Press inquiries now at full flood.'

He could say that again! Between getting out press lists of competitors' names and addresses, accepting changes to completed entry forms and dealing with communications problems affecting the London check-in station and control point, we carried out an analysis of the entries.

On 24th April the 397 entry forms showed that some 226 competitors intended to start from London, compared to 171 from New York. There were no dates or times on 23 entry forms, even though all but 7 had sent in an entry fee. Of the other 374, the majority opted for a first-day start: 114 from London—including the 54 from the Capitol International Airways party—and 68 from New York. Prestige was partly the reason—30 people wanted to be first away from either New York or London—but many chose Sunday for practical reasons. Weather was a vital factor for light aircraft, and a 4th May start gave them the maximum safety margin; they could always change to another day. Predictably, light Sunday traffic, in both New York and London, was another reason, competitors expecting to put up better times than during normal weekday traffic conditions. Ground traffic considerations also accounted for 30 competitors deciding to leave New York on the final Saturday. They expected to hit the least London traffic congestion of the week on the Sunday morning. Inevitably, as the Race week progressed, many changes were made in timings, following lessons learned in practices by competitors. In the light-aircraft classes, 19 competitors opted to fly from London and 24 from New York, including some doing the round trip.

With one exception, the quest for entries had been an overwhelming success. That exception was in the executive jet category. Only one had been received, from Sir William Butlin. It was a bitter blow and presented an immediate problem, for technically Sir William had a walkover and was entitled to one of the two £2,500 ($6,000) prizes and, since only one prize could be won by any one person, the other £2,500 prize would have gone to one of the competitors travelling with him in the plane on the other leg.

Amidst triumph, Brian Harpur sat dejectedly for a moment as he studied the consequences of the entry list. After deep deliberations, a new category was decided upon. It would have a reduced prize of £500 ($1,200) each way, and would be thrown open to competitors using aircraft which had been chartered for either professional or business reasons. Only competitors already entered for the Race would be eligible. This immediately threw an extra prize open to the teams travelling on Capital International Airlines, Stirling Moss using Crosse & Blackwell's chartered VC 10, Ted Drewery's businessmen's charter flight, Ohio millionaire Paul Vaughan's group and the Indian Pilots' Guild of Bombay.

However, Sir William's Hawker Siddeley 125 was unable to fly the Atlantic non-stop. Obviously, some form of handicap had to be worked out to enable his 8-seater executive jet to challenge the 250-seater stretched DC8, the VC 10s and the Boeing 707s now pitted against him. The Royal Aero Club officially refused to work out a formula for such an unusual 'race within a race', but following unofficial advice by one of their members, and by working on a similar basis to the original executive jet handicap—taking range and speed into account—a formula was agreed: solely for the purposes of the two new categories, the HS 125 was given a bonus time of 6 hours for the London–New York leg and 4 hours 50 minutes for the return journey.

Sir William was delighted. 'I am going to enjoy taking on the big jet set,' he declared on hearing the news.

His delight was not shared by the original New York-London leg executive jet category sponsor, the London *Financial Times*, one of the most prosperous newspapers in the world. A daily, readily distinguished by its pink paper and made bulky by an abundance of business and general advertisements, it is mainly devoted to financial matters. Getting it to be a co-sponsor was a masterstroke of initiative in the first place. What now irked the *Financial Times* directors was being associated with a failure. They wanted to quit the Race immediately. Blow though it was, the lack of support had not come as a surprise. For seven months they had been worried by the lack of entries.

As soon as the parlous state of their promotional enterprise was realized they contacted Charles Ranald, chairman of the Castle Britannia Group of Unit Trusts and the original sponsor of the London-New York leg. They wanted to find out if he was ready to withdraw. Ranald was not in so much of a hurry. He saw the value of remaining associated with the Race. While unhappy at the collapse of the executive jet category, when Brian Harpur put the proposition for the new category to him, he accepted.

But the *Financial Times* were resolute. When they formally notified the *Daily Mail* that they were withdrawing, they magnanimously left the timing of the announcement to the *Mail*. They did so to enable an additional sponsor to be found to take over their place in the new category. Quickly Brian Harpur got Grovewood Securities to fill the gap, and news of the reshuffle was announced.* By dropping out, the *Financial Times* forfeited a lot of publicity. But there was no question of their being anti-Air Race, and eagerly they went ahead with arrangements for one of their writers to compete.

His taking part was typical of the decision of many newspapers and magazines not only to cover the Air Race but also to become totally involved. More than twenty journalists from the world's press, radio and TV had been entered by the 18th April deadline. They included Tim Heald of the rival *Daily Express*, who was down to make the run both ways; *Sports Illustrated* entered a two-man staff team; *Life* magazine entered—but failed to take part; the *Sunday Times,* the Sydney *Morning Herald* and *Vi* Magazine from Sweden were all represented. *Flight International's* Humphrey

---

* To keep the prize total at £60,000 (£144,000) it was decided to add in the £3,500 ($8,400) insured value of the trophies.

Wynn took part, carrying a letter from the Lord Mayor of London: Thames TV and the BBC's '24 Hours' both put in runners, and Liam Nolan made live BBC broadcasts from a radio car during his attempts. Most intriguing of all, 80 per cent of the Capitol International Airways Race contingent were staff members of IPC, the International Publishing Corporation, publishers of the world's largest-circulation daily newspaper, the *Daily Mirror*.

Meanwhile the task of preparing for the start of the Race had to go on. Norman Heath's face came to be an all too familiar sight at 3 o'clock in the morning—sometimes it was 4 o'clock. Only an occasional full burst of laughter at the ludicrousness of the situation saved our sanity and kept us even-tempered. And yet there was nothing that could be done about it. To train additional staff would have been impossible in the short space of time available. It was easier to do the bulk of the work ourselves. We had excellent day-time support from our colleagues and the secretaries used to be in at 9 a.m.—we were usually back at our desks by then—and they would stay until 9 and 10 in the evening.

The problem was that we were geared up to handling about 150 to 200 entries. We also misjudged the intense rivalries that the Race was creating. Hundreds of competitors were timing and retiming their routes and asking us to shave off minutes from their starting times to enable them to have a better chance of obtaining a prize. As many as forty changes a day were recorded, and some of the competitors revised their times and methods almost daily. This competitiveness was heightened by the vast amount of pre-publicity the Race was given in rival newspapers and on radio and television. It augured well for the actual event. But before that stage was reached, there was still much to do, including the final meetings with the Post Office. Communication-system checks had to be made, and installations ranging from the timing clocks to closed circuit television had to be tested. Arrangements for crowd control and the organization of the operational nerve centre at the base of the tower had to be scrutinized and approved.

The final meeting for formal Post Office discussions was held on Friday, 25th April. Amicably it drew to a close after all the loose ends had been brought together. Just as we were about to break up, Fred Joyce raised the question of Tina the Brooke Bond

Tea chimpanzee. Raised! Dropped a bombshell would be a more appropriate description. For in a matter-of-fact voice he quietly pointed out that 'Animals are strictly prohibited from being taken up the Tower'. He said he only raised the point because he understood there were plans to put a chimp in the Race!

Tom Gibson, the Central Area Telephone Manager, who was chairing the meeting, simply raised an expressive eyebrow and looked at me. So did the others. To allow a chimp up the Tower would break a strictly enforced rule, and they were not anxious to set precedents.

Purposely, I adopted a matter-of-fact tone, because pressure tactics could easily have led to an impasse.

'Gentlemen, I don't want to persuade you to do anything. We, of course, faced a similar dilemma when we received Tina's entry form. But checking up, we found that a thumb print is a legal signature in Britain, so we had no alternative but to accept the entry form as valid. You may also like to know that your sister state-owned corporation, BOAC, have broken their rules and agreed to carry Tina on a regular passenger flight.

'Normally, this would not affect the issue but, as you know, the press and television have already publicized the chimp. In fact, you could say she has become something of a celebrity.

'It's not for me to tell you what to do. But if the Postmaster-General wants to explain to the world's press just why he banned Tina, then I am afraid he will have to do it without our help. We couldn't be seen to support such a ban.'

No one said a word. There was no indication of whether the point had been taken seriously or not. Lamely, I ended my speech with a flourish: 'Gentlemen, I await the Postmaster-General's decision with interest.'

I didn't dare tell them about the parrot the Navy were going to carry up and down the Tower in a cage. Luckily, at that point, none of us knew about the tortoise, hare and budgerigar that were to take part. Just as well, perhaps; for not knowing, we couldn't seek to overcome rules. It would have been a difficult task to achieve *carte blanche* for animal contestants. In fact, the duty staff used their discretion and no snags occurred. But the publicity given to the chimp had made the formal raising of the problem necessary. As was to be expected, the Postmaster-General gave his formal approval and the way was clear for Tina to steal the headlines.

However much advance planning takes place, the final week before any event tends to be chaotic. The count-down to the Air Race proved to be no exception. If it had been difficult to reach us by telephone before, it now became quite impossible; so much so that Tony Ellis of Hodgkinson Partners, acting for Brooke Bond Tea, was driven to sending me a telegram:

HOW DOES ONE GET TO SPEAK TO YOU A FORLORN CRY FROM THE WILDERNESS = TONY ELLIS

I phoned immediately.

Eric Fielding, the Vickers public relations chief, sent a message by hand asking me to telephone.

Our lives became dominated by the 'speaking machine' and we began to wish Mr Bell had never invented it. To escape, if only momentarily, from their urgent bleatings, Brian Harpur, Norman Heath and I used to hold quick policy-making sessions in the Feathers Bar, next door to the *Evening News,* for during the pre-Race period, extemporization was the order of the day.

Messages flashed backwards and forwards between London and New York on the telex. Many queries were routine, following a set pattern and getting a rapid answer. Others were more complex and needed legal interpretation—for where vast sums of money are being given away, you have to be doubly careful, or the legal repercussions can be costly.

Sometimes the queries were unusual. Jeffrey Blyth cabled from New York:

> He is an Englishman working in the United States, a resident of New York State, but also with residence still in Britain and of course still on British passport.
>
> Question is: Does he qualify for Butlin Prize!
>
> He does qualify for ESB prize, as he is resident of New York State and ESB do not impose any nationality qualifications—but at same time Butlin prize is more attractive.
>
> Question might be merely academic if it weren't for the

H

fact that he does, I think, stand a chance of an 'originality prize'.

He aims to be the cheapest competitor.

In fact, he hopes to make the trip without spending a penny. . . . Secret is that there is a little-known loophole in the airline regulations—if you organize a charter flight of at least 160 people you get 2 free seats in a charter plane.

He says anybody can do this if they know the secret. . . .

Can you give any advice on whether he is or is not eligible for the Butlin prize. Regards.

The ruling went against this entrant as he was not normally resident in the United Kingdom. But as well as the ESB £1,000 ($2,400) prize, he was in fact eligible for the £2,000 ($4,800) Brooke Bond prize, by virtue of the fact that, although living outside the U.S., as a British citizen he was automatically a member of the Commonwealth.

Such a query was typical of dozens received during the immediate pre-Race period. Confusion over the twenty-one classes of prizes was rampant. In fact the organizers automatically considered every competitor for all the categories they were eligible for, whether or not they had marked them on their entry form.

To forestall difficulties over a one-day print union strike an eight-page Air Race Supplement had to be prepared on the Monday. This resulted in many competitors being left out, and a large number of changes were not included. The result was a fresh burst of telephone queries from often irate competitors.

Alerting official organizations on either side of the Atlantic about what they could expect during the Race week was a hectic task. But by 2nd May it was possible to transfer the London and New York Bureaux to their Race Control Centres and test out the systems at each check-in station. Everything worked.

Competitors had also been getting ready. Many came up against bigger problems. Among these, Mira Slovak and Neil Stevens* faced the task of getting their unusual aircraft to the New York starting line from the west coast of America—in the case of Mira Slovak from California; and in that of Stevens, from Bellingham in Washington State.

* See page 33.

Undeterred by the 3,000-mile journey, Czech-born Mira Slovak had set off to fly his Volkswagen-engined powered glider to New York from Los Angeles via Texas, Windy, Oklahoma, and Kansas the week before the start of the Race.

Over in Bellingham it took nine days to convert the 1940 open-cockpit bi-plane De Havilland DH 28A Tiger Moth to its Atlantic-crossing role. An extra 75-gallon fuel tank was fitted in the front cockpit, with a hand pump by the pilot's seat. Stevens would continually have to work the hand mechanism to drive the extra fuel up to the top fuel tank so that it could drip down to the engine. An extra oil tank was installed, gravity feeding to the main tank through a transparent plastic pipe and a control valve. There were two new compasses, artificial horizons, air-speed indicator, transistorized direction finders and portable VHF and HF radio sets. Also stashed away in the cockpit was a complete survival kit including dinghy, lifejackets, wet suits, rescue locator beacons and emergency food rations. But it had not been practical to cover in the cockpit because during the flight Stevens would frequently have to lean out and clear the ice off an intake which captures the air to drive the instruments.

Time was running out and Stevens didn't want the task of piloting the Tiger Moth 3,650 miles to Moncton, where it would be checked out to fly the Atlantic by the Canadian authorities, before reporting to New York to start the Race. So it was decided that his publicity man, Harry McPhee, should take the Tiger Moth to Moncton and Stevens would join him there after clocking out.

That's how Stevens came to be watching on Saturday, 3rd May, as former World War II pilot McPhee lined up for take-off on the grass at the side of the normal runway to avoid wearing out the metal tail skid. He opened the throttle and the heavily laden Tiger Moth went into its customary waddle-like take-off run. But as the speed increased, instead of straightening out into a comfortable ground posture, the Tiger Moth began to weave. Stevens watched, horrified, as the tiny aircraft first drifted off to one side in a huge semi-circle, and then to the other side in another gaping semi-circle. From where he was standing, it looked as though the plane went round in at least one complete circle. No sooner had that happened than it began running out of ground. Before McPhee could pull it into the air the plane hit soft ground. In agonizing seconds its wheels bogged down, forcing the plane into a ground loop. The propeller smashed as it went over, and the wing tips were damaged. There, on its back, in a bog at the end of Bellingham airfield, was probably the most comprehensively equipped Tiger Moth ever to be prepared, and the only one capable of flying the Atlantic. Quick inspections showed that McPhee was all right, and that there was nothing fundamentally wrong with the aircraft, except for one thing. The propeller. It was damaged beyond repair.

Where in the whole of America was Stevens going to find a Tiger Moth propeller, particularly on a Saturday? Undaunted, he began phoning known Tiger enthusiasts all over America. Finally, one single-blade propeller was located hanging over a mantelpiece in Seattle. Stevens drove 180 miles through the night to pick it up. He got back at 3 a.m. on Sunday morning, and began fitting it to the now serviceable aircraft.

Stymied by air regulations which would not allow them to fly the aircraft by night, there was not enough time to fly to Moncton. Simple. Drive it there by road. A boat trailer and a half-ton pick-up truck were produced. McPhee set off on the 3,651-mile journey to Moncton with the Tiger Moth divided into two parts: the wings on the truck and everything else on the boat trailer. Meanwhile, Stevens headed for New York to check in at the Empire State Building for the start of the Race.

About the same time as Stevens's problems reached their crescendo, an urgent cable was sent to me from Gander. It arrived at 5.56 a.m. on 2nd May. Its cryptic, and disturbing, message said:

```
FDZ GANDER NFLD 39 1 830P NDT
PETER BOSTOCK DAILY MAIL FLEET STREET
LONDON ENGLAND

NOTIFIED BY DIRECTOR AIR TRAFFIC OTTAWA ALL PILOTS
WITHOUT INSTRUMENT RATING WILL REPEAT WILL
CONTRAVENE CANADIAN LAW DESPITE ALL ADVICE TO
CONTRARY STOP SITUATION CRITICAL PLEASE CLARIFY
URGENTEST THROUGH BLYTH

WILSEY
```

It was a heart-stopping plea from Captain John Wilsey, who was taking the Sandhurst Piper Aztec out to New York from where 20-year-old Cadet David Wynne-Davies would fly it in the Race from New York to London.

If what he was saying were true, it would immediately debar 80 per cent of the light-aircraft competitors from taking part. For to get an instrument rating* costs about $2,000 in tuition and licence fees in America, and about £1,500 in Britain. Our understanding of the regulations was that instrument ratings were not required when a twin-engined aircraft—like the Sandhurst Aztec —was used. But from Captain Wilsey's cable it looked as though the Canadians at Gander were insisting that pilots have instrument ratings even for twin-engined planes capable of sustaining altitude on one engine.

If that was so, the only hope for the majority of the light-aircraft competitors would be to re-route themselves via the French island of Grande Miquelon in the Cabot Strait, just off the Newfoundland coast. Doing so could be hazardous, particularly in uncertain weather conditions.

In response to my frantic cable messages Jeffrey Blyth and Ken Corney began working on the Canadian authorities, while I approached them through civil aviation contacts in London.

Within a couple of hours, back came Jeffrey to say he had talked with the Canadians and it looked as though they were going to rule in our favour.

'PROBLEM is,' cabled Jeffrey, 'THERE ARE MANY WAYS OF READING the REGULATIONS, THEY DOING BEST LEAN OUR DIRECTION. SO KEEP YOUR FINGERS CROSSED,

They came out in our favour, explaining that a highly technical point had been wrongly quoted by the Gander authorities, and gave an immediate go-ahead for the Race to proceed.

The tempo of anticipation was building up on both sides of the Atlantic, for in London the RAF were ready to show their hand. But how they did so was breathtaking.

Saturday morning, 3rd May, had been quiet. Suddenly the eating stopped. Only a solitary popping champagne cork broke

---

* An instrument rating is given to pilots who can navigate by instrument readings when weather conditions make it impossible to fly visually.

the involuntary silence. Caviar, *avocado aux fruits de mer*, steaks and lobster were all forgotten as a hundred pairs of eyes watched a helicopter slide past the revolving Top-of-the-Tower Restaurant. Propelled by threshing blades the ugly 'bird' was soon thrust away to the north-east, where it hovered expectantly about 600 feet above the ground. Moments later, it was joined by another RAF helicopter, which let down towards the assembled array of orange flags just at the edge of St Pancras station. In a puthering mushroom of disturbed coal dust the gawky machine settled on the ground.

Alert eyes spotted another shape appearing over Parliament Fields, to the north-west of the Post Office Tower. It was the Harrier. The dart-like jet scurried along at 120 mph towards the hovering helicopter. Just short of the hangar-like building of St Pancras station, the jet stopped. Almost motionless, it turned around slightly until the engine air intakes looked like bulbous eyes. Then, with outstretched wheels hanging from its fuselage and wing tips, it began descending gently towards the orange flags.

With a thunderous roar the Harrier thumped down on a 40-foot-square aluminium pad in St Pancras station's disused coal-yard, to become the first jet ever to land in the heart of any city. As it did so, its engines' hot blast stirred up a black pall of coal dust and routed an army of rats who had remained undisturbed for fifteen years. Crowds watching from near by rooftops stopped clapping to thrust their hands over their eyes, as swirling granules of coal were thrown over a vast area. BBC commentator Brian Johnston, resplendent in white suit, suddenly looked like a chimney sweep, but his commentary never faltered! A short distance from the landing site a family wedding group posing for photographs outside Old St Pancras Church with bride Jean Phillips were forced to scatter. But even though she got coal spots on her dress and neck, 24-year-old Jean did not complain; she was too proud of the British achievement.

Yet all the swirling coal dust was quite unnecessary. The RAF were forced to use the coalyard only because of the refusal of the Ministry of Public Building and Works to give permission for them to land in near-by Regent's Park. To have done so would have shown off the Harrier in a much more favourable light.

But then, the MPBW seemed not to be interested in selling jets for export!

Before the dust had settled, the jump-jet pilot, 34-year-old Squadron Leader Tom Lecky-Thompson, had clambered to the ground. 'It was easy and safe. Nothing to it really,' he declared.

Among the vast crowd waiting to greet him, after rubbing coal dust from their eyes, were twelve scientists. They had been checking on the noise level and observing what could be the first step in setting up vertical take-off city hop services. For Hawker Siddeley, the Harrier manufacturers, were already at work on designs for a two-hundred passenger jump-jet.

The first, and in many ways the most critical, phase of the RAF 'Exercise BLUE NYLON' had been completed. The Harrier was ready for the Race to begin.

Chapter Eleven

BLAZE OF GLORY

'It is an awful thing to be told one has made history or done something historic.'

Sir Arthur Whitten Brown, May 1920

WITH SMOKE AND flames streaking from its wheels, the Mark F4K supersonic Phantom jet snaked across the runway, an arrester parachute billowing from the tail. Both main tyres burst. The anti-skid gear failed. But, steering with the nose wheel, the naval pilot controlled the hurtling machine. So, in the stench of burning rubber, the jet ended the fastest-ever flight between New York and London. As it thundered along the runway, a giant Wessex helicopter closed in. Even before the seconds-saving braking could halt the Phantom, its twin cockpit cowlings rose and out from one popped Observer Lieutenant Paul Waterhouse. Free of his harness, disconnected from his oxygen, he scrambled onto the wing before the jet stopped. Seconds later he had leapt to the ground, dashed across the Wisley runway and jumped into the Wessex, which instantly surged into the air.

Escaping disaster was the last thought in Lieutenant Waterhouse's mind—in fact he was oblivious to its nearness. His thoughts were firmly fixed on the Post Office Tower, 20 miles away.

A last-minute change of naval plan had singled him out, instead of Lieutenant Drake, to be the first Air Race competitor to reach London from New York. Standing in the helicopter whirling towards the Tower, he was determined to turn their world record transatlantic flight of 5 hours 3 minutes 18·8 seconds* into an unbeatable city centre to city centre Race record.

* Beating by 29 minutes 14 seconds the record set in 1958 by a USAF Boeing Strato tanker.

He had left New York's Empire State Building check-in station 16 minutes after it opened on Sunday, 4th May. A motor-cycle got him to his helicopter, which switched him to the Floyd Bennett Air Station. There the Phantom, piloted by Lieutenant-Commander Doug Borrowman, was ready to take off. Touching 1,000 miles an hour for forty minutes on leaving Nantucket Sound, the jet was making good time. But there was a setback. According to Lieutenant Waterhouse, 'We were shooting for five hours but head winds stopped us.' In flight they were refuelled three times by Royal Air Force Victor tanker jets in a skilled navigational operation which, Waterhouse declared, 'went perfectly'. The only mishap was the landing trouble.

After leaving Borrowman to cope with the crippled Phantom, Waterhouse changed in the helicopter from his heavy rubber flying suit into a regular light-weight flying overall and donned his orange Race identification jacket as the Wessex approached the Post Office Tower.

Tilting past a forest of giant cranes towards the specially constructed helipad beside the Tower, the helicopter crew could see the crowds waving Union Jacks and scrambling for a position on the route that Waterhouse would take to cover the 60 yards from the building-site landing spot to the Tower entrance. Standing at the open doorway, Waterhouse saw them in focus for the last time before the Race end. After that, they were a blur.

Surprisingly, it was also the last time one eager spectator saw him. For a girl tugging her small brother homeward from the helipad just before the Wessex touched down was heard to say, 'No, you can't watch. You've seen helicopters.'

So they missed Waterhouse's spectacular leap from the Wessex before the wheels touched ground. Running like mad he bounced along the temporary ramp to the street. Past cheering, clapping crowds he surged; up the seven steps of the Tower entrance, along the marble corridor, up another ten* steps, past a reception desk and into the foyer before skidding round the curved passageway to the open elevator. Instantaneously the doors closed and he hurtled upwards to the 33rd floor. A cheering throng greeted him as he burst out of the elevator. Surefooted, he thrust himself

* There are 798 steps to the top of the Post Office Tower.

towards the timing clock, race card at the ready. The button froze the mechanism to record a time of 5 hours 31 minutes 24·4 seconds from the ESB check point.

A delighted First Sea Lord, Admiral Sir Michael Le Fanu, toasted him in champagne, while Waterhouse's wife Nancy, between kisses, whispered that it had taken her over five hours to drive from their Somerset home to the Tower.

Going in the opposite direction, ground traffic snags had not affected the performance of Flying Officer William Fuller, who had taken only 6 hours 28 minutes 9·01 seconds early that day to race from the Post Office Tower to the Empire State Building. Like Waterhouse, Fuller was able to avoid traffic jams, cut through the customary airport red tape and highlight the sort of times that would be possible if as much effort was put into tackling ground problems as to turning out faster and larger civil aircraft.

Instead of a 50- to 60-minute journey to the airport, which confronts the regular airline passenger, Fuller clocked out from the Tower at 8.27; reached the temporary Service helipad, 60 yards away, in two minutes; arrived at Wisley—20 miles from London —11 minutes later and was airborne in the Handley Page Victor at 8.41—just 14 minutes in all. A repeat performance at the New York end had him jumping 6 feet from a Wessex helicopter, which landed sideways on the 30th Street heliport. Then he sprinted off the pad so fast that he overshot the 750 cc. BSA Rocket motor-cycle waiting to whip him to the Empire State Building.

'It was all such a mad rush,' he said. 'At one point my legs were dangling out of the Victor which was still doing 40 or 50 mph as we touched down at the US Navy Base. Before I had a chance to jump clear and spring for the helicopter somebody booted me out—that's how keen the boys were to win.'

Predictably, the Services had taken the lead in the two prize categories for the fastest times in either direction. But in the other nineteen categories the Race was still wide open, and excitement mounted with each new contestant setting off or arriving on either side of the Atlantic. For as well as being a pace-setting spectacular, the Race was a colourful extravaganza of individualism, testing ingenuity as much as personal skill and daring. Even the weather added a touch of drama, being totally unpredictable, with winds blowing in directions quite contrary to the expected patterns. No wonder it was a cliff-hanger till the final hour.

The build-up for the Race began in London just before 7 a.m. on Sunday, 4th May. Competitors began arriving at the ground floor Control Centre to carry out documentation which allowed them to go up to the check-in station. Every contestant was required to report at least 45 minutes before the off, to enable the Royal Aero Club to check them out and issue them with time-cards and the bright orange identification panels which slipped over the head like a sleeveless jacket. By 7.45 more than 60 people had registered, including the majority of the 50 competitors travelling on the Capitol International Airways charter flight. Because of the heavy load and desire for increased speed, the airline decided to leave from Stansted, 30 miles north-east of London, instead of from the smaller runway at (London) Gatwick Airport in the south.

Shortly before 8 a.m. the first batch of competitors were lined up at the top of the Tower. They included Anne Alcock, Stirling Moss and Edward Drewery, resplendent in grey morning suit and grey bowler hat, representing his 139 export-minded British businessmen; a handful of light-aircraft contestants including Julia Turner and Stephan Wilkinson; and Lieutenant-Commander W. G. Boaks, a publicist for unusual causes who campaigns much of his time from a bicycle adorned with a framework of notice-bearing boards. The bicycle had been left chained to a post while he turned up for the start, to make the first of several attempts which never got him farther than an airport. Diligently the retired naval commander had paid four separate entry fees. He had caused a mild sensation on the first day of the London to Paris Air Race by roller skating to the Thames Embankment from the Hyde Park starting point with a rolled umbrella firmly clutched in one hand. But he never flew to Paris. For the 1969 event his bicycle had replaced the roller skates and he never took off for New York. His aim was to draw attention to the dangers to children from motor vehicles. With that he was satisfied and he went back to his campaigning.

Ten minutes to go. Covered by the Union Jack and the Stars

and Stripes, the centre-piece plaque of the starting platform stood ready for the ceremonial unveiling. This was done to a fanfare of applause, by Britain's Postmaster-General John Stonehouse, and Philip Kaiser, Minister at the American Embassy in London. Just before the 30-second count-down began, Stonehouse handed a package to Anne Alcock. It contained a letter of greetings to the U.S. Postmaster-General, the Hon. Winton M. Blount, and a presentation pack of stamps, including a block of the 50th Anniversary Alcock and Brown stamps depicting the flyers and their Vickers Vimy. Anne was appointed a licensed mail carrier by the GPO for the purpose and was charged with delivering the package safely to the Manager at the ESB.*

Down below at the entrance to the Tower a vast crowd had gathered, in spite of its being a 'ghost hour'. Motor-cycles were noisily moved into position, exhaust-blaring cars hugged selected starting spots and passing taxis got tangled in the bewildering mêlée of machines and men which spanned back along three roads converging on the Tower.

Precisely at 8 a.m. on Sunday, 4th May, Anne Alcock punched her time card to start herself and the Race. She was closely followed by Mrs Julia Turner and her light-aircraft flight companion Vivian Wales. They rushed for the elevators and moments later were out into the streets cheered on by enthusiastic crowds, Anne headed for Warren Street Underground station for the first part of her leisurely journey to Stansted.† She was to be joined there by the 50 other, later starting, competitors of the Capital International Airways charter group.

Favourite runner among the charter jet set, Stirling Moss went off at a cracking pace over a carefully rehearsed route, after a momentary setback when he just missed an elevator. Sprinting from the Tower, he flung himself onto the back of a 750 cc. Norton Commando motor-cycle. Five minutes and two and a half miles later he leapt from the Norton, sprinted along the police pier at Waterloo Bridge and jumped into a 45-hp Penta inflatable

---

* A British postal plan to license all the London-New York contestants as mail carriers to take special Race covers for auction later for charity had to be scrapped when the U.S. postal authorities refused to co-operate.

† Anne planned to make a fast return run later in the week. Her symbolic start had made it impossible for her to return a fast westward time.

speedboat as it headed out to the centre of the Thames. A helicopter was in mid river, sitting on an 87-foot barge, specially filled with 200 tons of wheat to get her low enough in the water for Moss to climb aboard easily. As the rubber-nosed boat touched the barge side he scrambled aboard. Less than sixty seconds after Moss had shot from the motor-cycle, ace pilot Mike Orme was airborne. At 8.26 Moss landed at Gatwick. Whisked by car to the terminal for a quick customs check, moments later he raced back across the tarmac to a BUA VC 10. The jet engines flared into life the moment he stepped aboard. Seated waiting for him were the other 110 passengers in the Crosse & Blackwell party, who had been on the aircraft since 7.50 a.m. The carefully rehearsed co-ordination had paid off. Only 27 minutes after Moss clocked out from the Tower the giant jet was airborne. Everyone settled back; Kennedy Airport was the next obstacle.

Although he sprinted through American customs and immigration at Kennedy Airport in 90 seconds, Moss said he lost a minute when an immigration man 'looked my name up in the big black book of banned foreigners. He had never heard of me and must have thought I was a Commie.'

More valuble seconds were lost when he charged full tilt into the heliport gate. Someone had locked it. Just as he was about to fling himself over the top, he spotted the barbed wire. Fleet-footedly switching direction, the white-uniformed figure scooted around the heliport and dashed through another gate. A swift helicopter ride to Manhattan and a switch to a motor-cycle for the last lap to the Empire State Building. It went so fast that even ex-racing champion Moss admitted: 'I had my eyes shut tight the whole time.' His reward—a Race time of 7 hours 31 minutes 45·63 seconds, compared with the usual westbound city centre to city centre time of nearly 11 hours. But Moss's elation was short-lived.

Hot in pursuit was 23-year-old Tony Drewery, front runner for the 139 bowler-hatted businessmen. Like Moss, young Drewery clambered aboard a motor-cycle at the Tower. But unlike Moss, Drewery stayed with it all the way to Heathrow Airport and it got him there in 20 minutes. BOAC staff, wearing orange fluorescent armbands, created a passageway through No. 3

terminal. Within 25 seconds Drewery cleared all formalities (15 minutes is the norm for regular passengers) and raced to the charterd BOAC VC 10. He was cheered on board by the business-men, led by his father who had arrived a few minutes earlier at a more leisurely pace. In flight the pilot, Captain Mike O'Sullivan, spoke from mid-Atlantic to BBC's Cliff Michelmore, who was broadcasting live on a TV show. Millions of viewers had a prac-tical demonstration of the possibilities of aircraft being fitted with air-to-ground passenger phones, to fill in some of the tedious flying hours. As a result of the link-up, Michelmore was able to keep the Drewery team posted on the latest Race news.

At New York the Kennedy Airport staff were overwhelmed by the bowler hat brigade and shot them through all formalities in record time. Leaving the bunch of umbrella-swinging exporters, Tony Drewery and team-mate London solicitor Peter Brooker jumped into an ambulance. At the heliport Drewery switched to a helicopter, leaving Brooker to continue by road. Young Drewery hit the ESB check-in station 7 hours 25 minutes 14·03 seconds after leaving London. He was elated at beating Moss; likewise the bowler hat brigade, who hurled their headgear aloft on hearing the news that their man had beaten the racing star by four minutes.

The ambulance carrying Brooker moved fast enough for him to return a Race time of 7 hours 48 minutes 53 seconds. Breathlessly he explained at the ESB, 'The ambulance really carved up the Sunday drivers. We didn't see any policemen, and there were no problems over wailing sirens and flashing lights.'

If the police were turning a blind eye in New York, at least one policeman in London wasn't. He flagged down BOAC driver Jock Little on the M4 motorway and wrecked his first Race attempt—though he went on to make two later attempts, the fastest of 7 hours 35 minutes 19·42 seconds, beating by just over 2 minutes Clem Whitlock, a rival BOAC syndicated runner.*

Over in New York, still elated at his time, Tony Drewery was storing up trouble for himself on the return journey when he boasted to radio men that he had hurtled through the centre of London at 60 mph, twice the permitted speed. But even such dashing motor-cycle speeds were not enough to keep Tony

* Little was fined £70 ($168) at Acton in September.

Drewery in the lead for the rest of the First Day. Hustling in to lop another 2 minutes off his time came Dave Kolozy, the 38-year-old public relations officer for Capitol Airways. He had been aided by a near record-breaking Atlantic crossing, during which the 250-seater DC8 touched 604 mph. Olympic sprinter Mary Rand travelled on the same flight for a time of 7 hours 37 minutes 23·24 seconds, compared with Kolozy's 7 hours 23 minutes 23·81 seconds.

Her effort had been something of an ordeal following a pre-Race dilemma when she found she had lost her passport photograph. She made a quick abortive run round Euston and King's Cross Stations before finally locating a coin-operated booth at Baker Street. With the photographs safely pinned to her Race card she clocked out of the Tower, made a 45-second Olympic sprint to Warren Street Underground station, then at Charing Cross switched from the train to the river. Cutting upstream with savage swiftness, her launch got her to Battersea heliport where, linking up with Thames TV personality Monty Modlyn who had arrived minutes earlier, she leapt aboard a helicopter. They touched down at Stansted Airport with 6 minutes to spare before the take-off for New York. During the wait Dave Kolozy hurried aboard, all set for his record run. His plans had worked with satisfying smoothness.

Precise planning also paid off for motor-cycle dealer Ray Wilson from Preston in Lancashire. He had motor-bikes lined up at strategic spots on the 15-mile route to Heathrow Airport so that he could 'leapfrog' at traffic signals. When halted by red lights he raced on foot across the road to another bike; he had to switch bikes fifteen times. Such tactics enabled him to reach the New York check-in station in 8 hours 24 minutes 28·73 seconds.

Not everybody had such good timing. Attractive Danish-born Marie Louise Cohen, wife of a Brighton solicitor, was almost reduced to tears by a string of frustrating incidents. They began the moment she arrived at the control point. She was barred at first by the Royal Aero Club officials. The vivacious 29-year-old mother of three children was crestfallen when they told her she had to wait until they checked the validity of her flying licence. Her Danish licence had expired, and although she had been flying since her teens, her British licence did not altogether satisfy the Royal Aero Club stewards. Eventually it was agreed that she should travel to New York as a competitor on a scheduled airliner and let the NAA decide if she should be allowed to fly back to London in the Cessna 310 which she had christened *Suffragette*. Dejectedly she went to the Top-of-the-Tower Restaurant to join the official send-off party who were noisily devouring a champagne breakfast after seeing the first batch of competitors away.

She looked businesslike in a specially created one-piece Race suit with a Union Jack decorated crash helmet by her side.

'Don't worry,' she told me, 'I shall win something.'

She was all set to do just that when she clocked out at 10.15 on her revised programme. She pulled away from the Tower in an open-top vintage car and reached the River Thames below Waterloo Bridge on schedule. But her speed launch would not start. Frantically she switched to an overcrowded press launch. It went too slowly. So she waded towards an RAF launch that was busily refuelling. Seeing her plight the RAF hauled her aboard and set off for the Battersea heliport one and a half miles up the Thames. Realizing she was desperately short of time, Mrs Cohen again leapt from the launch and plodded through the mud to the helicopter. It whisked her to the northern side of London Airport —the nearest spot the Airports Authority were willing to allow helicopters to land at. A motor-cycle was waiting. But she reached the terminal just too late. Her BOAC VC 10 had left two minutes before she arrived.

'It's terrible,' she said as she settled down to wait for the next flight. Her frantic 40-minute escapade had been in vain. But she persevered and reached New York for a Race time of 9 hours 36 minutes 33·18 seconds.

Frustrations at the New York end had slowed down Anne Alcock. She was the only competitor of the day to get in a real tangle with the U.S. customs and immigration, which caused her to miss her helicopter connection to Manhattan. But, as she explained after her late arrival at the ESB, it was not really their fault. 'I could not find my passport and my immigration form,' she said dejectedly, looking at her Race time of 11 hours 34 minutes 23 seconds.

Breaking speed records was the last thing Donald McNab was worried about, for he had set himself a novel task. He was going to work his way to America. He clocked out from the Post Office Tower at 0808. It took him until 6 p.m. on Tuesday to raise the cash to get his ticket and board the aircraft at London Airport. In doing so he washed cars, worked in a night club, collected half a dozen product samples, moved cases of tinned food and sacks of potatoes, and picked up some Decca radar equipment and other parcels for urgent delivery to America. Getting his commercial priorities right, before checking in at the Empire State Building on Wednesday he made export sales to Macy's and Gimble's, America's two largest stores. He was well satisfied with his time of 81 hours 34 minutes 10·08 seconds.

Time was also unimportant to a competitor headed in the opposite direction, a man spotted by an unbelieving TWA official. Wearing the *Daily Mail* Air Race markings, he ambled from one of the arrival corridors at Heathrow Airport. The official couldn't make it out. Twelve times that day he had been almost bowled over by competitors dashing madly for the immigration lounge. Only this time the man patiently took his turn in the queue leading to the immigration checkpoint and customs hall. Hurrying over to him and offering to speed up the airport controls process, he got as a reply, 'No thanks, I'm in no hurry.'

'Have you a car or motor-bike waiting for you outside?' asked the bewildered airline man.

'No,' said the contestant. 'I'm going into town on the airline bus.'

'The airline bus!' he almost burst with amazement. 'You mean you don't mind waiting around?' was all the baffled TWA man could think of saying.

'I'm used to delays,' came the philosophical reply as the competitor moved up one more place in the immigration line-up. 'I'm an American Air Traffic Controller.'

That wry remark was the first anyone in Britain heard to indicate that there was more to 'The Jumbo Jet Economy Class Tourist Committee' than first met the eye. For the nominated competitor of the Committee was Nick Kleiner, an Air Traffic

I

Control specialist, and his backers were fellow controllers from Kennedy Airport.

Originally the group had intended to set out to snatch the prize for the fastest time. But they hit snags with the Federal Aviation Authority and had to change the whole concept of the entry. The four, who shared all expenses, decided to prove that 'the frustrations, inconveniences and delays of vacationing tourists on a limited budget result from poor surface transportation, inadequate airports and airport services'. They had decided that 'Poor roads, slow trains, no mass transportation facilities direct to and from the airports, inadequate ramp space and room for unloading baggage make "ground time" a miserable ordeal for the "happy holiday-maker".' And they sent Nick Kleiner off to prove their theory.

So as to leave no one in doubt as to what they were getting at, Nick's luggage bore the sign:

```
WE JET TO LONDON AND NEW YORK IN THE 'GREAT
AIR RACE OF 1969'
```

```
WE KNOW THE SWIFT SERVICE IN THE AIR WILL BE
JUST FINE. BUT THE TRIP TO AND FROM THE
AIRPORT IS A TERRIBLE GRIND. OUR THEME, RELIEVE
THE JET TRAVELLERS OF THESE BINDS, AND JET-AGE
THE GROUND-TIMES.
```

His single suitcase weighed 33 lb. and he decided to check out from the ESB at 5.30 p.m. on Sunday to simulate an ordinary passenger setting off from a hotel or home to meet the airline's standard check-in times of an hour before take-off. Jim Ean, an Oceanic Air Traffic Controller, decided to walk along with Nick. They agreed it was safer to travel in pairs on the New York subways. John Staut, the Oceanic Air Traffic Operations officer, had driven the pair to the Empire State Building and the fourth team member, Jim Scorse, a domestic Air Traffic Controller, had positioned himself in the JFK Air Traffic Control centre to see that the team's eager-beaver colleagues didn't give Nick's aircraft any unwanted priority take-off treatment.

After leaving the ESB check station, Nick walked along to the Sixth Avenue subway. When the train arrived, the door nearest to them didn't open and he and Jim Ean just managed to squeeze through the next one, which opened only half-way. The subway passengers shied back; one thought they were 'protesting some-thing' or about to take up a collection. Since it was the first day of the Race, not many New Yorkers knew much about the event.

Getting out at Kew Gardens station, the pair switched to a Green Lines bus which deposited them at the PAN AM Airport terminal 1 hour and 39 minutes after starting the race. Nick checked in at the airline counter 51 minutes before the scheduled take-off time—9 minutes later than the stipulated time. At 7.36 p.m. he boarded the aircraft. By 1 minute past 8 the plane began to move and it took off at 8.20 p.m. Nick had been travelling for 2 hours 50 minutes and he had only just lifted off from New York.

As the PAN AM jet touched down at Heathrow after a flight of 6 hours 31 minutes, the crew tried to insist that Nick—who had been given VIP treatment on board—be first away. But Nick stepped aside to make it possible for Bill Rodger and his 15-year-old son Martin to scooter off first. They chose scooters to speed them along the airport corridors at London and New York. As a result Bill Rodger reckoned that 'we spent less than ten minutes in airport buildings all told'. That was quite something, for when Nick waved them ahead, they were returning to the Post Office Tower on their second Race leg. The round trip was completed in just under eighteen hours.

They had disappeared by the time Nick, walking at a leisurely pace, reached the immigration line-up and met the baffled TWA man. No sooner was that encounter over than a British passport control officer spotted the *Daily Mail* Race jacket, rushed over and tried to hustle Nick to the head of the queue. When he wouldn't move, saying he was prepared to wait his turn, the official switched the two people ahead of him to another line-up, grabbed his passport, gave it a quick stamp and told him to run.

Getting out of customs, Nick spotted his pal Addie Johnson (the FAA representative at the American Embassy in London), stop-watch in hand, also urging him into a run. 'He was so funny with the stop-watch, and all excited, he forgot I was not trying for the fastest time,' recalled Nick. 'We no sooner got on the bus—a No. 91—when it takes off like a racing car. It seemed like a couple of minutes and we were at Hounslow West Tube station.' In fact, everything on the public transport system went perfectly.

What impressed him most were the upholstered seats on the Underground trains. 'They would not last a day in New York because of the vandals,' was his surprised comment.

Thanks to the assistance from Johnson, Nick reckoned he did better by travelling on public transport than he would have done in a rush-hour taxi. As the pair strode from Warren Street Underground station, people again urged them to run, and shook their heads in wonderment when they didn't.

Nick Kleiner finally checked in at the top of the Post Office Tower 10 hours 55 minutes 20·92 seconds after starting. It took him 91 minutes from leaving the aircraft at Heathrow to finish the Race. Altogether he had spent 6 hours 31 minutes flying and 4 hours 25 minutes on the ground in New York or London.* His return trip a couple of days later took 11 hours 49 minutes. Some 4 hours 53 minutes were needed to cope with the ground legs, partly due to TWA requiring passengers to check in at their new London terminal 80 minutes before flight time. He also experienced a 1 hour 4 minutes delay to the take-off time because of a technical fault. The most baffling part of the return journey came when, pleading ignorance, Nick asked the Kennedy Airport staff where he could pick up a Carey bus to the airlines terminal in Manhattan. He was misdirected, which meant that he had to carry his bag an extra quarter of a mile. En route to the spot—which turned out to be non-existent—he bumped into another passenger off the same flight who had been similarly misdirected. Both eventually got a bus, and Nick's ordeal was almost over. His effort certainly proved that although the *Mail* Race competitors were being aided all along the line to cut corners and turn in record speeds, things were not so very good for the regular airline passenger during non-race times.

Time on the ground is diluting the advantages of speed in the air, and it looks as though things could get worse. Some airlines, to cope with jumbo jet-loads of passengers, are even thinking of imposing a reporting time two hours ahead of take-off. In spite of experimentation with computerized systems at a few airports, passenger processing and documentation is apparently unable to keep pace with the growth in size of aircraft. Few of the world's

* See Appendix I for full times.

airports will be ready for automated luggage handling of the advanced design necessary to cope with the jumbo-jet age when the first 500-seater giants go into regular service. Until then, Nick Kleiner's times are going to be the norm, with the tendency to get worse, not better.

Unlike Nick, the majority of competitors were out to win. But as Captain John Alcock said: 'The winners will be the ones with luck. You can have the finest aircraft in the world but if the luck's against you, you won't win.' He could have mentioned another ingredient that was to speed competitors along—unexpected help, like that which came to a BOAC Speedbird aircraft headed towards Kennedy Airport during the early days of the Race. There were seven jets converging on Kennedy some 60 miles out from New York. The Air Traffic Controller was watching them on his radar screen, instructing them which altitudes to take in readiness for their descent. This is a normal process which means the jets slow up ready for the final let-down. Such changes in speed and altitude are carried out under the watchful guidance of an Air Traffic Controller, who keeps a safety distance between the aircraft to avoid the possibility of a mid-air collision. Under his control, each aircraft was called on to cut speed and drop down to 6,000 feet. The first five aircraft did so. When the Controller gave instructions to descend to 6,000 feet to the sixth BOAC aircraft, back came an urgent request from the pilot. 'I have some Air Race competitors on board, can I possibly hold a higher altitude for a while and keep up my speed?'

'I'm involved in it too,* came back the reply. 'So maintain your present speed and altitude of eleven thousand feet.'

Gratefully the BOAC pilot acknowledged these instructions, which allowed him to pass the five aircraft in front before having to descend to 6,000 feet ready for the Kennedy approach controller to talk him down onto the runway.

Even with such co-operation, and with superb co-ordination on the ground, actually boarding the aircraft can be the vital factor. Last on, first off, was without exception the rule for every airline. But for some competitors that was not enough. Careful preliminary investigations had revealed that the door-closing,

* He was one of Nick Kleiner's partners.

steps-away operation eats up vital minutes in any flight plan where shaving seconds off total times over the 3,250-mile course is important. It was as a result of this that quite a number of competitors had hit on the idea of entering aircraft when they were all clear for take-off, with engines running and ground chocks away. To do so they had to get in through the belly hatch, normally only used by the crew, and then only occasionally.

One competitor who believed he could do without such subterfuge was Green Diamond Club entrant Peter Hammond. Acting on the findings of their earlier detailed research, Hammond decided to aim to link up with the 8 p.m. BOAC VC 10 flight from Kennedy Airport on Sunday, 4th May. Precisely as planned, he punched his time card at the Empire State Building check station at 7.44 p.m. While he was racing for the elevator a club member was telephoning instructions to the ground floor to alert team members to stop the traffic on Thirty-fourth Street. Hammond dashed headlong onto the back of a motor-cycle which roared away to the West Thirtieth Street heliport at 7.46 p.m. Alerted by more telephone calls, the Bell Jet Ranger helicopter was slowly lifting from the pad as Hammond leapt aboard. It took only 6 minutes for the helicopter journey. Another 4 minutes for a car to sweep him to the aircraft. A final sprint up the steps and the door closed and the aircraft was moving away just 10 seconds after 8 p.m.—16 minutes after leaving the ESB.

In spite of unusual head-winds, the BOAC pilot and navigator —both former Green Diamond Club members—managed to push the VC 10 along for a flight time of 6 hours 20 minutes. But they had been hoping to do it well under the 6 hours.*

As the VC 10 rolled to a halt, Hammond went scurrying out of the already open door, raced along a quarter of a mile of corridors, past immigration and customs—who waved him through—and jumped onto the back of a motor-cycle. It took him to a second Bell Jet Ranger helicopter, positioned at the north apron. Hammond was lifted skywards just 6 minutes after his VC 10 had touched down. At 7.33 a.m. the helicopter dropped onto a river

* In 1965 a TWA Boeing set up a record flight time from New York to London of 5 hours 11 minutes.

barge anchored 40 feet from Waterloo Bridge. It touched only long enough for Hammond to spring out then it shot away. Hammond ran across the barge top as a launch swung into place to form a link with the bridge. Scaling the bridge wasn't necessary, for like an impatient giraffe a hydraulic lift, of the type used for repairing lamp posts, collected him and swung him 40 feet up to the road. Jumping on the back of a motor-cycle, he raced across Waterloo Bridge and on to the Tower, with club members fixing every traffic light. A radio-alerted club member had the Tower elevator at the ready and Hammond hurtled up to the check-in station to record a breathtaking 6 hours 54 minutes 56 seconds. He had broken the 7-hour barrier; something none of the 95 people before him had been able to do, except for the Phantom and Victor competitors.

Hammond had certainly set a cracking pace for the civilians. It had been no idle boast at the outset when he said, 'We want to challenge the military people in organizing ability.' Indeed, 75 of the London members turned up at 6 a.m. on Monday morning to smooth the path for Hammond's triumphant arrival.

The Services were ready for any such challenge. Ready to stake not only their own reputation on the outcome, but that of one of the most revolutionary projects ever to be turned off a designer's drawing board: the Harrier. Not for it the semi-secrecy of a military transatlantic flight, but a performance before a critical world audience, watching each dramatic step on television via a Telstar link-up.

Monday, 5th May, was selected as the big day. The revolutionary Hawker Siddeley Harrier was about to be put through its paces, pointing to the future abolition of land-hungry airports sited miles from the cities they are supposed to serve. But the British weather is notoriously no respecter of historical occasions, and 5th May was no exception. The Harrier was grounded. Not because it couldn't take off in a thick fog—that would have been child's play for the pilot, Squadron Leader Tom Lecky-Thompson; but because the conventional Victor Tanker jets couldn't get airborne to refuel the 600-mph Harrier over the Bristol Channel. Fog had clamped down on their RAF Marham, Norfolk, base making it impossible for them to take off.

Probably the least nervous person of all those who waited anxiously for the Norfolk fog to lift was 34-year-old Lecky-Thompson, who looked far too small to be piloting the amazing jet which can fly backwards, sideways, turn circles within its own length and touch near supersonic speeds in conventional flight, as well as take off and land like a helicopter.

Personally, his main regret was that PAN AM's abandonment of the helipad at the top of the central New York skyscraper meant that the Harrier couldn't land there and prove that it was as gentle as it was versatile. Historically also, it was a lost opportunity. For the Harrier to have set down on the PAN AM building would have proved the full civil potential of the vertical take-off and landing technique, alerting architects and civil engineers to the idea of incorporating such landing features into projects for the late 1970s.

Finally, after two postponements, the go-ahead was given and Lecky-Thompson arrived at the check-in station, time-card at the ready. His first warning to get set came when the throb of a helicopter was heard outside the glassed-in observation platform. A quick flash from an Aldis lamp signalled the helicopter to approach the temporary pad on the Moss Construction site immediately alongside the Tower. At the same time 'Now!' came the yell from the Aldis lamp operator which sent Lecky-Thompson into action. He punched his card. Skipped to the elevator. Shot down the exit route into the street. After a lung-bursting sprint arrived on the helipad just as the giant Wessex was stroking its wheels gingerly on the staging. Helping hands grabbed him aboard. Then, pulling sharply upwards, clear of the construction cranes and buildings, the helicopter carried him less than three-quarters of a mile to the St Pancras coal-yard. Lecky-Thompson leapt 4 feet from the helicopter, as lithe as a cat. He sprinted for his machine, which stood incongruously in the great coal-yard. There was no pilot waiting primed in the cockpit of the single-seater aircraft, as with the Phantom and Victor. Everything was up to Lecky-Thompson.

Hundreds of schoolchildren had taken an unofficial day off to see him leave. They crowded the surrounding roof tops. And, in spite of the threat of choking coal dust, dozens of housewives were hanging from their windows for a better view. The roads around the site were clogged with traffic waiting for the take-off.

Strapped into his narrow cockpit, Lecky-Thompson gunned the jet engine into life. Black clouds shot skywards, unchecked by the two thousand gallons of water optimistically sprayed on the ground to keep the dust damped down. For a second the Harrier engine faltered. The sound died away. In the momentary silence, most people caught their breath. Was it going to be a flop? As the engine shot into life again, they started to cheer. A crescendo of thrilling noise rose up. Then, through the swirling black clouds of grit and chips of coal, the needle-nosed jet began to rise. Slowly at first, almost hesitantly. Then, as though shaking itself free of all the grime and squalor which had been its launching pad, it broke into the clear air. Still rising vertically, its nose pointing northwards in the direction of the railway tracks, it made a proud sight. When the Harrier was poised like an expectant eagle above St Pancras Station, the pride of Victorian Gothic architecture, Lecky-Thompson switched the four jet nozzles—two on each side—into a half backward-facing position. The re-directed jet stream pushed the Harrier forwards as well as upwards. With the airflow beginning to build up over the wings, he switched the jets fully backwards. The Harrier became a normal jet, rocketing ahead over the railroad tracks. Seconds were all that were needed to perform the manœuvres. As the Harrier soared up and away, past the grimy entrails of St Pancras freight yard, Brian Harpur enthusiastically sent off a cable to the New York Bureau:

```
BRITISH RAIL ARE PROUD TO ANNOUNCE
THAT THE 1032 HARRIER JET FROM ST
PANCRAS STATION LEFT ON TIME.
```

Getting it airborne after such a delay was no mean feat. To switch the start time involved team chief Group Captain Peter Williamson in mounting a massive operation at RAF Strike Command HQ. Flight clearances all along the route—civil and military—had to be obtained from the Air Traffic Controllers. The Victor tanker's flight plans had to be reformulated, H.M.S. *Nubian* and the Canadian and American radar tracking stations had to be fed revised data, weather forecasts had to be re-computed. But the 3,500-mile flight went off without a hitch. The Harrier, with its angled feeder nozzle poised expectantly out over its nose, didn't miss a single refuelling rendezvous. Throughout most of the flight it continually supped fuel at nearly 600 mph from accompanying Victor tankers. The topping-up operation was necessary in case any emergency caused a supporting tanker to miss a rendezvous or the Harrier had to make a dash for land. With maximum fuel the jet would have been just able to cope.

Nothing went wrong. On time, Lecky-Thompson sighted the American coast. Following his Air Traffic Controller's directions, he moved close in towards the skyline of Manhattan. He flew the last leg to the United Nations riverside plot of ground visually. Effortlessly the Harrier swept towards the target. Stopped. And while incredulous Americans looked on, it made a perfect let-down; it would have been just as easy on a tennis court or along the centre of Broadway.

As Lecky-Thompson hurtled on his last lap towards the Empire State Building in a Jaguar sports car, the New York *Daily News* received dozens of calls from readers reporting 'There's a plane down in the East River'.

By the time everyone had discovered there wasn't, Lecky-Thompson had checked in to set up a true city centre-to-city centre, London to New York time of 6 hours 11 minutes 57 seconds. But he was disappointed. 'It should have been under six hours,' he said, grinning all over his face as he was swamped by enthusiastic New Yorkers. Thanks to the Harrier the Americans, just like the British, were beginning to take to the Greatest Air Race of them all. Exercise BLUE NYLON was starting to pay off for the *Daily Mail* as well as for Hawker Siddeley and the RAF.

Chapter Twelve

DEDICATED IDEALISTS

'By night on swift enchanted wings I fly,
Bright stars above become my Rosary . . .'

Max Conrad, May 1969

WHAT WITH THE Harrier, the Phantom, the Victor and hot foot jet-setters like Peter Hammond and Dave Kolozy, the event, even before it was forty-eight hours old, made Atlantic-hopping seem routine. The public suddenly awoke to the fact of the immediacy of jet-age travel. The ocean really did appear to shrink in size in face of the onslaught.

Competitors were not content merely with breakfasting in London and chasing the time differential to have another breakfast in New York; they were turning right round and making a double Atlantic crossing in the day. Speed had become synonymous with adventure, with success. Undoubtedly it was the ingredient that turned the Race into a spectacular spectator event, for races which begin and finish in one day seem to have greater impact for the public than those which take weeks or months to produce results. Such immediacy was the *raison d'être* for the Air Race. It had also much more: extroverts, gimmick merchants, nut cases, do-gooders, competitors simply out to prove a personal point or win a private wager; and always there were the Services battling among themselves, a class apart. Each facet provided a race within a race. In a blaze of world press headlines and images captured on thousands of feet of TV film, ingenuity, sometimes misplaced, was seen to triumph.

Sharply in contrast to such high jinks were the exploits of the dedicated band of light-aircraft enthusiasts. They were men and women who found themselves confronted by conditions similar to those faced by Alcock and Brown fifty years before, and many were flying smaller aircraft. Weather, which played such a dramatic part in the 15 hours 57 minutes, 1,880-mile flight* of Alcock and Brown, was a vital factor with the Air Race contestants in May.

Prevailing winds had been the obvious reason why most light aircraft competitors decided to start from the west. But in the event the winds did not turn up. There never were any really strong westerlies at any height to push them along, saving fuel and precious time. Quite the reverse happened on several days, with the best wind conditions favouring those flying in the opposite direction—from London. At one point the weather was so contrary that a low across the whole area produced unexpected tail-winds for westbound light aircraft on the Greenland route with a quite reverse—though weak—jetstream far south of the Great Circle Route for the Navy Phantom. As a result of the unpredictable and often alarming weather, the majority of light aircraft starting from America were held up for considerable periods.

Flyers setting out from London capitalized on the advantage, and on the first day Britain's best-known woman pilot, Sheila Scott, set up two records in her Comanche 260, clipping 4 hours 22 minutes and 26 seconds off her own Shannon—Gander record with a time of 12 hours 51 minutes 35 seconds. She completed the London to New York leg of the Race in 26 hours 34 minutes 1 second. Impeccably dressed and wearing a red coat, trousers and a blue hat, she arrived exhausted in New York after two days without sleep.

'For eight hours I had a mass of ice on my Piper Comanche, *Myth Too*. There was no way I could get rid of it and it was affecting the controls. The radio was out of action, and also the airspeed indicator. It was worrying but exciting at the same time. I feel as if I've been flying for three weeks,' she said.

Headed in the opposite direction was Vladimir Kazan, a refugee Czech flyer with sixty-six solo Atlantic and Pacific crossings to his

* From St John's, Newfoundland, to Clifden, Ireland, their time from coast to coast was 15 hours 57 minutes; their take-off to landing time 16 hours 28 minutes.

credit. Arriving in London in a single-engined Piper Comanche in 23 hours 58 minutes 18 seconds, he took three cups of tea and within 52 minutes was on his way back to America. Astounded officials protested at his plans. But removing his sunglasses and rubbing red-rimmed eyes, he retorted:

'Whatever you say, I am going straight out again. My mind is full of my flight plan. I mustn't be distracted.'

He wasn't. And he headed back to his plane. What fascinated him was the wind blowing from Britain to America.

Such a turnabout with the weather brought with it a greater hazard—ice—which caused havoc with many light aircraft plans. Vicious weather conditions over Greenland forced Britain's Julia Turner and Vivian Wales to change plans.

They were greeted with the bad news when they arrived at Keflavik, Iceland. Icing and turbulence over southern Greenland, with gusting winds up to fifty knots, meant diverting to Søndre Strømfjord on the west coast, instead of making for Narsarssuak on the southern tip, as planned.

'What a wretched nuisance,' exclaimed Julia Turner. Wearing an eye-catching blue trouser suit and red jumper, she told *Evening News* reporter Harry Jones in Iceland:

'We are really enjoying the Race. We had a bit of icing on the way, but nothing serious. We had stew, fresh fruit and coffee for lunch, and chicken salad for supper.

'About the only serious thing that has happened so far is we ran over a policeman's foot outside the Post Office Tower. But he didn't seem to worry too much,' added Vivian Wales, who sells ladies' corsets for a living.

The couple had been the second and third competitors to leave the Post Office Tower on the first day. With only 1,000 flying hours between them, they reckoned they had less experience than anyone else in the Race. But they had lots of guts. And the weather forecast couldn't deter them. After a brief thirty-one minutes refuelling stop, they took off in their white Comanche.

Already ahead of them, by over ninety minutes, was Stephan Wilkinson of *Flying* magazine, once more teamed up with Jim Kieffer in a Beagle 206-S.* This time they were setting a cracking

* See page 18.

pace. There would be no repeat of the 97 hour 58 minute 7 second marathon. For a start, Jim had the long-range ferry tanks fitted at Shannon before departure time. He was positioned at Heathrow Airport raring to go as Stephan clocked out from the Post Office Tower only four and a half minutes after the Race started. The Beagle, the tenth to be delivered to the U.S., was the first aircraft in the competition to reach Iceland, only 5 hours and 25 minutes after leaving London. With a twenty-knot tail-wind the pair didn't think anything could catch them. They still thought so when they arrived in New York after a flight which they said had been 'as smooth as silk'. Stephan turned in a Race time of 20 hours 23 minutes 31 seconds.

Later, heading in the opposite direction, things were far from smooth for Fred Clauser.[*] First came news from Gander that thick fog in mid-Atlantic had forced him to change his flight plans. During a refuelling stop, he announced his decision not to fly direct to London but to refuel again at Shannon. 'The weather has suddenly closed in and there is a forecast for headwinds and fog. This is going to gobble up more fuel than I had figured', he said just before leaving Newfoundland.

Not until an urgent telex message arrived at the London Control Centre on Monday did anyone realize something might be wrong.

```
HAVE YOU ANY NEWS OF 655 CLAUSER ESB
START 0800 NEW YORK TIME YESTERDAY.
INQUIRES COMING IN THICK AND FAST.
```

The last word from him had been his decision, just before he left Gander, to switch plans and fly to Shannon instead of directly to London. From that moment he was out of contact with the Race Bureau. A quick check round Air Traffic Control centres produced a negative response. Clauser was missing.

Suddenly the spectre of disaster loomed large.

Out in mid-Atlantic the frail 180-h.p. Mooney aircraft was caught up in a wild storm. Lashing rains and buffeting winds cascaded down as Clauser put up a desperate fight to stay in the air. Constantly driven off course, blinded by squalls of rain and

[*] See page 70.

hemmed in by fog he suddenly found ice building up on the wings. Then his radio began to overheat. He was in trouble. Desperately he tried to force the aircraft to climb. He knew that if he could only get high enough, he could ride out the storm and the upper warm air currents would free his plane of the dreaded ice.

But as he defiantly began to edge his way slowly upwards, the rapid ice build-up continued. It began to affect the controls, making it almost impossible to keep the aircraft steady.

Trouble had stalked him ever since he had left Gander, for he had been heavily loaded with fuel.* Now this worked against him. The extra weight held him down, preventing his reaching his planned altitude of 9,000 which might have saved him from getting into the grip of the ice. But he tried hard. Slowly, the Mooney edged up to 6,000 feet. The icy grip tightened. The controls became almost too heavy to operate. Yet Clauser instinctively realized that somehow he had to free himself from the icy area. To drop down was inviting disaster. Visibility was so bad that the ocean was out of view. And there was no telling how low the cloud base was. It could go right down to the wave tops, or be a dozen or a hundred feet above. Yet an ocean-hugging flight might be the only alternative to disaster. As he pondered the possibility, Clauser's radio came back to life. Over it he heard the reassuring voice of one-legged veteran pilot Bill Guinther, flying ahead of him in a Beech Bonanza. Though they had never met, the two were near neighbours.

'What do I do?' asked Clauser over the radio link. 'Should I climb?'

'Can you?' Guinther asked, already fearing the answer.

'No.'

'Then you had better go down,' replied the experienced pilot. He himself had encountered the icing, found he couldn't 'top it', so had been forced to go round the area. Clauser was in the middle of the thunderstorm area. For him there was no going round. He had to get out from under it.

Clauser bravely set about the task. Going down is no simple

* Overloads of fuel caused several of the early pioneers to crash on take-off before their Atlantic flight attempts.

manœuvre with an aircraft whose stability is already threatened by masses of ice which destroy the very aerodynamic characteristics which keep an aircraft airborne. Easing the Mooney into a shallow descent, he began to 'sweat it out'. At 3,000 feet above the sea the ice stuck fast. It still had not moved at 2,700 feet. At 2,500 feet Clauser began to be worried. No break in the cloud gave him a sight of the ocean. And in those conditions a pilot can never be sure that ice has not affected the altimeter, causing wrong readings.

Anxiously he peered out at his wings at 2,000 feet. Still the ice refused to give. His plight was desperate. The point of no return had been reached. With a superhuman effort Clauser could have pulled the aircraft out of the immediate descent, but the ice build-up was so heavy he would never be able to climb again. Courageously the American persisted with the dive, scanning the air below him to try to spot the waves.

He was experiencing a repeat drama to that played out fifty years earlier by Alcock and Brown during their pioneering flight across the same wild stretch of water. Alcock recounted that they 'rarely saw the sun, moon or stars'. As they throbbed along at 120 mph in the converted Vickers Vimy bomber they were either in the middle of fog or flying between banks of it.

At one point they began 'having a very rough time' in thick fog. Sleet jammed the air speed indicator. The intrepid pair's aircraft did some 'comic stunts', 'looping the loop', according to Captain Alcock. He said: 'We had no sense of horizon. We came down quickly from four thousand feet until we saw the water very near. That period only lasted a few seconds but it seemed ages. It came to an end when we were within fifty feet of the water with the machine practically on its back.' For a moment it looked as though they were going to share the fate of H. G. Hawker, and Kenneth Mackenzie-Grieve who came down in mid-Atlantic a month before their flight.* Then: 'The air speed indicator began to work. We climbed up to eleven thousand feet. It was hailing and snowing. The Vimy was covered with ice for four or five hours,' declared Captain Alcock.

'Brown had continually to climb up to chip off the ice with a

* Hawker and Mackenzie-Grieve were picked up safely 750 miles from Ireland on 19th May 1919 by the steamship *Mary*.

knife. We came down to three hundred feet again. To the sea. We flew along the water and we had doubts about our position.'

Clauser was having similar doubts. But unlike Alcock, he had no one to go out and chip ice off the wings of the much smaller Mooney, which had but one engine instead of the Vimy's two.

Still he dropped down, searching for the white-crested waves, hoping he would spot them before they engulfed him and his gallant machine. The altimeter showed 1,800 feet. It was still dropping. Then suddenly he saw chips of ice beginning to break from the wings. He was going to be all right. He sensed it. But he was still not out of danger, even when the ice all came off. He was hundreds of miles away from land. The ice drama had caused him to lose his bearings. But Bill Guinther kept talking to him and so did a dozen airline pilots sitting comfortably thirty thousand feet above him as they scurried at 600 mph across the Atlantic in their modern jets. Everyone tried to help. A TWA pilot flying west-wards picked up the conversation between Clauser and Guinther and relayed radio calls on his more powerful set to help Clauser work out a fresh altimeter setting and a new compass route to steer along to safety. When he passed out of range, an SAS pilot took over. It was like that all through the night. And Guinther kept on talking 'like a Dutch uncle'. But Clauser's radio began to overheat again. As he was going to need it when he got close to land, the squad of airborne advisers recommended the young American to switch off for a while. He would need the radio to make his final approach to land. Clauser dutifully went off the air.

That was when Bill Guinther lost contact, but he didn't worry. He believed Clauser was out of his worst trouble. Only when he hobbled into my office at the end of his 24 hour 15 minute 1·34 second journey from the Empire State Building did he discover that Clauser had not turned up safely at Shannon. Bill looked as though he had popped over from a party rather than flown the Atlantic. He wore a red cardigan, striped blue shirt with a button-down collar, open at the neck, and dark blue trousers. Not a piece of flying gear in sight! By this time I was urgently calling the RAF Search and Rescue Co-ordination Centre. Bill listened to my conversation, and when he saw me shaking my head he offered to talk to them. The RAF boys were delighted to have someone at

K

hand who had been directly in touch with the lost pilot. His complicated routing information, with its altitudes and compass bearings, gave them new clues. But what was more important, Guinther was able to reassure them that Clauser had taken on board an extra load of fuel. That meant he could still be airborne. On a quick rule-of-thumb calculation the Wing Commander and Guinther worked out that at worst Clauser had enough fuel left for several more hours.

That was a relief. But I had to cable Jeffrey Blyth immediately to say that there was no positive news, adding as reassuringly as I could that the Search and Rescue Centre were not unduly worried at not making recent contact, because Guinther's explanation of Clauser's radio trouble fitted in with the last broadcast they had picked up from him.

But I was worried. It was 7.30 p.m. and it would be dark, windy and very lonely out there in the Atlantic. Having reconciled myself to the Rescue Centre's assurance that there was no real cause for alarm, I was taking Guinther next door to Ken Pragnell in the BBC radio studio when I was besieged by an anxious group of journalists.

'What's this aircraft that's down in the drink?' they asked.

Before I could recover from the blast they added 'We have a tip-off that it's Wynne-Davies, the Sandhurst Cadet'.* I was shocked. But I was positive that if there had been any doubts about the young army flyer the RAF would have told me immediately.

'That's not true,' I said, stung to an immediate response on realizing that for several of the morning papers, first edition deadlines were fast approaching. Once the news is in the page it is almost impossible to stop it for that edition, even if it is incorrect. One thing to avoid was speculation about disaster, particularly where it concerned a young British officer cadet. 'There has been confusion over Davies and an American flyer, Clauser, who has been having radio trouble and hasn't been in contact for a couple of hours. Let me do a re-check for the latest position.'

---

* The journalists confirmed later that evening that a freelance had sent in an incorrect story; having heard that a pilot had lost radio contact, he assumed it was Wynne-Davies and that he had crashed in the sea.

Immediately I phoned back to the Rescue Centre. The suggestion that an aircraft was 'down in the drink' was news to them. Double checking while I was holding on to the phone proved the rumours groundless: they reported 'all oceanic stations are happy that no aircraft are overdue. Only communications checks are being carried out.' For the moment the press were satisfied.

I knew they were wrong about Wynne-Davies, but as the minutes ticked away—and it's surprising how that trite-sounding phrase becomes meaningful in times of emergency—I became terribly afraid for Clauser.

But as I waited in the Control Centre puzzling out the next move, RAF Rescue Centre phoned. They had a radar fix on an unidentified aircraft which could be Clauser. They were not positive because of other aircraft in the area and the fact that he was several hundred miles off course. But all their checks pointed to its being Clauser. They had given him a course to steer for Vagar in the Faeroes, believing he could receive radio messages even though he could not transmit.

With great relief, I put out a brief announcement to that effect at 9.25 p.m. But our troubles were not yet over. Messages of concern were pouring into Jeffrey Blyth's office in New York because Clauser's family and friends had calculated that he was sixteen hours overdue. Was the radar sighting good enough to reassure them?

The phone rang. It was RAF Rescue again. The news was good. Immediately I telexed details to Jeffrey:

```
HOLD FAST. AIR TRAFFIC SEARCH AND RESCUE
HAVE HAD HIM ON VOICE AND RADAR A FEW MINUTES
AGO BUT THEY CAN'T REPEAT CAN'T GET HIM INTO
VAGAR.
```

Why, I didn't know. By now I had the phone to the RAF Rescue Centre in one hand and was scribbling out messages to be telexed to New York with the other.

My pen involuntarily jerked upwards in a movement of sheer horror. The telex operator caught the sense of shock in my expression. Then as I began to write, he rattled off the message to New York:

CLAUSER DISAPPEARED OFF THE RADAR SCREEN DU-
RING AN APPROACH TO THE AIRFIELD OF VAGAR IN
THE FAEROES. HE WAS COMING INTO THE AIRFIELD
AND DISAPPEARED. THEY ARE NOW CARRYING OUT A
RADAR SURVEILLANCE SEARCH.

One could almost feel the impact of the message at the other end. I only hoped that the relatives were not in the same room as the telex machine.

'They've got him again,' came the call over the telephone. 'It's all right. He must have gone round again. The mountain would have blocked out the radar.' Immediately I alerted New York:

RE CLAUSER. NO REPEAT NO ANNOUNCEMENT YET
PLEASE HE'S IN TROUBLE BUT STILL FLYING

That was an understatement. Vagar airfield, stuck in the middle of the ocean over 400 miles north-west of Prestwick, lies in a valley surrounded by mountains rising to 2,590 feet. Both the mountains and the airfield were shrouded in cloud that came down to within 300 feet of the sea. Clauser was having trouble lining up with the runway. Three or four times he made approaches, abandoned the idea and went round the island. Vagar was his last chance of safety. He was 700 miles off his original course. If he overshot the Faeroe Islands there was nothing in front of him but vast tracks of empty ocean.

He was facing the loneliest moments of his life. He was tired and exhausted after his twenty-hour vigil. Safety was only a few miles away, but flying conditions were almost impossible. Even a helicopter couldn't take off, the cloud base was so low.

Grimly the young pilot set the Mooney on an approach to the asphalt runway he had never seen before. It lay 283 feet above the sea. There was less than 30 feet between it and the cloud base. For an experienced pilot, getting down would have been a near miracle. Slowly Clauser flew the Mooney towards safety. The islanders, alerted to the emergency, could hear the drone of the engines.

Suddenly Clauser's radio crackled urgently. 'You are headed directly at the mountain. Repeat directly at the mountain.' The warning came from the radar controller.

Instantly Clauser made a brave decision. He decided to land on the sea, in the icy fjord, rather than risk crashing on a mountainside. In the water he had a chance. Crumpled against an unknown cliff there was none. Bravely he pushed forward the controls of the aircraft he had bought three months earlier for $12,000 (£5,000) and for which he was still paying. The ocean rushed towards him. . . .

CLAUSER IS SAFE BUT INJURED AFTER CRASH
LANDING. WE DON'T KNOW HOW BADLY WILL ADVISE
YOU SOONEST.

I instantly dictated the news from the phone. Minutes later we were able to tell New York:

HE IS ALL RIGHT AND IS IN BED. HE CAME DOWN
IN THE SEA AND WAS RESCUED BY THE FAEROES
RESCUE BOAT.

He had made a perfect landing on the waves and climbed into a life raft from which he was picked up by local fishermen within five minutes of his touch-down. Within minutes he was in the care of the island's doctor, Peter Reider. Next morning, it was found that the Mooney was not badly damaged except for the electrical system in the under-carriage. As for the rest of the aircraft, all it needed was a good drying out. From hospital Clauser said: 'I was hoping against hope that I would be able to complete the course, but it looks as if I shall not see London this time.'

But he did. Going via Copenhagen on a scheduled air service, he arrived at the Post Office Tower to clock in. His time: 153 hours 17 minutes 17·95 seconds.

When news of Clauser's escape came through, New York were already involved in another major Air Race drama, for they had lost another light-aircraft competitor. Ben Garcia was missing. In his frail canvas-covered Colt, he had turned up at the Canadian Aviation Centre at Moncton, only to receive a complete turn-down on his request for permission to fly solo over the Atlantic. The Canadian authorities ordered the 32-year-old pilot not to proceed. They decided that neither his plane—which didn't have the range to cover the gap between Iceland and Shannon—nor his flying experience met the requirements for transatlantic flight. The Canadian Government's Department of Civil Aviation inspectors said the Piper Colt's navigational aids were simply not acceptable.

Then, overnight, Garcia disappeared.

He had flown from Moncton to Portland, Maine, taken off two hours later and vanished. His last message: 'If anybody calls from New York, tell them I'm still going to make London.'

His wife Carol, from their New Jersey home, said: 'Ben wouldn't live with himself if he didn't accomplish what he set out to do. He's that kind of man. No one seems to have any idea where he is, but it's my bet that he is going to do it. He has put his whole life and soul into this trip. It would be just like him to go ahead when he had been told not to.'

That's what worried us in London. After a quick consultation with John Blake of the Royal Aero Club, Brian Harpur decided that Garcia should be disqualified if he had decided to proceed in defiance of the Canadian authorities.

The only problem was how to communicate with him and let him know of the organizers' decision.

Maine Air Traffic Control were the last people he talked to and they said: 'Mr Garcia taxied on to the runway and asked for taxiing instructions, which we gave him. We haven't any real idea where he was headed—but he told us he was still going to London.'

Ben Garcia, wearing Red Baron flying helmet and goggles, was intent on doing that. Only he had a couple of things he wanted to do first, like getting some extra fuel tanks fitted and adding a HF radio to his navigation equipment. The Canadian authorities had convinced him that Atlantic-hopping without the right instruments was suicidal. And though Garcia admitted he was a dreamer, he was no fool. But no one back in New York or London had any idea of what he had in mind.

While we were all baffled by his disappearance, Garcia was sleeping in an abandoned airfield, oblivious of the world's concern. Bright and early he got airborne again and headed for his home.

Somehow his do-it-yourself navigation book let him down. He

got lost. His fuel was running low. Peering past his single propeller Garcia spotted a chicken farm. Breakfast! The thought electrified him. No chicken farmer would mind his dropping in for bacon and eggs. So he did just that.

Neatly dipping the wing, he lined up with the chicken farmer's field and coasted in for a perfect landing. . . . Well, not quite. He misjudged the terrain. Though the three wheels touched down perfectly, the ground gave way under them. The Piper Colt did a somersault, ending on its back with the wheels pointed skywards.

Garcia was left hanging upside down.

Bob Schwartz and his father, stunned to see a plane upended beside one of the chicken coops, hurried along to find out what had happened. They discovered Ben hanging like a bag of beans. They seized his leg. He yelled: 'Hey, stop pulling my leg. I'm alive! They jumped back. With great tugging and heaving, which Garcia said 'almost broke me in half', they eventually got him free.

By the time local state trooper Ralph McAllister reached the scene, Garcia was crawling from the plane. Said McAllister:

'He kept burbling to me about some race across the Atlantic to London. Well, we never get to hear about these things in a place like this. It's pretty quiet, you know. Frankly, I had a suspicion that maybe he had been drinking or something—maybe he had stolen the aircraft.'

But along with his navigation book, Ben Garcia carried a pile of newspaper cuttings, including ones about himself, and convinced the law he was okay. He refused to go to hospital, even though he had a sore back and an aching arm.

Although the plane was a write-off, Garcia was more determined than ever to win a prize—only this time he would use a regular airline to cross the Atlantic. So, soon after a Civil Aeronautics Board inspector reached the scene of the crash—just outside the town of Lykens, Penn.—Garcia headed for the Empire State Building. The volunteer helpers, from the Ninety-Nines Organization of women pilots, were stunned when he turned up still wearing his orange suit, helmet and goggles, and carrying a giant parasol 'to protect me from the London rain'.

Unshaven, he signed in at the Empire State Building, intending to use roller skates and a motor-cycle to get to the airport. His big snag; what to do at the London end?

His plea, passed on to the BBC, was heard by Simon Goodman when he was driving along Finchley Road after he had been to see *The Mikado*. He was listening to the 'Late Night Extra' programme on his car radio, when they broke in with the news of Ben's plight. Goodman, who had taken part in the London–Paris Race, stopped the car and phoned to offer to meet Garcia at Heathrow. Battling Ben was delighted, and back came his telex acceptance. The Garcia Saga was about to enter its zaniest period.

He was to dart to and fro across the Atlantic, without sleep and unshaven. At one moment he would appear in a bathing costume, a rubber duck around his middle and walking on skis. The next he would be travelling by Rolls Royce garbed in an impeccable morning suit. Another time he feigned poverty and made the Atlantic crossing from London to New York wearing a pith helmet and naked except for underpants and boots, hiding his modesty inside a cardboard cigarette carton plastered with his press cuttings and fastened over his neck by string. Like some magical Disneyland figure come to life, Garcia captivated the hearts of millions of newspaper readers and television viewers. He became such an instant personality that women would grab hold of him in the street and kiss him; children used to trail him around in London and New York, and airline passengers and staff loved his antics, which were never spiteful and always harmless. As his wife said: 'Ben is a changed man. He has found a new meaning in life. It's as though he has come alive again.'

As Vincent Mulchrone wrote in the *Daily Mail*: 'Had there been a category called "Dreamers" in the Race, it would have been won by a gutsy little Yankee called Garcia.'

Guts, indeed, seemed to be the characteristic shared by all the light-aircraft entrants. Even as Garcia was making his 'chicken farm' début, a mini aeroplane, powered by a Volkswagen car engine, was dodging what its pilot, Mira Slovak, called 'ice cubes' in mid-Atlantic. The 'cubes' were icebergs which were too tall for the powered glider to fly over when it was brim full of fuel. Slovak didn't mind; he was in his element in that tiny machine, sitting in a rubber survival suit because there was no heater to keep out the icy winds. The 43-year-old Boeing 707 pilot, with 15,000 flying hours to his credit, was content to chug along at 75 mph—his top speed was only 90. Occasionally he had to open the cockpit of the Furnier FR4 and scrape ice off the windshield with his hands, but he wouldn't take chances flying at night. He used to sleep during darkness at the nearest air-strip, then set off 'island-hopping' the next day.

While all the excitement over Clauser and Garcia was being played out, Slovak—an American citizen born in Czechoslovakia —was in mid-flight, en route from New York to London. He was doing it 'because it is a terrific way, in this confused and troubled world, of paying a respect to great people who did the flight fifty years ago. Doing it my way, I can appreciate a bit more what Alcock and Brown went through.

'It's a poor man's way of paying tribute to those two great aviators.'

His flight was also a way of paying respect to the Czech people in their struggle for freedom.

Slovak had flown the powered glider across the Atlantic before, from Europe to America, but as he came to make his final landing he half 'spun in' and hit a ditch. He broke eleven bones in his back, opened up his kidneys, lungs and left arm, broke both hips and cracked his skull. All because of what he said was his mistake, and not a fault in his beloved plane, *Spirit of Santa Paula*. Probably more than for any other reason, he was flying in the Air Race to prove that he, not the aircraft, had been at fault.

Confidently Mira Slovak headed for England, content in the knowledge that he would be able to arrive some time on the final day.

Getting into cloud-shrouded England wasn't proving all that easy for David Wynne-Davies, the 20-year-old Sandhurst Cadet whose previous experience of flying over water had been to cross from England to the Isle of Wight, a mere half-dozen miles. Now, with civilian flying instructor Derek Johnson beside him, he was trying to pick out the Scottish coastline from a cloud-filled sky. The coastline would help guide them into Prestwick, after a hectic flight from Teterboro Airport, just across the river from New York.

From the outset things went wrong. Every New York traffic light was against them. Then they had fifteen minutes of frustrated waiting at Teterboro before being allowed to take off. Next, the expected tail-winds turned into 35-knot head-winds, but the flight to Gander was fine. Getting the Piper Aztec Twin to start again after the refuelling stop wasn't quite so easy. For twenty minutes there was no spark of life. Finally, a $10 tip secured the use of a power starter unit. The engines sprang into life. The trouble was the first hint that the generators were about to black out.

Unknowing, they flew on, only to discover that the key weather ship *Bravo* was 400 miles off its normal station, and as a man was up the mast servicing the radio beacon in any case, they had to navigate by dead reckoning*—an additional strain. No food or drink was available at Narsarssuak and they decided to push over the mountain to Reykjavik in Iceland.

All this time David was gradually becoming icy cold. The temperature in the aircraft seemed little different from the 20 degrees below zero registered outside, as they flew at 12,000 feet to clear the mountains. It was then that the generator finally failed. To help him speed up his ground work from the check stations to and from the aircraft, David was wearing only a light flying suit and canvas shoes. For six miserable hours they flew on, a spare flying suit wrapped around the cadet's feet to give him some protection from the icy blasts of air. The first tinges of frostbite began to gnaw at his toes.

At Reykjavik the generator was repaired whilst the pair grabbed some food. But while they were working out details of the next leg, both David and Derek Johnson involuntarily fell asleep over their maps. They had been on the go for thirty-seven hours. Utterly exhausted, they had a short fitful sleep before climbing back into the aircraft for what they thought would be the last lap to Northolt on the northern outskirts of London. Although the generator was working, the heating system did not come on. The radio wouldn't function properly because it hadn't enough power,

---

* By taking into account compass bearing, speed, wind direction and point of departure, you plot your exact course by mathematical calculation.

and they never were able to get the longer-range radio to respond. Just to add to their problems, they again encountered severe icing conditions.

Thick cloud shrouded the Scottish coast on their approach, but they managed to work their way down south as far as Liverpool. Then, unable to raise anyone by radio, and running short on fuel, they decided to turn back and make for Prestwick. Alarm mounted at Northolt, where the Sandhurst team were waiting with a helicopter ready to rush Wynne-Davies to the Post Office Tower. The Aztec was well overdue. The Operational H.Q. Land-Rover outside the Post Office Tower sent out an urgent relay of messages to try to trace the missing plane. But there was silence.

Up in the clouds, battling his way over unfamiliar territory, with a dead radio and fuel running low, David was getting 'a bit agitated'. He climbed to 15,000 feet and still the cloud persisted. Without the ability to check his position, because of the defunct radio, David became disorientated and flew round in wide circles. But the only time he was 'frightened to death' was when he went down through the clouds and he 'thought we might break cloud too low'. It's like rushing along at a hundred miles an hour in a thick fog not knowing where the next turn of the road comes.

But he made it. Five hundred feet from the ground the cloud was clear and the Aztec crawled into Prestwick.

Only when David phoned through to the Academy at Sandhurst did the other cadets realize what had happened. A quick telephone consultation resulted in the decision to change the final landing spot from Northolt to Blackbushe, just outside Camberley, Surrey. The farther south they flew the more the weather improved. Over Oxford they came out of cloud, and shortly afterwards Derek Johnson brought the little green plane over the hedge at Blackbushe, his home airfield. As he did so David prepared to leap out, in spite of his frostbite, and dash for the Army Scout helicopter which whisked him to a barge on the River Thames. From Waterloo Pier a Land-Rover hurried him to the Post Office Tower where hundreds of people turned out to greet him at the end of his marathon. He punched his race card 44 hours 3 minutes 10.43 seconds after leaving New York.

With cheers ringing in his ears, he was led to a press reception, with champagne provided by the journalists themselves led by Keith Thompson of the *Daily Express*. The press were disgusted that there was to be no Army Top Brass reception* for the young hero. Spontaneously they felt that if the First Sea Lord could turn on the champagne for the Phantom pilots, and the Air Staff turn up for the Harrier arrival, then the press were not going to let his feat go unsung because no one of equivalent General rank from the Army could bother to turn out.

Recounting his experiences as he relaxed in the comfort of the Post Office Tower VIP lounge David, who had shared the flying with Derek Johnson, said: 'My feet feel like corned beef. ·I suppose I'd better get a doctor to look at them.' But: 'It was a fabulous experience for someone who has been flying for only eighteen months.'

That was an understatement.

* The Sandhurst C.O., General Philip Tower, had been at Blackbushe to meet David, but no senior Army Officer from the Ministry of Defence turned up or sent a message of congratulation.

Chapter Thirteen

RACE FEVER

*'There are occasions when the Gods of travel are out
to amuse themselves, and when all travel booking
clerks are unquestionably in their pay.'*

Nigel Buxton, *Travel '67*

IRISH MOTOR-CYCLE sprint champion Dan Keany decided to do
the seemingly impossible: connect with his New York flight at
Shannon by flying from London on a BEA jet which was not due
in Shannon until fifteen minutes *after* his connecting flight for New
York was scheduled to leave. Relying heavily upon the natural
'luck of the Irish', his plan was daringly simple. It depended upon a
clear record-breaking flight by a BEA Trident; on his wife, a
former Aer Lingus-Irish air hostess, pre-clearing all his documentation at Shannon; and on the co-operation of the Aer Lingus-
Irish Boeing 707 captain on the connecting flight.

Dan Keany, who had spent part of his honeymoon checking out
his New York route arrangements, was confident he could pull it
off and win the £5,000 ($12,000) Aer Lingus prize. The 29-year-
old importer finally committed himself to the plan on 2nd May.
Then he withdrew the reservation he had made in another name
on the Aer Lingus-Irish flight for 7th May, on which the bulk of
the competitors aiming to lift the same prize would be travelling.
In February Keany had done a dummy run on the Aer Lingus leg
from London to Shannon, and decided that it was the weakest link
in the plan. One inhibiting factor was the insistence by Aer Lingus
that competitors must be at a specially established pavement
rendezvous at Heathrow Airport ten minutes before the aircraft
began taxiing for take-off. Use of the BEA flight gave greater

flexibility, as Keany would be the only Air Race competitor o
board, instead of one of a large party. He could rely on spli
second timing rather than be stuck with a ten-minute reportin
time penalty.

Precisely at 12.55 and 58 seconds p.m. on 5th May, Dan Kean
stamped his time card at the top of the Post Office Towe:
Within seconds he was astride a motor-cycle and flashing towar(
the motorway to Heathrow. Rising to the occasion, the pilot c
the BEA Trident 1 opened up the big bird and clipped 18 minut(
off the advertised flight time. He touched down at Shannon an
rolled to a stop at 2.20 p.m. The Aer Lingus Boeing 707, due t
depart at 2.15 p.m. was still standing on the loading area.

No sooner had the Trident doors swung open than Keany's wi:
thrust his processed passport, air ticket, boarding card and custon
clearance into his hand. BEA had arranged the ramp transfer an
Keany, victory within his grasp, dashed across to the Boeing 70:
But the Aer Lingus duty station officer had other ideas. Becau:
the doors were closed, he blocked Keany's way and refused to l
him pass. Then took away his papers, twice ignoring the Boein
pilot's call that it was all right to let Keany on board. Not und(
any circumstances was the duty station officer going to gi
permission for the competitor to go up through the 'lower doo:

Heartbroken, Keany argued but got nowhere. Ironically, tl
Boeing 707 sat motionless for fifteen more minutes, held at i
loading point by Air Traffic Control delays. There was ample tin
for the regular passenger door to be opened to allow Keany to g
inside.

Angrily Keany declared: 'I believe that if I had made the journe
from London on Aer Lingus, there would be no problem. I had a
this worked out, I took a long shot on the speed of the Trident
it worked, but I would not be let on. It is not unusual for the do(
to be reopened for a passenger. Nobody could have touched n
for time, as I had eliminated the refuelling time.'

Somehow, the 'luck of the Irish' hadn't held good. Kean
almost in tears, stayed firmly on the ground.

The view of officials of Aer Lingus at Shannon was that to ha
allowed Keany to get on the Boeing would have given him 'a
unfair advantage over other competitors'. They denied the act w

one of bias because Keany was not travelling with the main party. Said an official: 'It is not our policy as an airline to open the door for anyone.'

In London, the question of boarding procedures was exercising the thoughts of Douglas Kelly, Aer Lingus Publicity Manager for Britain, even though he was blissfully unaware of the Keany saga. A telephone call at midnight on 6th May from Clement Freud warned Kelley that if one of the special cars cleared for taking competitors to the aircraft side was still around at the Heathrow pavement rendezvous after the 3.50 p.m. deadline, the car would 'constitute an aircraft with its doors open and steps in position!' Which meant that Aer Lingus would not legally be able to refuse to allow a late-arriving competitor to get in the car and go on board the aircraft. Up to that point, Aer Lingus had worked on the principle that their decision—not availability of vehicles—was the only rule necessary for closing the rendezvous. Freud's message was a major blow, as the airline had worked out the system as an impartial way of giving competitors the maximum of assistance and enabling them to skip normal boarding procedures.

The 'disruptive call' came as Kelly's team were busily sorting out final plans for the 7th May exodus. By 2.30 a.m. they had worked out a solution and an emergency staff order was produced, duplicated and distributed. It called for the rendezvous controller to scramble all staff and competitors from the rendezvous at precisely 3.50 p.m., under the supervision of Cyril Audrey, the timekeeper from the Royal Aero Club. A new sign had been prepared saying 'FAILED COMPETITORS TRANSFER', and this was to be unrolled at 3.50 p.m., thus effectively covering the 'anomaly' raised by Freud. With that, the Aer Lingus team grabbed a few hours' sleep in preparation for the main ordeal which would begin at 11 a.m., when the competitors arrived at the Poland Street headquarters to draw lots for the seats they would occupy during the flight.

Such detailed organization was necessary because Aer Lingus were in the unique position of carrying the bulk of the competitors in their category on one flight, on 7th May. It was a race in the truest sense. Competitors would be pitted directly against one another, rather than impersonally racing against the clock.

Additionally, as a result of travelling on the same aircraft, each would have precisely the same airborne time, so that the ground leg times were critical. A half-minute saved by drawing a seat near the exit could mean the difference between winning £5,000 ($12,000) and getting nothing at all, or just scraping in with the second fastest time to take the westbound *Daily Sketch* (£2,500 ($6,000) prize.

Travelling en masse on the two key flights on 7th and 8th May, was the oldest competitor in the Race, 75-year-old London cab driver Edward Beaton, sponsored by Mrs Hazel Guggenheim McKinley of the famous American Guggenheim family; and the two youngest, 10-year-olds Dominic Faulder and Dominic Freud, who were travelling with Clement Freud. Also seeking a prize were Edinburgh bus conductor John Trotter, a veteran of 208 world flights; Christine Turnbull, a 20-year-old balloonist; two naval ratings, Leading Seaman Stewart Dow and Leading Mechanician Howard Evans from the frigate H.M.S. *Nubian*, that controlled the Phantoms; Sandhurst Cadet Mark Hugo Fraser; a captain in the Irish Air Corps, John Kelly; and 74-year-old pioneer aviator and current licence holder 'all-weather Mac', Wing Commander Robert McIntosh, who has flown 23,000 miles. Joining them were Welsh café proprietor Romeo Basini, one of the first to enter the Air Race; Tony Appleton, who trained by running three miles every morning, taking sauna baths and leaping up and down stairs; Lord Montagu; and Lady Hermoine Thompson.

There were also a stockbroker from Jersey, Channel Islands, Terence Rory Conolly; a couple who had won their flight in an *Evening News* competition, Ellen and Frederick Cullwick; BBC commentator Liam Nolan, who was going to do broadcasts directly into sound programmes from radio cars at the London and New York ends; Eddie and Joey Freudmann, partners in a London travel agency; Luton travel agent Peter Odell and Taunton Round Table nominee Peter Hill.

Included in the original 6-strong American contingent were social worker Marvin Louis Gathers; Robert Schmeer, a piano tuner; PAN AM engineer William Hustler Allen, who just kept chasing back and forth across the Atlantic; and battling Ben

'Up Guards and at 'em!' is the battle cry of ex-Guardsman Captain Alan Clark who, in spite of being confined to a wheel-chair, put up a cracking time with the help of Guardsmen on both sides of the Atlantic.

Hold on to your hats is the order of the day as twelve-year-old Gail Shepherd races for her BOAC VC 10.

'Hop on a balloon!'
was the cry of at le
three competitors.
this one twenty -
year-old Christine
Turnbull heads for
London's Heathrow
Airport.

Below: *A refuelling stop and
quick documentation for world
record breaker Sheila Scott.*

Tony Samuelson gets away in his World War II Spitfire on his way to New York.

Ben Garcia was only looking for a quiet breakfast when he ended upside-down on a Pennsylvania chicken farm.

Ben Hur might not have approved of Michael Wellings's take-off in a chariot but the spectators certainly did—though he startled strollers in New York's Central Park on the other side of the Atlantic.

Dressed in a replica of Alcock's uniform, Derick Williams sets out in vintage style.

Marie Louise Cohen was full of smiles until her speed-boat got swamped.

The top hat will be kicked off the top of the Empire State Building if Sir Billy Butlin doesn't get a prize.

Prince Michael's attempt was very much a team effort by the 11th Hussars. Here is the briefing of the team in front of some of the equipment (Prince is on extreme right).

Prince Michael does the *Air Race* rope trick.

This wasn't the only mishap that WRAF Sergeant Heather Robinson experienced.

After braving impossible conditions Sandhurst Cadets' light-aircraft entrant David Wynne-Davies prepares to leap onto a barge in the middle of the Thames. As dusk approached his marathon of 44 hours 3 minutes 10 seconds was nearly at an end.

It's surprising what U.S. Naval Commander Bill Martin can do in a hood, even though a try-out ended up with him in the Hudson River.

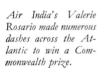

Air India's Valerie Rosario made numerous dashes across the Atlantic to win a Commonwealth prize.

Garcia—who booked even before his famous chicken farm pile-up. Strike-bound Air Canada employee Wolf Graunitz from Bolton, Ontario, was also signed up to take part.

By 2 p.m. on Wednesday the Control Centre at the Post Office Tower was besieged by competitors travelling on the Aer Lingus-Irish flight. Although Ann Robinson of the *Sunday Times* and Britain's only licensed woman balloon pilot, Christine Turnbull, had already left, 31 competitors crowded into the Centre. Outside, the roar of dozens of motor-cycles could be heard, practising and being tuned for the 'off'. A line-up of vintage cars began to form. There was a bad omen for the Navy when the motorized rickshaw, brought all the way from Singapore in the torpedo compartment of a submarine for use by a naval rating from H.M.S. *Nubian*, broke down during a try-out. But a 1927 Volvo, shipped especially to London from Sweden for Jan Sundfeldt, a journalist on *Vi* magazine, was working perfectly. Many of the contestants were garbed in old flying kit or traditional costumes, and Derick Williams and Brian Lathey made quite a stir when they arrived as Alcock and Brown. The majority of the contestants exuded an endearing spirit of jocular rivalry, though most were already resigned to the fact that they would not be present at the prize-giving ceremony on 14th May or be presented to Prince Philip.

First away, hours ahead of the others, was law student Christine Turnbull, in a flowing 1902 outfit. She had set off in a 1902 Panhard car for Farnborough, in Hampshire, to board a balloon for Heathrow, where she would link up with the main party.

Time of start was critical. As a result, pulling off a prize depended as much on nerve as on detailed organization. Nerve was needed to judge the precise moment of punching the timing card at the start: too early, and the advantage would go to the competitors who clocked out after you; too late and you would never reach the pavement rendezvous on time. Although each competitor had been allocated a start time, the chief timekeeper, Bill Fairley, accepted last-minute—sometimes last-second—changes. The Freudmann brothers decided as a precaution that each would clock out at different times and that only the one reaching the Heathrow pavement rendezvous with the minimum time to spare would actually go on the flight. Clement Freud, wearing a deer-stalker hat and dark blue track suit, had arranged that both his son and Dominic Faulder should start. But as he could take only one of the boys with him, he decided that which-ever reached the speedboat first would go all the way. He planned to do an immediate about-turn at the Empire State Building, arrive back in London at about 9 a.m. on Thursday and take whichever 10-year-old was left behind back to America on the afternoon's Aer Lingus flight. Before the start, Freud jokingly announced: 'We have arranged for some of my son's school friends to be on a zebra crossing so that traffic will be held up and allow us through to the speedboat.'

With cheering crowds to urge them on, the Aer Lingus con-tingent began to pour out of the Post Office Tower. At first there were stately exits by veterans like McIntosh, but with the rendez-vous deadline time drawing nearer, the atmosphere got decidedly tense. Bearded Howard Evans, one of the Naval ratings, hurried past the ground-floor controller out into the street, a parrot in a cage swinging menacingly from his hand. Then in a flurry of snapping feet Joey Freudmann hurtled out, hotly pursued by white-helmeted Marvin Gathers.

But incredibly, with only 23 minutes left in which to reach the Heathrow pavement rendezvous 15 miles away, 5 contestants still waited at the top of the Tower, time-cards at the ready. They were the remaining Navy man, Dow, Eddie Freudmann, and the three members of the Freud team, Clement, Dominic and Dominic Faulder.

Clement Freud, with slide rule, stop watches and wind gauges, had calculated that to get from the Thames Embankment steps into the speed boat, then onto the helicopter, to Heathrow, and from the helicopter to the pavement rendezvous would take at least 11 minutes 15 seconds. The inevitable conclusion was that he had to step into the boat no later than 3.38 and 45 seconds p.m. That left traffic and elevators as the only imponderables. But his plan was simple. One of the boys would leave by the first elevator, Freud would get into the next and the remaining boy would use the third one. Precision timing required the first to leave punctually at 3.30 p.m., the next at 3.31 p.m.

An act of God caused a rapid switch of tactics. Three-quarters of an hour before the plan became operative, the winds outside the Tower reached the level at which the speed of the elevators had to be cut by half. This threw everyone—except, that is, Clement Freud. The next lift after 3.30 was actually ready to leave at 3.32·45 seconds.

With Freudmann and Dominic Faulder already in the elevator, Clement Freud made a split-second decision to take it. After punching his time-card he just squeezed in beside them before the doors shut. Left behind were Dominic Freud and Leading Seaman Dow. Young Dominic Freud put up a remarkable performance. He dashed out of the Tower straight on to a motor-cycle and made up over a minute, to reach the Thames steps in under 3 minutes. But he was just 40 seconds too late to catch his father and Dominic Faulder. Their boat was in midstream when he appeared. Somewhat dejectedly, he had to be content with making a successful attempt the following day, but he gave a rousing cheer as his father's Jet Ranger shot skywards.

Freudmann by this time was already airborne, on his way by helicopter from a Thames barge helipad to Heathrow Airport. So was Navy man Evans, whose helicopter went from the much nearer St Pancras coalyard site. Quiet returned, momentarily, to the Tower, where for over half an hour the throaty roar of motor-cycles had drowned the send-off ovations. Risking it all the way by road was late starter David Cumplen, entered as Mr Festival of London Stores. The 20-year Aquascutum salesman, six foot three inches tall, wearing a bowler hat and a royal blue tracksuit, hit his first snag when the elevator was delayed for two minutes. Trying to pick up lost time, his motor-cycle-driver Jim Poskett overshot the speed limit by a good margin and was stopped by police. When he finally arrived at the pavement rendezvous at Heathrow, he was 14 seconds after the deadline and out of the Race.* He wasn't alone. Nine other competitors failed to get there by 3.50, including one whose plans were wrecked when he lost 3 minutes because of a wait for an elevator. Then his ingenious device for scaling down part of the Tower was vetoed moments before he reached it. In spite of a fast motor-cycle trip, covering the 15-mile

---

* The following day he reached the aircraft on time, but lost his time-card in the rush and was again disqualified. But he carried on to New York.

distance in 21 minutes, he arrived a minute too late. Leading
Seaman Dow, Graunitz and Scottish salesman Edward Clapperton
were also counted out. Yorkshire businessman Jim Thomson
arrived 15 seconds too late. As a result, instead of spending a night
tucked up in a luxury New York hotel, he had to sleep in a pair
of overalls in London; his clothes and luggage had gone to New
York on the flight he missed.

Freud hustled home just on the deadline and Eddie Freudmann
got there with 2 seconds to spare after a 14-minute dash from the
Tower.

Thanks to two schoolboys, Christine Turnbull also reached the
aircraft. Her blue and silver hydrogen balloon, which flew at 1,000
feet, made an almost perfect landing on West Dean Common,
near Camberley, after a 30-minute cross-country dash. But she
got disorientated and, surrounded by small hills, she didn't know
in which direction to head for the road. Then Steven and Mark
Cannon, who had been chasing after the balloon on their way to
school, came over a hill and directed her back to the road to wait
for her vintage car. Said an excited Mark: 'Cor, it was ever so
exciting. We chased the balloon for miles. But I don't know what
my dad's going to say when he finds I've missed school. Still, I
bet he never chased a balloon,' he added philosophically as
Christine, united with her vintage car, chugged off towards Heathrow, her straw boater pulled firmly on her head and her trailing
white chiffon scarf and ankle-length gown billowing in the
breeze.

On board the aircraft, Freud and Freudmann had been drawn to
sit next to each other. Everyone was in good spirits and the big jet,
as well as carrying regular passengers, was overflowing with
television teams from the BBC, Thames, Southern and Channel
Islands companies, as well as the Post Office Film Unit and
journalists from the *Guardian*, the *Daily Mail*, the *Daily Sketch* and
the *Evening News*. The Boeing made a record flight from London
to Shannon in 43 minutes.* It was so fast that the pipe band
arranged to meet the Race party had to spring onto the apron and
were only just lined up in time when the first competitor popped

---

* Pilot Gordon Wade thus beat the record established by the BEA Trident used by
Keany on Monday.

out and claimed his glass of Irish coffee during the rapid turn-round before the flight continued to New York.

On the final leg of the flight to America, Eddie Freudmann began to ponder the notes he had received from John Harlow, a New Yorker who was handling all the details of getting from Kennedy Airport to the Empire State Building. John's last-minute letter was crammed full of instructions. 'I must ask you to show absolute confidence in me and my team,' he wrote. 'With due respect to you, we are placing you in pretty much the same position as the chimpanzee Brooke Bond Tea are entering. The chimp will be carried over the entire course of the race in a travelling bag,* and will not have to make any decisions of her own. Likewise we will be carrying you from point A to point Z and will be telling you exactly what to do, and when. Please trust in us, let us do all the work and the prize money is as good as won.'

Eddie was prepared to do just that. John Harlow's team had been working on the Air Race plans for months for another would-be competitor who pulled out at the last minute. As the Aer Lingus jet approached the Kennedy Airport runway, well ahead of schedule, Eddie Freudmann, like the other 23 competitors on board, was anxiously wondering if the New York planning would work. Several competitors who had left earlier in the week had complained that the New York end, particularly at Kennedy Airport, was disorganized, with an apparent communications system failure which made it impossible to discover if a flight was going to arrive ahead of time.

Freud, Faulder, Freudmann, Kelly and Evans hit the terminal so fast that they were outside almost before anyone realized the Aer Lingus flight had arrived. Just as promised, Harlow, wearing a bright red parka, was waiting for Freudmann. As soon as recognition between the pair was mutual, Harlow started running. Freudmann followed, instinctively, across three busy roads to the inner expressway. As he did so, Harlow called up his motor-cyclist on a walkie-talkie. By the time they reached the expressway he was waiting to rush Freudmann to his helicopter.

But Clement Freud and young Dominic made the mistake of

---

* This in fact wasn't so; Tina only travelled in a cage in flight. Elsewhere she got VIP, including Rolls-Royce, treatment.

going through the same customs and immigration channel, and having to wait for each other cost them dearly. When they emerged from the arrivals terminal, the Navy man, Evans, had a three minutes' start on them, and Freudmann was ahead by a minute and a half. Luck turned for them when they were in the air. Freudmann's helicopter took a wrong turning when it was half a mile in front of them. The result was that Clement Freud and Dominic Faulder dropped down past the Manhattan skyscrapers only fifteen seconds behind Freudmann. Evans was nowhere to be seen.

Freudmann was onto a very fast motor-cycle within seconds. Freud and Dominic leapt into an ambulance in hot pursuit. When they started getting into heavy traffic the ambulance swept over to the wrong side of the street, mounted the pavement and with lights flashing and sirens blaring pulled ahead of Freudmann, leaving him in its slip-stream.

At the Empire State Building Freud and Dominic dashed for an elevator. Freudmann, following instructions, leaped off his motor-cycle as soon as he saw a five-foot-eleven, slender, attractive girl dressed all in black, with long brown hair hanging over her shoulders. She was Holly, the guide. Blue-uniformed Freudmann hot-footed it after her into the entrance hall. He reached the elevator. But before the doors could properly close, they were pushed open and in stepped Captain Kelly. Even then the elevator couldn't get started. The doors opened again and in rushed Freud and Dominic. The four of them arrived at the 86th floor together. In the rush to get out, Dominic was sent stumbling and an unsuspecting spectator was brushed aside as, arms flailing, lungs bursting, Freudmann led the others in a frantic last-minute spurt to the check-in station area. The timing clock was almost knocked over by a flurry of bodies. As amazed officials grabbed it to stop it falling, Freudmann pushed in his card, waited a few seconds,* then banged the button to freeze the clock and withdrew it immediately. Within a fraction of a second Freud pushed the card into the machine and pressed the button, in one continuous movement. Dominic Faulder followed immediately.

* Had he punched the button and held his card for a few seconds the man behind would have been that much slower.

Leading Mechanician Evans was calmly giving a victory press conference as the trio hurtled in, but his elation was premature, even though he had arrived minutes earlier. For, in an incredible finish to a 3,500-mile transatlantic dash, only two and a half seconds separated the winner and the runner-up, while the first four competitors had times within 90 seconds of one another. The Race had been won and lost on the 33rd floor of the Post Office Tower. For the last man of the four to clock out there, Clement Freud, won. His Race time was 8 hours 4 minutes 18·63 seconds. Second was Edmond Freudmann, 8 hours 4 minutes 21·19 seconds; third, Dominic Faulder, 8 hours 4 minutes 40·55 seconds; and fourth, Leading Mechanician Howard Evans in 8 hours 5 minutes 56 seconds. Captain Kelly was fifth with 8 hours 15 minutes 18 seconds, followed 4 minutes later by Lord Montagu.

As there were only two prizes—and the next day's flight time turned out to be slower than the one on 7th May—it meant that Clement Freud walked off with the £5,000 ($12,000) Aer Lingus prize, and Edmond Freudmann took the £2,500 ($6,000) *Daily Sketch* London-New York prize.

Victory celebrations were not the order of the day for Wing Commander McIntosh. His 1922 Dodge car hired to bring him from Kennedy Airport broke down half way.

Going in the opposite direction Hubert Georges, a 32-year-old from New Jersey who arrived at Heathrow Airport on the Thursday, had similar bad luck. The motor-cycle he was banking on didn't show up, so he grabbed a taxi. But when they approached Central London the driver claimed he did not know the location of the Post Office Tower, Britain's tallest building. Eventually he dropped Georges off at the foot of Tottenham Court Road, at the Centre Point Building, half a mile from the Tower. Unscrupulously he then charged him £6 ($15)—twice the correct amount. Frustration was haunting another American, Hobey Vance, who arrived in London on Tuesday. He spent most of the 36 hours before the return trip searching for a bowler hat. He couldn't find one! But he did 'manage to get to see the inside of an English pub'. In fact, English beer tasted so good that airline pilot Tom Shelton of Olympia, Washington, decided to spend most of his time going round 'tasting the stuff'.

Everyone had a different reason for going in for the Air Race—that's why it was so much fun. Often it was a spur-of-the-moment decision that attracted some competitors; occasionally it was enthusiasm tinged with luck—at least, that is how Air India pilot Ram Sastry came to enter. During a regular flight from Cairo to Bombay the 32-year-old pilot, when talking to the chairman of Air India, was so enthusiastic about the Race that the chairman decided Sastry and an Air India team should enter. Captain Sastry made the first of his two attempts on Tuesday 6th May, and returned a time of 7 hours 38 minutes 37 seconds, gaining valuable minutes by entering the aircraft through the crew hatch after the passenger doors had been closed for take-off. With their chairman behind them, Air India also entered a strikingly beautiful air hostess, 23-year-old Miss Valerie Rosario. Dashing backwards and forwards across the Atlantic, at one point she led the Rothmans New York to London category with a time of 7 hours 15 minutes 31 seconds.

It was after jumping from an Air India aircraft on the Friday that round-the-world hitch hiker Kenneth Crutchlow left Heathrow chased by irate customs and passport officials. He forgot to check with them before dashing for the road and hitching a lift to the Post Office Tower. He returned a time of 8 hours 42 minutes 17 seconds.

By-passing immigration and customs caused a momentary furore, too, over an attempt by New Yorker Jim Bailey. One of the most persistent competitors in the Race, he led one of the categories for most of the week, only to be pipped on the final day. What happened was that on one of his eight attempts Jim leaped from the PAN AM aircraft at Heathrow, skipped customs and dashed for his ground transport to take him into London. In fact he had done nothing illegal, for on that flight he had been registered as a crew member of the aircraft and his name appeared on the crew list for regular customs clearance. He is a PAN AM engineer.

Using PAN AM commercial flights, plus motor-cycles, helicopters, taxis, buses and private cars, Bailey raced back and forth across the Atlantic in partnership with fellow engineer Bill Allen, attempting to take various prizes. Throughout the eight-day race period the only sleep he got was snatched propped up in an aircraft seat or lolling in a chair at one or other of the Race check-in stations. His slowest time was 10 hours 30 minutes when he tried for the Empire State Building prize awarded for the 'Most Meritorious Resident of New York State'. In sharp contrast, his best time was registered on Saturday 10th May, during a trip from New York to London. Grabbing a motor-cycle lift from the ESB to the East Sixtieth Street heliport, he found Bill Allen had taken his helicopter. A quick chase round and he was soon airborne and headed for Kennedy, although precious—they turned out to be vital—minutes were lost. The PAN AM Boeing hurtled across the Atlantic in 5 hours 58 minutes air time. On touch-down at Heathrow Bailey leaped into a Royal Navy helicopter (as a former USAF officer he is still in the active reserve). The Wessex sped him to the St Pancras Station coalyard site. From there a Royal Marine motor-cycle, with outriders, raced him to the Tower. His time, 6 hours 57 minutes, consolidated his position as leader of the *Daily Sketch* category.

On his last try on Sunday, 11th May, Jim Bailey met with his final frustration. This time, when he reached the Sixtieth Street helicopter pad no helicopter was available. Hopping on the back of a motor-cycle, he reached Kennedy Airport in 20 minutes. The Boeing pilot made up the lost time in the air. It looked certain that he was going to better his Saturday time and make sure of a prize. Then things went wrong. His motor-cycle began to falter, finally spluttering to a dead halt. Within minutes a car picked him up and Bailey raced to the Tower. But his time was an inadequate 7 hours 3 minutes.

Another motor-cycle blew up on competitor Peter Howard, an El Al Air Lines duty officer, and threw his plans haywire. But it was a helpful airport official who grabbed Kathy Kopf's passport to speed her through Heathrow who added 1 hour and 34 minutes to her Race time—she forgot to pick it up, and it contained her time-card. So, while her sister Rayna clocked in at 7 hours 48 minutes 13·64 seconds Kathy, 18, a partner in the Small World Travel Agency in San Francisco, waited for her card to be retrieved.

It took 26-year-old Beat Studer just 50 seconds to sprint from his plane to the air terminal door, waved through by customs and immigration men. But his car was missing when he got there, probably because he switched flights to BOAC after his PAN AM jet went unserviceable. Frantically the Swissair steward rushed around asking the waiting line of taxi drivers if they could get him to the Tower 'in twenty minutes'. They weren't interested. In desperation he began stopping private cars. But when they heard the kind of time he wanted to make, they shook their heads.

Defeated, he took off his orange competitor's jacket and declared: 'I give up. It's too late now. But I'll try it again if I can.' He already had a 7 hour 51 minute 53 second London to New York time to his credit, in his bid to win the *Blick* prize for the fastest time put up by a Swiss national. On that occasion luck favoured Studer. He had chosen a flight piloted by Bob Pfaff, who was all geared up to turn in a fast time for Esso's entrant, Edwin 'Gillie' Potter. Bob, who between flights had been helping to prepare late light-aircraft entrants Nancy and Kerwin Kelly for their attempt, is one of PAN AM's most experienced pilots. By choosing to fly at 28,000 feet, he escaped certain restrictions imposed on the higher-flying commercial jetliners confined to the regular air lanes. The one disadvantage of low flying for jet aircraft is that it increases fuel consumption; its great advantage is that they can fly much faster and get closer to the speed of sound without inconvenience to passengers or damage to the aircraft.

For a long time no one tumbled to what the PAN AM skipper was doing. Then a BOAC VC 10 pilot woke up. He had got competitors on board also. But by then it was too late and the Boeing streaked ahead into Kennedy Airport nearly 70 minutes ahead of time. Potter, with the prospect of a prize looming in front of him, dashed for the helipad. The pilot of the first chopper he jumped into turned him out—it was waiting for someone else. The same thing happened at the next, and the next. After he'd had 30 minutes of frustrating scampering around, one pilot took pity on him and whipped him along into the skyscraper citadel of Manhattan. The helicopter pilot who had been hired to fly Potter didn't check on the early arrival of the PAN AM flight. Undoubtedly it cost Potter a £4,000 ($9,600) prize. Bitterly disappointed at throwing away his advantage, Potter checked in at the

Empire State Building for a Race time of 7 hours 38 minutes 17·23 seconds.

Helicopter problems thwarted Stirling Moss on his return to London on Thursday in a chartered BUA VC 10. When he reached Gatwick, the Jet Ranger helicopter which should have taken him to a Thames barge wasn't there. As he waited forlornly on the runway, Moss saw that it had taken him only 6 hours 19 minutes to reach Gatwick from the top of the Empire State Building. With the helicopter, the check-in station could have been reached comfortably under the 7-hour mark, even if he got snarled up in traffic from the Thames to the Tower.

But the helicopter stayed grounded at its base, unable to reach Gatwick because of the weather. Despairing of its ever getting airborne, Moss jumped into a Lotus Elan and then transferred to a Norton motor-cycle. But the traffic blocks were incredible, with the buses so close it was impossible to squeeze through. It took 55 minutes to reach the Tower. He finally clocked in for a Race time of 7 hours 16 minutes 57·19 seconds.

Biggest delay of all seemed to be that encountered by BOAC navigator John Cowell. He was held up for 30 hours by a faulty engine, but altered his check-out time as soon as a new engine was fitted in the Boeing 707 freighter, which was carrying a cargo of strawberries to London. The delay meant that he hit the rush-hour traffic and his car got so bogged down in a bumper-to-bumper jam that the driver of a follow-up motor-cycle belonging to another competitor took pity on him and gave him a lift to the Tower. His time, 7 hours 59 minutes 13 seconds.

Of all the hard luck stories, none was quite so heart-breaking as that of 21-year-old Women's Royal Air Force Sergeant Heather Robinson. Her job, Air Quartermaster, is similar to that of a civilian Air Stewardess but with a few extra, Service, responsibilities. Derby-born Heather was chosen by the No. 10 Squadron Commanding Officer, Squadron Leader Robert Hill, because she could be relied upon to use her initiative. Not only that, she was plucky, as she clearly showed when she was accidentally pitched off the pillion of her motor-cycle as it skidded to a halt beside an RAF Wessex helicopter standing in St Pancras coalyard.

Heather picked herself up, brushed down her scarlet anorak, and jumped into the helicopter. It took her direct to Wisley Airfield, where the RAF Air Support Command VC 10 was waiting, engines running, at the beginning of the runway. But the Wessex pilot had to hop over a fleet of fire trucks, busily engaged in watching a repair to a fuel panel, and land 15 yards from the VC 10. It took Heather only 40 seconds to race across the ground, sign customs forms, then scramble up a 15-foot ladder to the plane. During the flight she fulfilled her usual role and served refreshments—no alcohol—to fourteen RAF men on a routine training flight. She donned her crash helmet again just before touch-down in America. A fast helicopter and a motor-cycle ride helped her to a time of 7 hours 17 minutes 52 seconds. But she was beaten by 13 seconds by Sandhurst Cadet Simon Langdon, travelling in the same RAF Air Support Command VC 10.

On the return journey Heather made a brilliant run. Everything went right. When, glowing with exertion and pride, she arrived at the top of the Tower, she had achieved a remarkable time of 6 hours 29 minutes 11·03 seconds. Only the Phantoms, Harrier and V bombers could beat her. That, as it turned out, was the heart-breaking point. For, worried at the effect on the civilians if all the top prizes were snatched by the military, the Ministry of Defence and the organizers had a rapid consultation.

As a result, Heather had to forfeit her £4,000 ($9,600) Rothmans prize for the fastest eastwards subsonic time. For it was decided that the RAF would waive all claim to the Rothmans prize.* One of the reasons given was that Heather had inadvertently used a form of ground transportation in America which had not been specified on the official entry form; hardly a justifiable reason, for many winners could have been similarly faulted. Rothmans immediately stepped forward and offered to make a silver presentation to Heather at the official prize-giving to commemorate her superb feat.

It was an official mix-up that landed Heather Robinson without a prize. But an unofficial hitch nearly put the ten fancy-dressed, fund-raising London University students out of the Race, thus

* Like all prizes won by the Services, the money is given to deserving Service and civilian charities. Only the tophies are retained either by individuals or by the units.

wrecking their chances of winning a prize for the MacIntyre Schools for the Mentally Handicapped.

Oblivious to the problem, they set out from the Post Office Tower to parade down Chelsea's King's Road in stage coaches and 'old crock' cars. They aimed to be the most imaginative losers and collect the Butlin £5,000 ($12,000) prize. At a steady three miles an hour they reached Heathrow. Then they made four laps of honour round the airport, during which one of the cars caught fire. Arriving at the check-in point in a stately and dignified procession, their smiles suddenly vanished, and some of the seven girls almost burst into tears. For during their dawdlings around the countryside a misunderstanding over their intentions convinced the airline that the students had been forced to abandon their plans to fly; whereupon the tickets were sold.

Only two seats were left when the party arrived. The whole project was in jeopardy. Flabbergasted, the airline made panic calls to the Board of Trade. Their pleas set a sympathetic civil service machine into operation. Quickly permission was granted to Loftleidir, Icelandic Airlines, to re-route one of their aircraft from Europe for a special non-scheduled stop at Glasgow. From there the students could be taken to Iceland, and get back to their itinerary. Grateful to the Board of Trade, the remaining eight students hustled aboard a BEA flight to Glasgow. Luck still evaded them, for bad weather prevented the Loftleidir jet from landing at Glasgow and it was diverted to Prestwick. Undeterred, the students hightailed it to Prestwick in a taxi. Finally, after more technical hitches—due to a systems fault on the aircraft—they got airborne, en route for New York via Keflavik. After some of them had travelled from the airport in a Model T Ford, they clocked in at the Empire State Building 26 hours 30 minutes after leaving London.

Panic of a different type had caused Jack Webster to telephone me from Vancouver, Canada. An old friend, Jack was calling me live from his CKNW open-line radio programme, with an SOS; or rather, a Save Our Stevens plea. In his familiar Scottish brogue Jack, who befriended me a decade ago when I arrived broke in Vancouver, unfolded the tragic sequel to the Stevens Tiger Moth escapade.

Although it survived the bent prop mishap at Bellingham, the aircraft just couldn't take the 86 hours, 3,651-mile road journey. While it was being trucked through Montreal on its way to Moncton in readiness for pilot Neil Stevens, a huge gust of wind bounced the trailer hard—so hard, in fact, that the impact cracked two key longerons on the fuselage. It wasn't until it was unloaded at Moncton, with only five hours to prepare it for take-off, that one of the engineers discovered the worst. The key structures near the tail were damaged so badly that it was impossible to get the machine into the air.

'Impossible' isn't in Jack's vocabulary. So there he was, asking for help. 'This is what we want to do. We will get Stevens on to a regular airline flight from Montreal to Prestwick, because we're determined he will finish the Race somehow. Obviously his own Tiger is useless. But can you line him up with a Tiger Moth when he arrives? Then he can make a symbolic flight from Scotland to London in time to finish the Race on the last day. It means he will have started out and finished in a Tiger,' Jack's enthusiastic voice boomed out the plan. 'Can you do it, Peter?' he asked.

'I can't. But I know just the man who can. Give us an hour and we'll call you back.'

Within the time limit John Blake, the Royal Aero Club stalwart, had arranged for Tiger Moth owner Bill Meynell of Richmond, Yorkshire, to pick Neil up at Prestwick on Sunday morning. He was delighted to let Neil fly it to London. An overjoyed Jack Webster, before relaying the good news to Stevens in Moncton, said: 'Tell Bill he can't miss Neil. He'll be carrying the Tiger Moth prop with him!'

The successful execution of Air Race plans often hinged on the unpredictable weather. Starting off with contrary winds across the Atlantic, the predicted May sunshine often gave way to heavy overcast skies, ground mist and occasional fogs. The fickleness of Tuesday's weather spelled good luck for TWA air freight sales director Clifton Cooke and disaster for U.S. Navy Commander Larry O'Toole. Both flew into London on the same scheduled TWA flight, which clipped 36 minutes off its time. Once on the ground O'Toole knew he would have the advantage, for as a serving officer he was able to use the military helipad at St Pancras. Cooke had to stick to the river.

Cooke got clean away. But within seconds the weather clamped down and grounded O'Toole's helicopter. So he switched to the back of an RAF motor-cycle, but met snail's-pace traffic conditions. Instead of bettering seven hours for the New York–London leg to gain an almost certain prize, O'Toole clocked 7 hours 34 minutes 21 seconds. Already Cooke, by achieving 7 hours 16 minutes 36 seconds, had taken the lead in the £4,000 ($9,600) category. There was one consolation for the American Naval Commander: he found himself competing with an old friend, PAN AM pilot Richard Selph.

Ironically, a 'miraculous' tail-wind sent Richard Selph scooting across the ocean to New York in 6 hours flat on a regular PAN AM cargo flight, which clipped 10 minutes off an old BOAC record for the east-west crossing. Selph, a 29-year-old Dartmouth graduate from Sandy Hook, Conn., got off to a bumper start from the London end, thanks to weeks of meticulous planning. Peter Fornara, of PAN AM's London crew office, rode 200 miles around the city plotting the motor-cycle route through the back alleys; Jim Toomey, the airline's ramp operations superintendent, buttoned up the loading of the cargo flight 15 minutes early. Handled like a piece of express freight, Richard Selph was plucked from his motor-cycle and whipped through the airport tunnel by Brian Woosey in a Land-Rover cleared to dash out onto the airfield. Captain Dick Mayhew waited with jet engines running. Up through the crew hatch popped Selph, and the giant Boeing 707 freighter began hurtling down the runway.

After the record ocean crossing Captain Mayhew faced surface winds at New York, and had to put the plane down on Runway 22 at Kennedy Airport; it was almost a disaster, for it took 15 minutes to taxi in. To Richard Selph, waiting to spring out and make a fast getaway to his helicopter, 'it seemed like an eternity'. But in spite of the setback, he hit the Empire State Building clock 7 hours 6 minutes 24 seconds after checking out from London. It was good enough to win him the £4,000 ($9,600) Rothmans prize for the fastest westbound time in a subsonic aircraft.

Two days later there was another PAN AM assault on the New

York–London prizes. But their key contestant, who sat kicking her heels atop the Empire State Building observation platform before the off, looked like a high-school bobby soxer who had turned up to watch the others run. That was part of the disarming charm of fresh-faced 17-year-old Susi Scribner. Then she donned her orange *Daily Mail* race bib and safety helmet. One thing was wrong, decided her partners, yellow-jacketed Bob Ottum and Jerry Cooke of *Sports Illustrated*: Susi had leather-soled shoes. They popped over the Ohrbach's store and got her a substitute pair of sneakers—essential equipment for breaking Peter Hammond's record time of 6 hours 54 minutes 56 seconds.

Booked on PAN AM's Flight 104, due to take off at 10 p.m., the trio stoically waited to check out long after two other contestants had sprinted to catch a rival 10 p.m. BOAC flight. Not until word by phone from Susi's father, PAN AM pilot Captain Kim Scribner, told them the regular passengers were on board did they attempt to move.

At 9.28.24 p.m. Susi punched her time-card, followed by Bob and Jerry. With Jerry yelling 'Contestants, look out, contestants!' the team raced into the elevator after *Sports Illustrated* picture editor George Bloodgood, who had master-minded the ground leg. Spilling out at the ground floor, they hit the Manhattan night air and jumped into the waiting ambulance, its engine already running and the emergency roof light swirling around impatiently.

Two white-coated ambulancemen held up the traffic on Thirty-fourth Street to let the ambulance spurt by, tyres screeching and siren blaring. While they were jumping red traffic lights and careering from side to side down traffic-filled streets, Captain Scribner was already taxiing away from the loading area with his planeload of passengers.

The ambulance spun onto the pad with the helicopter already beginning to lift off the ground. The trio jumped in and were airborne just as Bloodgood was interviewed alongside the ambulance by a speed cop.*

Precisely at 10.10 p.m. the 'copter sank on to the Port Authority landing pad at Kennedy. Dressed in civilian clothes, a PAN AM

* He got two summonses that set him back $50.

representative hustled them into an International Scout vehicle. Slipping out past a bank of parked jets the driver pulled out towards the runway, where Captain Scribner was already lining his Boeing up for take-off. After a pre-arranged headlight signal from the Scout, the vehicle rushed out to the plane and skidded to a stop under the nose. Mindful of the roaring jet engines Susi, Bob and Jerry ran single file under the belly. With a click the little hatch opened, just as had happened at rehearsal. Hands snatched them up one by one into the heart of the Boeing 707. The hatch closed. The Scout screeched back to safety. Instantly the jet began gathering speed for take-off.

In mid-Atlantic, cruising along at 700 mph at 29,000 feet, Captain Scribner joyously announced that the rival-carrying BOAC flight was 4 minutes behind. It stayed that way. Captain Scribner made a smooth touch down at 9.33 a.m. London time— 7 minutes ahead of schedule. Off the aircraft they ran, down long tedious polished corridors towards the arrivals lounge. The escorting PAN AM representative, running like fury, snatched their passports. Immigration officials instantaneously stamped them. Helter-skelter they went through customs straight into a PAN AM station wagon. Still breathless, they jumped out and charged into their helicopter. As they took off Lavinia Scott-Elliot, from *Sports Illustrated*'s London Office, handed each a crash helmet.

The pilot, spotting the 10-foot-square splash of silver paint on top of a barge, settled the 'copter neatly on the waterborne pad. A motor launch carried them to the Embankment where three motor-cycles were waiting, engines already emitting a shattering crescendo of impatient noise. For Susi, it was her first motor-cycle ride, and she was scared. Bob Ottum was going great guns when his driver inadvertently swept the wrong way up a one-way street, had a quick brush with an oncoming lorry, bounced off the side of the road but somehow kept going. At the Tower steps London staffman Gwil Brown hustled him to the elevator. It had disappeared with Susi aboard. She had arrived first, even though on the final stretch her motor-cycle driver jammed on his brakes and shed a chain, leaving her to leg it to the Tower. She still clocked 6 hours 55 minutes 48.43 seconds.

Jerry Cooke, whose motor-cycle driver had got lost, achieved

M

6 hours 59 minutes 1·27 seconds, and Bob did it in 6 hours 57 minutes 24·39 seconds. Susi missed beating Peter Hammond by just over a minute. But jubilantly she saw her name go up alongside the Rothmans £4,000 ($9,600) prize, even though Peter Hammond's name filled the slot for the £5,000 ($12,000) BOAC prize.

Susi did a little victory jig around the 33rd floor of the Post Office Tower. When asked what she was going to do when she met Prince Philip at the prize-giving, Susi deliriously replied:

'I don't know—faint I suppose.'

But that was on Friday and the Race had still three days to go. Anything could happen before the Sunday, 11th May midnight deadline.

Chapter Fourteen

AIRBORNE ADVENTURERS

*'The only life worth living is the adventurous
life. Of such a life the dominant characteristic is
that it is unafraid.'*

Raymond B. Fosdick

ICELAND HAS RARELY witnessed such a spectacle. Passengers waiting
in Keflavik's airport lounge stared; air hostesses chatted ex-
citedly, and American Servicemen stood back in disbelief. For
stepping jauntily from the eight-seater executive jet came a jubi-
lant Sir Billy Butlin, rigged out in Ascot togs, resplendent in
morning suit and grey topper. Sir Billy Butlin, Britain's 69-year-
old holiday camp millionaire, was guarding the topper with great
care. Before leaving London he had promised: 'If I am not in the
first three in my class, I shall kick it off the Empire State Building.'
Then he swung aboard a high-powered motor-cycle. Clutching
his RAF driver, and surrounded by a military escort, he swept off
to the South Bank of the Thames to pick up his helicopter.

The last time he had been on a motor-cycle was ten years before.
That was when he competed in the *Daily Mail* London–Paris
Air Race, commemorating Blériot's first crossing of the Channel.
In those days—plain Billy Butlin—he had dashed backwards and
forwards so frequently across the Channel that the French dubbed
him 'Puffing Billy', and thanks to an agile turn of speed and a
Spitfire, he turned in the fastest non-jet time and came fourth
overall.

He arrived in Iceland 3 hours and 4 minutes after commencing
his bid to win the £500 ($1,200) Castle Britannia prize for com-
petitors using a leased or chartered plane. Members of the Variety

Club had joined with friends to guarantee to make the sum up to £5,000 ($12,000) if Sir Billy won; then the money would all be given to the International Variety Club charity and to the Channel Islands Variety Club. Sir Billy, whose home is in Jersey, carried with him a message of greeting from Sir Robert Le Masurier, Bailiff of Jersey, to the Hon. Richard J. Hughes, Governor of New Jersey. So he hoped he wouldn't have to kick his topper off the Empire State Building.

After refuelling in a record 14 minutes, the Hawker Siddeley 125 jet headed for Søndre Strømfjord and Goose Bay, before touching down at La Guardia airport. A siren-wailing ambulance rushed Sir Billy to the Empire State Building, enabling him to record 11 hours 30 minutes 41·35 seconds. Deducting the 6 hours handicap allowance gave him an unbeatable 5 hours 30 minutes 41·35 seconds Race time.* The topper stayed firmly on his head. Unexpected tail-winds had helped to push the tiny jet along at 400 mph. Returning in 11 hours 48 minutes 56·6 seconds, Sir Billy carried with him Thames TV's Monty Modlyn and Ann Robinson of the *Sunday Times*.

On the day of Sir Billy's second flight, aviation's famed flying grandfather, 67-year-old Max Conrad, finally left the Empire State Building check station. Bad weather had delayed him for six days. The veteran of 136 solo Atlantic crossings took with him only a flask of hot water and tea bags because he doesn't believe in eating while he's flying. Still stalked by bad weather and with 560 gallons of fuel crammed into extra tanks, compared to a norm of 140, he set off on his non-stop flight to England. Although more winds were against him than were pushing the Piper Aztec along, he encountered few snags.

Clear skies and absence of icing problems gave him a good run. 'I flew real low. It wasn't very cold at 5,000 feet. In the aeroplane I never sleep. In fact most of the time I sit composing songs. Then every hour I took a sip of hot water with a little sugar.'

With such modesty Max, who at 63 crash-landed in Greenland and had to walk thirty miles across a glacier to safety, dismissed his 137th solo Atlantic crossing. He clocked 23 hours 13 minutes

---

* The handicap caused annoyance among most competitors eligible for the prize. But the handicap had been published before the Race and no one raised a query then.

32 seconds, but would stop only long enough for a couple of interviews. Dismissing his waiting taxi, I took him to Victoria rail station in time for his Gatwick train. Before stepping out of the car he turned and said: 'You know, one of the most exciting things to have happened to me was to get stuck for ten minutes in the elevator of the Post Office Tower when I arrived.'

With a smile and a casual wave, the father of ten children and grandfather to twenty-seven disappeared. His return time—27 hours 17 minutes 28·86 seconds.

Max was not the oldest light-aircraft entrant, for Gordon Blair was a year older. The 68-year-old Philadelphia businessman co-piloted his own 1948 twin-engined Grumman Mallard amphibian. With him was 40-year-old William Dalton, a commercial pilot. Blair, who learned to fly fifty-two years ago in London, commented: 'The slowest part of the journey was from Gatwick Airport,' adding with a wry smile, 'You have traffic problems just like us.' His time from New York was 27 hours 1 minute, which included 22 hours in the air. The biggest disappointment; they were not allowed to use an old seaplane basin on the River Thames near Tower Bridge as the take-off point for the return flight. The Mallard was just a few pounds over the light-aircraft ceiling of 12,500 lb., but Blair and Dalton didn't mind competing against the big jets.

Even though his Cessna was within the limits Robert Snyder from Moorestown, New Jersey, wasn't optimistic about getting a prize. Clocking 26 hours 45 minutes 36 seconds, he said: 'The best reason I have for doing this is to be able to tell my children that I took part in the Great Air Race over the Atlantic.' At least he reached London, unlike Sam Marshall of Dallas, Texas, who set off on 4th May in almost impossible conditions, and had to give up in Gander after meeting heavy snow and ice.

By inclination the light-aircraft competitors seemed to be a bunch of unassuming adventurers. So it wasn't surprising when tall, slim Lancashire businessman Tony Capper walked unobtrusively into the Post Office Tower on Thursday and clocked in at 22 hours 50 minutes 14·09 seconds. It gave him the lead in the eastbound class. Outward-bound he turned in a time of 21 hours 48 minutes. After a 7,000-mile round trip in his twin-seater Piper

Aztec with co-pilot David Antrobus, Capper said sleepily: 'It was lovely. We only did it for the fun of it.'

The sheer fun of it! That was the keynote for a multitude of contestants, some who had never flown before. Most amazing of the fun-set was Baltimore travel agent Cooper Walker, who began growing mutton-chop whiskers as soon as he heard the Race was on. Like Phineas Fogg in *Around the World in Eighty Days* Cooper Walker got involved in every form of transport from balloons to mules, from vintage cars to 50-year-old biplanes and twentieth-century jets.

In fact Cooper Walker, trying for the 'most meritorious non-winning entry', decided if the plan was not to win, then 'why not not win well?' At that moment the idea of a commemorative pilgrimage between St John's, Newfoundland, and Clifden, Ireland was born.

Using a 1919 Stutz Bearcat owned and driven by Henry Austin Clark of the New York branch of the Veteran Motor Car Club of America, Cooper Walker set out dressed in 1919 brown tweed jacket, knickerbockers, and a flapping, matching 'Henry Higgins' great-coat. They rumbled in stately procession to Rhinebeck, New York's World War I airport, and Cooper Walker climbed into a 1919 Jenny biplane for a single circuit. After travelling in a regular-type charter aircraft and then a hired car, he reached Toland, Conn. There, on Monday morning, he went solo in *Mark Twain*, a hot air balloon.

Weather problems prevented his landing at St John's, Newfoundland. The nearest he got was arriving overhead in an aircraft which couldn't land and had to be diverted to Halifax, and as a result he never got to use the horse hired to take him to the Vimy take-off site. Backtracking, because of the same type of fog that defeated many pioneer Atlantic flyers, he picked up an Aer Lingus-Irish flight from Boston to Shannon, where a 1910 touring Adler was waiting on the tarmac. After a symbolic ride he switched to a modern car to rush the 116 miles to Clifden and back within the six-hour stop-over. A BEA flight got him to London. From Heathrow a 1919 Rolls Royce took him to Dunstable in Bedfordshire for a 55-minute balloon hop with the British Balloon Club in *London Pride*. The intrepid adventurer then re-boarded the Rolls for Windsor and, after a sharp row on the Thames, the car carried him to the Post Office Tower, where he recorded the relaxing time of 144 hours 51 minutes 32 seconds. His partner Ogden Norman, the second man to arrive from New York on the first day, aiming for a speed prize, turned in a time of 7 hours 31 minutes 21 seconds.

Going the other way on a similar leisurely pilgrimage was Slim Hewitt of BBC's '24 Hours' television show. It took him 192 hours 33 minutes 3 seconds to reach the Empire State Building. Even so, father and son team George and Ralph Miele of Basking Ridge, New Jersey, robbed Slim of the honour of being last man home. He tried hard. In fact, it was amazing that Slim ever arrived at all. He left London sedately in a sedan chair carried by mini-skirted girls, changed to a bus, an Underground train, coach and horses, a normal train, and finally crossed the English Channel in a hovercraft. That's when things really began to go wrong. First, he got into a balloon which took off into fierce gusting winds and he lost contact with his ground party for four hours. Desperately a Beechcraft Baron was chartered to get Slim from Lille to Luxembourg, so he could connect with a special flight. The plane made it but Slim, in long raincoat, flying helmet and goggles, proceeded to get lost again, this time being stranded in Greenland trying to thumb a lift from the Eskimos. The USAF came to his rescue and flew him to America. Instead of heading directly for the Empire State Building, Slim decided to go on a 'meet the people' tour. By the time he plodded up Fifth Avenue in a covered wagon, he had made another balloon ascent, ridden a helicopter and a motor-cycle, got nowhere on a mule, pedalled wildly on a bicycle, rowed on the Hudson River, ridden in a sleigh drawn by two huskies, and somehow managed to arrive at the 86th floor check-in just before the Race ended.

At least he arrived under his own steam, unlike vivacious 18-year-old Rosemary Stanford Smith, who was dumped on the Empire State Building control table bound up in a plastic bag by air freight specialist McGregor Swire, 8 hours 27 minutes 7 seconds after being parcelled up at the Post Office Tower.

A 38-year-old U.S. Navy helicopter pilot, Commander Bill Martin, had his head covered by a black hood. Claiming he used magical powers to conjure up a tail-wind, he ended up leading the New York to London subsonic class with a time of 7 hours 20 minutes 10·7 seconds.

Refuting accusations that it was a cheap stunt, Martin claimed he had been given magical powers by a 100-year-old fakir fifteen years before in Singapore. When the fakir touched his head, 'a vibration passed right through my body, and the old man said he was transferring his powers to me. He died there and then'. Those powers, Martin claimed, included being able to see without eyes, resulting in his having 'my own built-in radar system. I can drive a car or even pilot a helicopter wearing a black hood'. To prove it was no spoof, he passed the hood round. No one could see a thing. Only once did the power let him down—during an Air Race try-out, when he leapt into the Hudson River instead of into a helicopter. Race time went off without a hitch. Martin leapt on and off motor-cycles, in and out of helicopters and aircraft without being able to see a thing. And he pounded along the sidewalks with vigour and ferocity.

Immigration officials at Heathrow had only just got over the shock of seeing Martin bound by when a dog-collared vicar raced past them at the double, an Air Race bib clasped tightly to his chest. A Norfolk Methodist minister, the Rev. Desmond Hall was returning from an American preaching tour. Fifth Avenue was treated to the spectacle of RAF Squadron Leader Groves, dressed as one of the Victorian Empire builders, weaving through the traffic pedalling his 1887 penny-farthing bicycle. His only problem had been getting the penny-farthing into a helicopter.

Back in London, champagne was the order of the day as the *Daily Mail* toasted Tim Heald of the rival *Daily Express*. Wearing his old school Rugby jersey, and the *Mail* racing bib, Tim made it from the top of the Tower to Waterloo Pier through heavy traffic—and red lights—in 7 minutes. In spite of the rain he dashed across the road, down the thirty-nine steps into a speedboat, which took him to a helicopter sitting on top of a barge. One minute and twenty-five seconds after reaching the pier he was airborne, and he was sitting in his BOAC VC 10 awaiting take-off less than 35 minutes after checking out, only to find that bad weather delayed the flight for 25 minutes. From Kennedy Airport, he switched from a helicopter to a motor-cycle—driven by an off-duty policeman, who attracted a friendly eye and was given a siren-blaring police car escort through a traffic snarl-up. Tim's Race time, 7 hours 50 minutes 42·85 seconds. He returned in 7:32:27·29.

Before starting, he received a postcard from his brother: 'Best of luck against the monkey.'

'That,' said Tim, 'is the competitor I'm most worried about!'

He need not have been, for Tina the chimp took 9 hours 52 minutes to get from London to New York, and returned in 10:40:31·9. But even if Tina had broken every speed record and snatched the prizes from the Navy and the RAF her reception, particularly in America, couldn't have been more sensational. A couple of New York television men actually attempted to interview her when she arrived in her glittering white outfit at the Empire State Building. The 5-year-old, 3-foot-tall West African chimpanzee mimicked the Race experts and got free television and press coverage for her sponsors, Brooke Bond Tea, worth £250,000 ($600,000). At the start, to oblige photographers, she frisked and pirouetted and cheerfully waved her time-card, showing her own photograph and thumb print. But when checking in, she became a model competitor. Unaided, Tina slipped her time-card neatly into the machine, and pressed the button to record her start. A sparkling new chauffeur-driven Rolls Royce took her VIP-style to the BOAC jet. There her dignity took a knock. Tina was bundled into the hold in her special cage for the flight to New York. After consuming six bananas and four cups of tea at Kennedy Airport, she was sped to the Empire State Building in a chauffeur-driven limousine.

George the tortoise, Beethoven the budgie and Harold the Handsome Hare didn't get that kind of VIP treatment. In fact they were smuggled in and out of America by Tom Ravensdale, usually in the false bottom of a suitcase, or hidden under his crash helmet. When Ravensdale was in a motor-cycle crash outside Kennedy Airport, which cost him a prize, George didn't raise an eyelid. During one of his six fund-raising trips for the *Spina Bifida* charity, Ravensdale spent only three minutes in New York. Unlike Tina, he didn't even have time for a cup of tea.

With six prizes open to contestants not putting up the fastest times, it was obviously a golden opportunity for gimmicks. ALITALIA salesman Michael Wellings left the Post Office Tower in a Roman chariot. A fresh chariot and horses met him in New York and, in full Ben Hur dress, he made a couple of circuits of parts of Central Park before clocking in at the Empire State Building, leaving the chariot parked outside. Once he had to draw his sword to prove to an American customs man that it wasn't lethal.

Suddenly the *Daily Mail* Air Race seemingly shrank the Atlantic to the size of a sports arena, with millions of world-wide spectators looking on. Even non-participants got caught up in the spirit of the adventure, including Norman Lamb, the 18-year-old assistant manager of the snack bar on the Empire State Building's 86th Floor. He loaned his hot dog machine to dry out the rain-soaked money and documents of two RAF Cranwell cadets, Ronald Handfield and Steven Mirrell, who used Jet Provosts to get from Northolt, on the London outskirts, to link up with their RAF VC 10. Arriving in New York on the one really rainy day, they got soaked, but managed Race times of 8 hours 17 minutes 22 seconds and 8 hours 19 minutes 2 seconds respectively.

Many competitors combined the fun of the Air Race with business. Outstanding were Ted Drewery's party, who arrived back in London bursting with export orders. In America, two of the men had phoned Drewery, saying, 'We can't afford to go home, we're too busy. . . .' Another sent a telegram from Montreal: 'Landed $30,000 order. Must go home immediately. Please bring my luggage back. . . .' Drewery reported, 'It's incredible—the publicity gimmicks that were used during the Race worked!'

He was even more enthusiastic about the hard sell: 'We took eleven paintings by a young British artist, Paul Taffs, who has never exhibited in Britain, and sold every one for $200 each . . . then ten $100 wedding dresses were snapped up. . . . But it's hard to put a figure on the orders. For instance, one man reported he had lined up a million-pound job in Afghanistan. But how do you put that over to the press? Would they understand that on a trip to America you could land an engineering contract in Afghanistan? It doesn't make sense. Does it?'

Lighter moments gave a fun side to the Drewery team visit.

They beat the Ohio Golf Club over 18 holes—but later lost a drinking match to an American team in Watney's Pub in Greenwich Village. To cap it all, on every American airline they used, they found the air hostesses wearing bowler hats while they served the meals. . . .

It was one-upmanship all the way.

In a crazy kaleidoscope of speed, humour, gimmickry and salesmanship, the Air Race drew to a close. Throughout the first seven days the BBC sound and TV programmes, the commercial TV companies and the press had given saturation coverage to the event. Late on Saturday night Brian Robbins, producer of BBC's 'Race You to the Top' TV programme, came up pencil in hand to ask:

'I would be right in saying that the final day will see changes in the leaders of some of the categories, wouldn't I?'

'Positive,' was my instant reply. 'It's still anybody's Race— Right across the board.'

Chapter Fifteen

GRAND SLAM FINALE

'What a gay and cheeky performance by the Navy and Air Force in the Daily Mail's *bumper Transatlantic Air Race ... That's real initiative. The Top Brass deserve a medal for enterprise. ...'*

London *Daily Mirror*, 6th May 1969

HARING DOWN THE motorway towards Central London at 110 miles an hour, the speed cops couldn't go any faster. If anything, the gap between their police patrol car and the E-type Jaguar was widening. Helpless, the two-man patrol car crew kept their eyes on the slowly vanishing vehicle in front, although since it was plastered with tell-tale Air Race stickers, there was no question of their losing it completely. From the moment they had set out to catch it, they realized that the E-type was bound for the Post Office Tower. And that is where they eventually caught up with the car and 22-year-old driver Simon Martin. His E-type was stationary. His passenger, Tony Drewery, was already at the check-in station. The 16-minute trip from Heathrow Airport enabled Tony, representing his father's 'BEST' planeload of bowler-hatted British businessmen, to return a Race time of 7 hours 3 minutes 5·01 seconds: good enough to oust Stirling Moss from the top spot in the Grovewood Securities prize for a charter business jet. As congratulations cascaded upon Tony Drewery for winning the £500 ($1,200) prize, his driver was being questioned by the irate speed cops.

'I didn't know they wanted to stop me, as I was a long way ahead of them,' explained Simon Martin. 'I don't know what speed I was doing on the M4 motorway, but the police say they were doing 110 and could not catch me!'

The final day had got off to a quiet start, as the first of the day's 52 competitors from New York arrived at the Post Office Tower. The early in-bound competitors ranged from one of the oldest, Wing Commander McIntosh, who took 7 hours 22 minutes 44 seconds for his return journey, to one of the youngest, 12-year-old Gail Shepherd from York. She had been entered by her grandfather, who had been one of the oldest competitors in the London-Paris Air Race. Her time of 8 hours 21 minutes 10·23 seconds did not put her among the winners, so bang went her hopes of buying a guide dog for a blind friend out of the prize money.

Some of the times of the early arrivals raised the possibility of a record-breaking day. First man into London on Sunday was Royal Marine Lieutenant Charles Smith of Cardiff, with 7 hours 22 minutes 43·99 seconds. Shortly afterwards Eric Wheatley, BOAC's Sales Manager East, from Eastchester, New York, arrived in 7 hours 11 minutes 7·99 seconds, a striking improvement on the 7 hours 34 minutes 27·25 seconds of Air India's Captain Ram Sastry. Each had left New York early on Saturday evening, when traffic conditions were still bad. The fastest times were expected from people leaving the Empire State Building late on Saturday evening or undertaking the complete journey on the Sunday. Conditions appeared ideal. At last the wind, which had been blowing in contrary directions for a week, seemed to have got firmly back on its predictable course over the regular air lanes. Tail-winds were again blowing for London-bound aircraft, a fact that could help them to clip more than half an hour off their scheduled flight times.

Peter Hammond, of the London Green Diamond Club, had been hogging the top spot in the prize-winners' list for six days with his time of 6 hours 54 minutes 56 seconds. But Hammond was convinced that his time could be beaten. Susi Scribner had come within a minute of doing so, and by his own reckoning it should be possible to clip off 20 minutes. Obviously, he must make another attempt.

Off he set for New York, puzzling over the problem of how to gear up the members of his American organization, who were unprepared for his second bid, apart from an SOS telex message. As he flew from London, Hammond set to work preparing a series of pocket-sized 'action cards' for five key personnel in New York. They contained exhaustive instructions and included telephone numbers and exact timings and link-up procedures. When he touched down at Kennedy Airport, Hammond had just four and a half hours to locate his five key helpers, hire a helicopter and rehearse the Empire State Building get-away procedure.

Hammond was booked on a BOAC aircraft. Some of his keenest rivals were flying later on TWA. They included Dr Ken Holden, a quiet unassuming Irishman who works as a Boeing 747 jumbo-jet projects controller for Aer Lingus. Purposely Holden and his backer, Ken Besson, owner of Irish Helicopters, had picked Sunday because, as Holden said, 'no one would expect a contestant on the last day of the race to make a really determined bid'. In that he was wrong. Blonde QANTAS employee Helen Lysaght was determined that she could better the time of 7 hours 48 minutes 49 seconds she achieved on the first day. On that occasion her jet met stiff head-winds and, after she had arrived at Heathrow Airport, her motor-cycle had broken down. Helen was positive she could break the 7-hour barrier on her QANTAS flight. So too was Rupert Lycett Green, whose white Norfolk jacket, light knickerbockers and white knee-length boots belied his determination to set up a speed record. Another hot favourite was PAN AM's Jim Bailey, making the last of his eight attempts.

All were competing for the £5,000 ($12,000) BOAC prize for the fastest New York–London time using a scheduled jet aircraft. If that evaded them, they had two other prize chances: £4,000 ($9,600) put up by Rothmans for the fastest time using a subsonic aircraft, and £2,500 ($6,000) offered by the *Daily Sketch* for the fastest eastbound time by an unsponsored individual.

Prince Michael, the Queen's cousin, was one who had to be beaten to take the Rothmans prize. Along with two sailors, two men of the Royal Regiment of Fusiliers and Captain Peter Tappenden of the Parachute Brigade, Prince Michael was using a VC 10 of RAF Air Support Command to cross the Atlantic. The Prince's Race attempt was almost wrecked at the start; disaster was only averted by quick-thinking Race Controller Ken Corney.

Doing his late night checks, he glanced down the list of the day's runners out of New York and his alert eye caught sight of a blank space against Prince Michael's name. He had not checked in. Spotting a sweater-clad spectator who looked an army type, Ken asked if he was anything to do with Prince Michael. He was.

'Then get him to check out or he will be disqualified. Don't you realize, 10 p.m. is the deadline for check out? If the Prince misses that, he will have to wait until 8 o'clock tomorrow morning!'

In a flurry of footsteps the man disappeared, and returned at top speed with Prince Michael who, oblivious to the drama, had been having a drink of coffee. His timing had been thrown out by the news that the RAF VC 10 was not ready for take-off from Kennedy Airport. With just one minute to spare, the Prince stamped his time-card.

Wearing a white crash helmet, a V-neck sweater, orange *Daily Mail* Racing bib, cream cricket flannels and rubber-soled shoes, the Prince shot off into the elevator. Ex-members of the Prince's 11th Hussars Regiment had organized the New York ground leg. Swiftly he was astride a motor-cycle and rocketing towards the helipad site. New York's traffic lights were no respecter of royal personages, and like 98 per cent of the other competitors, the Prince was held up at several. But since he was connecting with a military aircraft, his helicopter was able to land right alongside the RAF VC 10. His flat-out race from the check-in station was in vain. Somebody had bungled the loading procedure and the VC 10 was not ready for take-off. Air Freight was still being lifted aboard as the Prince arrived. Twenty minutes were needed before it was stowed correctly. The doors closed for take-off, but by that time the aircraft had lost its take-off slot. Just when Kennedy Air Traffic Control were about to give the pilot clearance after a frustrating wait, he was ordered to taxi clear. One of the jets which was airborne a few seconds before was suddenly instructed to return. Rejoining the take-off line-up took time. When the RAF jet eventually, screamed down the runway, Prince Michael had been sitting in it for 65 minutes.

Desperately the RAF crew tried to make up lost ground. But they didn't stand a chance. Luck was just not running the right way. In flight, the pilot twice had to change direction because of severe turbulence. Then harsh weather conditions forced him to take an unfavourable altitude, which cut his speed. But finally the plane touched down at RAF Brize Norton, Oxfordshire. As it did so, the six Air Race competitors were handed asbestos gloves. Dutifully they were put on by Prince Michael; naval ratings Howard Evans and Stewart Dow; 2nd Lieutenant Timothy Merritt and Fusilier Derek Clark, of the 1st Battalion the Royal Fusiliers; and the Para Brigade's Captain Peter Tappenden. Protection was needed, for they were about to do the Air Race Rope Trick. As the powerful jet engines were put into reverse thrust to act as an additional brake, the door was swung open and a long white rope was hooked to the top of the doorway. Almost before the VC 10 rolled to a stop, Prince Michael leapt into space, and slithered down the rope, his asbestos gloves protecting friction from burning his hands. The others followed. Moments later they were rushing for helicopters. The Prince was airborne first, as the naval ratings chased after their Wessex helicopter. The Fusiliers grabbed a third, and a fourth waited for Captain Tappenden and his three non-competitor paratroopers. After a mass exodus the helicopters headed for different vantage points in London. Prince Michael's destination was Waterloo Bridge; the Navy's, St Pancras coal-yard; the Fusiliers', Central London; and Captain Tappenden, having been denied the use of Regent's Park or Hyde Park, headed north of London to Hatfield, for a symbolic parachute descent before racing back to the Tower.

As he scrambled aboard the Alouette helicopter at Brize Norton, Prince Michael tore his trousers and gashed his leg. But that didn't stop his leaping from the helicopter onto a barge and then into a high-powered speed-boat across to the Thames Embankment. A hair-raising motor-cycle ride brought him tearing to the Post Office Tower the wrong way down a one-way street. When he reached the 33rd floor to check in 7 hours 45 minutes 42 seconds after leaving New York, there was an informal family reception committee waiting for him: his brother, the Duke of Kent, had driven to the Post Office Tower with the Duchess of Kent and their children, 5-year-old Lady Helen Windsor and 6-year-old the Earl of St Andrews. There was no pomp or ceremony for the royal visit. The family, with total informality, awaited arrival, chatting to other competitors whilst the children explored the public viewing gallery.

When he burst out from the elevator, Prince Michael had at least one consolation. He had beaten everyone else travelling on the RAF VC 10 by just under an hour. Of the frustrating 65 minutes sitting in the plane, which cost him the Rothmans prize, he said: 'We just sat twiddling our thumbs. The delay was just a piece of bad luck. But the Regiment organization was absolutely slick. Not a second's delay all along the route. Our experience just goes to prove that no matter how much planning one puts into it, one is in the lap of the gods.'

Gripped in freezing ice; with temperatures falling to 24 degrees below zero; and with a radio which suddenly packed up as they were flying their Riley Rocket near Greenland—husband-and-wife team Kerwin and Nancy Kelly were very much in the lap of the gods. They were temporarily lost in nightmare conditions. To top it all, the light aircraft's heater wasn't powerful enough to cope with the alarming temperature drop. Nancy, mother of four children, was freezing. Her warm flying kit lay out of reach at the back of the aircraft. Her husband, a former PAN AM co-pilot turned business tycoon, pulled off his jacket and wrapped it around her knees.

For a moment they had warded off frostbite. But for twenty tense minutes they flew on blind without their radio to give them a means of checking their direction. At that point Kerwin was ready to quit and turn for land. He looked at his wife, and she gave him a reassuring smile. Nancy was not going to give up the race of a lifetime. She decided to attack the defunct radio. Using her fingernails she unscrewed a panel and tightened up loose connections. Though she tore her nails, the radio miraculously crackled back into life. Deciding this was a good omen, they ignored the safety of Greenland and flew on to Iceland. The weather improved greatly and they hopped straight over to London. Oblivious to anyone else's timing, the pair made a leisurely trip to the Post Office Tower and Kerwin clocked in at 22 hours 31 minutes 48 seconds. His mini-skirted wife was 9 seconds slower. They gave each other a great hug when they discovered they had both shot into the lead—Kerwin for the fastest time from New

York by a man and Nancy the fastest time by a woman. It looked as though each member of the husband-and-wife team from Quakertown, Pennsylvania, was destined to walk off with a £1,000 ($2,400) *Evening News* prize.

Mike Fallon of Rickmansworth, Hertfordshire, had other ideas. He arrived unheralded to return 21 hours 31 minutes 57 seconds, ousted Kerwin from his top spot and gained the men's prize. His co-pilot, Anthony Samuelson, returned 21 hours 32 minutes 9 seconds. Outward bound, Samuelson had trouble with his Spitfire. He had to put in to Brawdey, Pembrokeshire, after he had a radio failure, and found the fuel was not transferring from his auxiliary tank. He switched to another aircraft to get to Shannon, from where he continued the Race in a light aircraft as planned. He reached New York in 34 hours 3 minutes 10·63 seconds. Now he had just missed a prize by eleven seconds.

Nancy and Kerwin were nevertheless deliriously happy just to have arrived in complete safety. And when Marie Louise Cohen, the last woman to arrive, checked in after flying her Cessna 310 across the Atlantic, Nancy was assured of her prize, for it had taken Marie Louise Cohen 24 hours 32 minutes 8 seconds to get from the Empire State building—nearly two hours longer than Nancy.

No one had really counted the Kellys as potential prize-winners and their mid-afternoon arrival caused quite a stir. But as the excitement died down, interest in the Air Race was not allowed to flag. Lieutenant-Commander Harry Lipscomb, the Royal Navy press man, alerted the Race Control Centre to the news that their third Phantom jet from No. 892 Squadron was fast approaching Britain. Flying it was the Squadron Commanding Officer, 35-year-old Lieutenant-Commander Brian Davies. And the Race competitor was the observer, 32-year-old Lieutenant-Commander Peter Goddard—the man largely responsible for master-minding all three race strategies.

The Royal Navy had opened the Air Race sensationally on the first day when Lieutenant Paul Waterhouse raced from the Empire State Building to the Post Office Tower in 5 hours 30 minutes 24·43 seconds; to do so, his Phantom, piloted by Lieutenant-Commander Doug Borrowman, established a world

speed record for an Atlantic crossing from America to Britain of
5 hours 3 minutes 18·8 seconds. Then on Wednesday, along came
Lieutenant Hugh Drake to drop the time to 5 hours 19 minutes
16·93 seconds after his Phantom, piloted by Lieutenant Allan
Hickling, had created a new world speed record from America to
Britain of 4 hours 53 minutes 10·6 seconds.*

Could the Navy produce a sensational grand slam finish to
eight days of daring and daffy exploits by a galaxy of air adventurers from all over the world? Certainly they were going to try.

Peter Goddard and Brian Davies were determined to become
the fastest men in the Race. The omens were good. Meteorological
forecast in New York indicated a tail-wind of 25 knots. Though
the weather was a little unstable, with luck they should have no
difficulty in making their three tanker connections to pick up fuel
in flight.

Drawing on the experience from the other two crews, Peter
Goddard made several slight alterations in their route. The main
decision was to arrange for the third, and final, tanker refuelling to
be farther away from England than before, which would give
them a faster run in. Learning that both previous crews had
experienced infuriating communications difficulties,† largely as a
result of having to juggle three different systems, the set-up was
slightly modified. Confident of success, and with Lieutenant
Hugh Drake back in New York to pass on tips and see him off
Peter Goddard punched his time-card. The elevators were waiting
as his small, eager figure darted past hundreds of sightseers for
the doors. Leaping onto the motor-cycle at top speed, he was
delighted to discover the Manhattan traffic was almost non-
existent; during the race to the helicopter pad they saw only
two cars. With three exceptions the traffic lights were green;
Drake had met eight at red, and each one stopped for fifty-five
seconds.

From the helipad, the 'copter thrust Goddard up and past the
Manhattan skyline to the U.S. Navy Floyd Bennett Air Station.

* The USAF record for a crossing from New York to Paris is 3 hours 19 minutes
44·53 seconds in a Convair B58A Hustler, piloted by William R. Payne on 26th May
1961, the average speed being 1,736·068 kilometres per hour,

† Drake had lost eight crucial minutes at one refuelling, due to a communications
failure.

Already Brian Davies was raring to go. He had tested the Phantom's Rolls Royce engines. They were tuned to perfection, the canopy was open and the sleek jet was lined up on the runway. Hopping in, Goddard took only moments to plug into his radio and oxygen and fasten his harness. By the time he had given the thumbs up, the Phantom was beginning to roll. As they streaked skywards, Goddard looked at his watch. He had already clipped a minute off the ground time.

RAF Victor tankers operating out of Goose Bay were airborne, ready for the first of the refuellings. Getting airborne and climbing to the right altitude for supersonic speed eat up enormous quantities of fuel. So the first refuelling came forty minutes after take-off. It was perfectly executed. So was the second refuelling, some forty minutes later. Then the Phantom faced the long, lone Atlantic leg, flying at speeds in excess of 1,200 miles an hour. Brian Davies, working from Peter Goddard's navigational directions, got every possible advantage from the tail-winds. They were edging ahead of schedule.

As the Phantom roared across the black-blue sky of the upper air space, two of the RAF's No. 55 Squadron Victor tankers took off from RAF Marham, Norfolk, one to refuel the Phantom, the other in reserve. Reaching 28,000 feet, they headed for the rendezvous area for the third refuelling. It was to be 400 miles northwest of Ireland, above the frigate H.M.S. *Nubian*, which was providing the vital radar guidance. Also airborne with the two tankers was an RAF Shackleton search and rescue aircraft, from St Mawgan, Cornwall, a precaution in case the hazardous and delicate refuelling operation turned into disaster. After the tanker made radio contact with H.M.S. *Nubian* when it was 85 miles away, it climbed to 33,000 feet.

Peter Goddard got his first radio contact with the refuelling tanker when he was 430 miles away. A quick check indicated they would make the rendezvous one minute ahead of schedule. The Victor tanker—call sign Papa Charlie—confirmed it.

Moments later *Nubian* reported sighting the tankers which, once in position, began to fly up and down a parallel track ready for the link up. A check with RAF Wisley for met. information on the last leg home got a reply of 'weather super'. So it was decided to put the refuelling forward by another minute. Goddard, still over 250 miles away, agreed.

Eight minutes before contact was due to be made, the Victor tanker began to trail its long central refuelling hose. When the Phantom was within 50 miles of rendezvous, the Victor pilot, Flight Lieutenant Peter Beer, put the giant aircraft spot on the pre-arranged course. Coming up from behind, at 20 miles a minute, Brian Davies could see the V-winged tanker and its trailing snout. He cut speed. There were still 32 miles to go. Precisely at the target time of 3 minutes past 5* the Phantom lined up 10 miles behind the trailing hose pipe. Both aircraft had now cut their speeds to around 500 mph. Like a slow motion film, the Phantom glided up towards the trailing hose pipe, aiming for the bell-like cup at the end. With perfect precision, Brian Davies guided the Phantom up under the tail of the tanker until his own refuelling pipe locked into the tanker's hose pipe. Linked together, like a man and his dog, the aircraft hurtled through the sky. The Phantom took two separate, mighty gulps, totalling 8,000 lb. of range-giving fuel. The twin operation took 17 minutes. Davies and Goddard were satisfied that they had enough fuel to get home. Breaking away, both aircraft picked up a message from *Nubian*: 'Very best of luck —see you at the party.' As the Phantom sped on to victory, over their intercom the tanker crew exchanged opinions on the refuelling. 'A couple of cool customers, that Phantom crew—very, very professional.' With that the tanker and the reserve tanker, which had not been needed, headed back to their home base, as did the Shackleton.

Meanwhile, the Phantom was screaming along at 1,200 mph towards the British coast. Within sight of it, though 40 miles away, sonic boom restrictions forced them to cut back their speed to below 750 mph—they weren't going to risk any broken house windows as a prelude to their victory. Roaring into Wisley, Brian Davies lowered the wheels, dropped the flaps and put the Phantom down with the same perfection as when carrying out the refuelling operation. No tyres burst and Peter Goddard was racing for the Wessex helicopter before he could turn round and say good luck.

* London time. It was 1603 ZULU, the international time.

As the Wessex whirled its way towards the Post Office Tower, Goddard slipped out of his pressurized flying suit, donned a pair of lightweight flying overalls and put on his orange *Daily Mail* Race bib. Spotting the approaching Tower through the open door, he sat poised on the edge and as the giant 'copter dropped down towards the temporary helipad, a tap on his shoulder sent him leaping out to follow a pacemaker already sprinting for the road and the Tower steps. Deafening cheers greeted Goddard as he hurtled along to the elevator, in too much of a hurry to check his watch to see if he was going to break the record and snatch the prize.

Turning right out of the elevator at the 33rd floor, he sprinted to the dais and banged the button for a sensational Race time for the 3,500 mile journey of 5 hours 11 minutes 22·98 seconds. He had clipped 7 minutes and 54 seconds off Drake's time. As he broke off from receiving a victory kiss from his wife Colleen, Goddard learned that the Phantom had set up a new 4 hours 46 minutes 57 seconds world record for a flight from America to Britain. The average speed had been 723·8 mph. As the victory champagne corks popped, a 'Well done all' signal arrived from the First Sea Lord, Admiral Sir Michael le Fanu. The Fleet Air Arm may have been under sentence of death by the Government, but it was certainly going out in a blaze of glory.

Indisputably it was the Navy's day. But the RAF were not going to let them steal all the glory. Not that Flight Lieutenant Derek Aldous was under the illusion that he could better the supersonic Phantom's time in his subsonic Victor reconnaissance bomber; he was out to prove a different point. His challenge was that though the Harrier might be able to hop from city centre to city centre, the V-bomber boys could out-race them from the Empire State Building to the Post Office Tower.

The Harrier had proved its paces again in mid-week. Squadron Leader Graham Williams, after being halted at every traffic light on New York's Twenty-Third Street, reached the United Nations building site in rain that was 'sheeting down'. Even helicopters were grounded. Undeterred, and shielded by a borrowed umbrella to keep from the cockpit the rain driving off the Hudson river, Squadron Leader Williams gunned the Harrier into action.

He hopped out of the heart of Manhattan, and put down in the St Pancras coal-yard just under 5½ hours later. His time between the Empire State Building and the Post Office Tower check-in stations was 5 hours 49 minutes 58 seconds.

That was the time Flight Lieutenant Aldous was out to beat. At the start no one was optimistic about his chances. On the outward leg to New York, Squadron Leader Lecky-Thompson had beaten the first V-bomber man by 17 minutes and the second one by 5 minutes. To cap that, Squadron Leader Williams's effort from New York to London had clipped 6 minutes off the time put up by Flying Officer Stevenson in a V bomber. Undeterred, the 25-year-old navigator set out from the Empire State Building in high spirits. Everything went perfectly—even the traffic lights turned green at the right moment. There were no air traffic control delays, and the V bomber roared out of Floyd Bennett Airfield slightly ahead of schedule. But then the winds let them down. They didn't find the hoped-for 50-knot winds along the course they were flying. Eventually, when they located one that would really have pushed them along at a hell of a lick, it was too far away. What they would have gained by flying along it would have been lost by going so far off course to reach it. When the V bomber touched down at Wisley, Surrey, there was only the slimmest chance for Derek Aldous to beat the Harrier man's time. But he was determined to try.

As news of his progress was given by Squadron Leader Olley Crooks, in charge of the landing pad next to the Tower, the crowds began to gather. Soon the heavy blades were whirling their way between the giant cranes to the bull's-eye spot on the pad. Making the biggest leap of all from the throbbing 'copter, Aldous shot out of the helipad enclosure as though he were sprinting down an Olympic track. Ignoring the burden of his flying helmet and flying suit, he pounded along the road, through cheering, clapping crowds into the elevator. When it reached the 33rd floor, he pounced out like a leopard, thrust his time-card into the machine and banged the button. There was a pregnant silence as everyone waited for the officials to convert the phase time into actual Race time. The news—5 hours 49 minutes 28·81 seconds—caused a great ovation to resound around the circular floor. The

V bomber boys had done it—they had pipped the Harrier by *twenty-nine and a half seconds.*

Once more seconds, not minutes or hours, were the deciding factor in the transatlantic dash. Indeed seconds, rather than the expected minutes, were all Peter Hammond was able to cut off his time on his second record-breaking attempt. Instead of slashing off 20 minutes, he had to be content with shaving his time by 56 seconds. His new winning time was 6 hours 54 minutes. Throughout the day it looked as though his luck would hold. Then came the final night.

At Kennedy Airport, earlier that day, a drama was being played out that was to have a vital bearing on the outcome of the final results. BOAC, QANTAS, TWA and PAN AM each had flights leaving at about the same time with Race competitors on board.

Helen Lysaght, under the patronage of New York's Francis X. Smith, President of the City Council, made a quick get-away with a Cadillac car from the Empire State Building to the helipad. As she sped towards it, accompanied by fellow QANTAS employee Peter Shilton, the traffic supervisor at Kennedy Airport was warned they were on their way. The helicopter took only 10 minutes to touch down at the airport. As it did so, Helen's son telephoned the airline's operation centre to warn them that Helen and Peter were only 2 minutes from boarding. From the 'copter the couple, having cleared customs the night before, dashed directly out to the aircraft loading ramp, boarding passes at the ready. Everything had worked perfectly—until they settled in their seats. Congestion on the ground forced Air Traffic Control to delay the take-off. Fifteen minutes went by. Also fuming, but aboard a PAN AM jet, was Rupert Lycett Green, who had arrived in record time on the point of the scheduled departure. But instead of the doors closing and the jet taxiing for take-off, nothing happened. With £5,000 ($12,000) at stake, there was a great commotion whilst an air stewardess and her baggage were taken off the aircraft. She had been put on specially to look after an unaccompanied infant. When the infant didn't arrive, PAN AM decided to take her off again, even though there were several Air Race competitors on board. The transfer operation lost 15 minutes.

While both the QANTAS and the PAN AM jets were sitting on the deck, Ken Holden, who left the Empire State Building at 9.42 a.m., scrambled up into a TWA plane 15 minutes later. It was already waiting to taxi out for take-off. To the annoyance of the competitors in the other aircraft the TWA jet jockeyed in front of the QANTAS and PAN AM jets and zoomed skywards ahead of the others. Ken Holden had a flying start.

Angrily the QANTAS team got airborne and gave chase. But they were pitted against George Duvall, one of TWA's most experienced pilots. Capitalizing on his lucky break of a quick take-off clearance, he was not going to lose the advantage. Scurrying across the Ocean he flew at 27,000 feet with the QANTAS jet 2,000 feet above him, trailing between one and three minutes behind.

On reaching Cork, only one minute's flying time separated the two giant aircraft. Approaching London Air Traffic Control, each captain asked permission to descend. But being already ahead of the QANTAS jet, George Duvall was allowed priority. Competitors on both aircraft were on tenterhooks as each pilot requested a 'straight in approach'. When they were given different runways for landing, the advantage was marginally with QANTAS. That was until a controller called George Duvall to see if he had the runways at Heathrow in sight. When he answered 'yes', they gave him permission to make a 'visual approach'. Immediately he capitalized on the situation and swung the giant jet sharply to the right and made a brilliant short approach, to put down well ahead of his QANTAS rival.

Untroubled by the Air Traffic Control technicalities Holden hopped off the jet and dashed for the arrivals building. Acting instantaneously, the customs and immigration authorities waved him through. Holden was roaring away from the airport before Helen Lysaght and the others had reached customs.

Officials at the Post Office Tower, oblivious to the airborne dramas, were relaxing after the hectic arrivals of the Service teams and the more sedate appearance of hot-air balloonist Bill Berry of Concord, California. Berry's Chitty Chitty Boom Boom balloon had been shipped over by air freight, to allow him to complete ascents on both sides of the Atlantic. His efforts were

o

sponsored by the Diablo Valley Junior College, Pleasant Hill in California.

'Competitor!' The elevator man's yell brought everyone on the 33rd floor up with a start. Around the corner sprinted a gaunt figure in a faded flying suit. No one recognized him. Without a sign of emotion—or excitement—he punched his race card. Calmly he handed it to the officials at an adjacent desk, for them to determine his Race time. Bill Fairley's powerful voice boomed out the time. 'Six hours forty . . .' the words hesitated for a moment. 'Forty-eight minutes and thirty-three seconds.'

A gasp of astonished delight went up from the crowd. I tugged at his sleeve. 'What is your name?' I asked.

'Ken Holden,' he said, a smile breaking across his angular features. 'Where from?' 'Ireland. I work for Aer Lingus.' 'My God,' I said, 'what a surprise for BOAC.' His time put him into the top spot for the BOAC prize. For with 6 hours 48 minutes 33·88 seconds he had clipped 6 minutes off Hammond's time and snatched the lead for the BOAC £5,000 ($12,000) prize. It meant Hammond dropping down to take over the Rothmans £4,000 ($9,600) prize spot, and Susi Scribner moving to the smaller £2,500 ($6,000) Daily Sketch category.

The applause had just died down when Helen Lysaght burst out of the elevator to clock 6 hours 58 minutes 21 seconds. She had come close, but not close enough to topple any of the prize-winners. Shortly behind her was Rupert Lycett Green with a time of 7 hours 1 minute 28 seconds. Both would have beaten Holden and Hammond if it hadn't been for the infuriating delays at Kennedy Airport. To add to the run of bad luck, Jim Bailey's motor-cycle broke down on the leg from Heathrow to the Tower and cut back his time to 7 hours 3 minutes.

Holden had won.

With all the excitement revolving around split-second timings, it was a refreshing change to see Neil Stevens turn up after his 108 hour 14 minute 38 second escapade. He flew down to London in the borrowed Tiger Moth, after crossing the Atlantic to Prestwick in a regular jetliner. In his excitement at finishing his marathon, he left the propeller of his original Tiger Moth in the back of the car at the foot of the Tower. For sheer endurance, he deserved a prize.

Endurance was certainly the key note of powered-glider pilot Mira Slovak's effort. He turned up just before the deadline, to record a Race time of 175 hours 42 minutes 7·1 seconds. Slovak had been flying for eight days. As his moment of triumph approached, the Czech-born pilot kept his sense of humour. He found time to stop off at an air display in Lincolnshire, because he just liked the look of it. He said: 'It seemed so inviting. They didn't mind at all. In fact they made me very welcome. But I had to press on if I was going to make London before the end of the Race.'

With his arrival at the Post Office Tower Slovak proved the merits of his beloved Volkswagen-powered glider. As for the future, he said: 'Now I am going to take the engine out and chrome-plate it and put it on my desk and look at it.'

Such a thought made him happy. So too did his successful flight which he said was 'a poor man's tribute to Alcock and Brown.'

Chapter Sixteen

FINAL TOUCH-DOWN

*'Those pioneer flights of half a century ago have
led from Tennyson's aerial argosies to the sounds
of tourists calculating currencies. It may be hoped
that one of the* Daily Mail's *new pioneers will
discover for us an easy and fast way to get to the
airport.'*

Washington Evening Star, 12th May 1969

SUDDENLY THE RACING was over. Plugs were pulled from the
timing machines at the top of the Post Office Tower and the 86th
floor of the Empire State Building. In the early hours of Monday
morning, 12th May, Ken Pragnell put out the hundredth Air Race
radio broadcast over the BBC network. Cliff Michelmore, after
completing his thirteenth stint as anchorman of the BBC TV's
'Race You to the Top' programme, passed round a celebratory
bottle of Scotch. But there were no glasses. So a quick raid on the
Brooke Bond Tea bar produced a pile of cups, just as Brian
Johnston, the BBC sound commentator, came over to join us.

Surrounded by unattended typewriters, silent television
cameras, batteries of telephones, piles of processed entry forms,
race stickers, baskets of telex messages that had been passed between London and New York, Atlantic maps and rows of sen-
tinel-like scoreboards, everyone began to relax. Tiredness, the
aftermath of having only three hours' sleep a night, swept through
my body in great waves. My mind suddenly seemed to seize up.
Everyone around me seemed to sag with exhaustion as tension
evaporated. They collapsed onto chairs, desks and even the floor
as Cliff Michelmore moved between them with the Scotch,

followed by John Blake, who had miraculously produced a supply of beer. It was one o'clock on Monday morning. Norman Heath took a deep breath and forced a tired smile. Wearily he said:

'Come on, chum. Let's get an early night. The prize-giving is only seventy hours away and we have to chase up the sponsors for their "most meritorious" winners.' We both burst out laughing.

For although the actual racing was over, seven prizes had still to be awarded. On both sides of the Atlantic, and in Switzerland, small committees were to meet to determine the distribution of £17,000 ($40,800) for efforts where speed had not been the criterion.

Garry May, the *Evening News* air correspondent, had meticulously charted the progress and performance of all the 26 light-aircraft flights. Armed with his recommendations his editor, John Gold, selected California's Mira Slovak for the £1,000 ($2,400) prize for the best performance for a competitor using a light aircraft under 5,000 lb. *Blick*, the Zurich newspaper, chose Beat Studer for their £1,000 ($2,400) prize. He had turned in the fastest time by a Swiss national, with 7 hours 45 minutes 45 seconds. The Empire State Building chose Nick Kleiner, the man who travelled as 'Mr Average Air Passenger' to take their £1,000 ($2,400). Ziff-Davis, the New York publishing company, after getting reports from London, including one from Don McNicoll of Associated Press, finally awarded their £5,000 ($12,000) prize to one-legged pilot Bill Guinther, who played a major role in helping to keep Fred Clauser flying during his long night of crisis.

Brooke Bond, in their search for the most meritorious Commonwealth entry, had no hesitation in selecting Tiger Moth pilot Neil Campbell Stevens from Vancouver, Canada, for the £2,000 ($4,800) New York–London prize, and Air India hostess Miss Valerie Rosario from Bombay for the London–New York £2,000 ($4,800) award.

Deciding the winner of the £5,000 ($12,000) Butlin prize for the most meritorious British effort was proving more difficult. A high-powered committee sat under the chairmanship of Robert Butlin. With so many courageous efforts to choose from, awarding the prize to one person seemed an almost impossible task.

After long deliberations, they narrowed the list down to three prospects: Sandhurst Cadet David A. Wynne-Davies, who suffered frostbite during his marathon of 44 hours 3 minutes 10 seconds in a light aircraft; Julia Turner, mother of three children, who also flew in a light aircraft but in the opposite direction, from London to New York; and the London University students who had set out to raise money for the MacIntyre Schools for the Mentally Handicapped. Realizing that three into £5,000 would not go, Robert Butlin added another £250 ($600) so that they could make three equal awards of £1,750 ($4,200). Miss Patricia Johnson was chosen to represent the students at the prize-giving.

David Monk immediately set to work re-organizing the arrangements for the presentation of winners to the Duke of Edinburgh at the Royal Garden Hotel before the banquet. So many dignitaries wanted to pay tribute to the success of the enterprise, that fitting two extra prize-winners into the spectacular gala occasion was a critical operation.

From a germ of an idea of Brian Harpur four years earlier, and encouraged by Angus Macpherson, the *Daily Mail* air correspondent, the Air Race had turned out to be the biggest promotional event ever staged in Britain. Moreover, it was an enterprise which captured the interest and support of the public throughout the world. It brought the *Mail* 130,000 column inches of press comment in other periodicals, and to have paid for the TV and radio coverage would have cost £3,000,000 ($7,200,000).

During the eight days in May, 345 attempts had been made to cross the Atlantic, 187 from London to New York and 158 from New York to London. Only one competitor failed to get through —light aircraft pilot Samuel Marshall of Dallas, Texas, who, faced by impossible icing conditions, had given up in Greenland. Fred Clauser of Pennsylvania who ditched his plane off the Faeroe Islands; Ben Garcia of New Jersey, who ended upside down in a chicken farm; and Neil Stevens were the only major casualties, but each continued and finished the race. Eddie Freudmann broke a leg and Tom Ravensdale sprained his ankle, and a couple of motor-cyclists were injured. Though vintage cars and motor-cycles had a habit of 'blowing up', the only sizable crash reported was when the 'Roman Chariot' scraped a passing car at a traffic light.

Disappointments were legion—most of all for the airlines who failed to recognize the publicity potential of the Race and woke up too late to get even an official 'flag carrier' entered in time. BEA, who did get a Trident entry submitted, pulled out after it had been vetoed by Henry Marking, their chief executive. Ironically, when the flight details and weather conditions of the actual day chosen were put through the computer Captain A. Angus, the would-be competitor, found that, on paper at least, the BEA team would have been clear winners and have walked off with a £4,000 ($9,600) Rothmans prize. Out of the 397 entry forms received compared to the 348 attempts actually made, some of those who failed to turn up for the start pulled out, like the two competitors from Hambros Bank, because they had left insufficient time to make winning preparations. Several of the light-aircraft pilots decided not to risk the perilous weather conditions, while poor Anne Conney of Trans Meridian Airways just failed to get a charter aircraft filled in time to enable her to take part in the Race.

Excitements, disappointments, all were part of the Air Race scene. In the final analysis, luck certainly played a key part in deciding the actual winners, and many times after the 3,500-mile dash only seconds separated the winner from the loser. But the event was also significant in the pointers it gave for the future of air travel. Certainly it proved that customs and immigration authorities—particularly in Britain—could be flexible. It underscored the difficulties and frustrations of getting to and from airports by using conventional ground transportation, and it proved the desperate need for a heliport in the heart of London. One important side effect of the Race was the way in which it got airlines and passengers working together in close harmony, both on the ground and in the air. For once, all those promises of special treatment, carried so monotonously in airline advertisements and which are so rarely put into effect, came true. During the eight days in May, Air Race passengers at least became VIPs, lavished with attention before, during and after the flight. What a welcome change! Usually concern is confined to the flight time.

Inevitably the Transatlantic Air Race highlighted the appalling problems faced by ordinary air passengers trying to get between airports and city centres. It focused attention on the absurdity, in an age when you can fly at ten miles a minute (600 mph), of spending an equivalent of a 600-mile journey on the ground going through tedious documentation procedures to get onto or off the jet. An hour wasted on the ground at the airport for pre-flight documentation and another hour getting to the airport, and an hour and a half at the other end before you get clear of customs and arrive in the heart of a city, is the equivalent in supersonic jet terms of losing 3,600 miles or a complete transatlantic flight. Though Concorde supersonic services are not due to start until 1972 (and American supersonic Boeings in the mid 1970s) the other aviation pace-setter, the jumbo jet, will be in regular airline service in 1970; when PAN AM, BOAC, and TWA will all launch the Boeing 747s. Though at first they will carry an average of only 350 passengers, it is inevitable that within a short time some operators will use them to their top capacity of 500 passengers.

It is already envisaged that during the summer months, between the hours of 6 and 7 a.m., six or more Boeing 747s will arrive at Heathrow Airport after overnight flights from New York. They will spill out 3,000 passengers, and about another 10,000 attendant friends and outgoing passengers will be at the airport. All these people will be imposed on top of the airport's ordinary traffic, which already has the airport bursting at the seams. It does not need much imagination to see that this spells absolute chaos, parti-cularly when it is realized that only two of the world's airports will be ready with special terminals to receive the jumbo jet influx. One is Kennedy Airport, the other Orly, Paris. Heathrow's jumbo jet terminal will not be ready until April 1970—more than three months after the start of regular jumbo-jet services. Worse still, the vital rail link connecting the centre of Heathrow with Victoria railway station in the heart of London cannot now possibly be ready until 1974, and even that is an optimistic estimate. It does *not* augur well for the passenger. Total transit times will almost cer-tainly increase rather than decrease. In view of this, the Air Race threw out some interesting statistics on total travelling times.

It is fair to take the average London to New York centre-to-centre journey time as being 11 hours, of which the flight time takes up 7 hours 40 minutes; and the New York–London time as 10 hours (flight time 6 hours 40 minutes). An analysis of Air Race times shows:

Total Journey Time	London–New York	New York–London
Under 5½ hours	—	3
„ 6 „	—	6
„ 7 „	3	15
„ 8 „	30	76
„ 9 „	84	119
„ 10 „	110	126
Over 10 hours	73	14
(Excluding light aircraft)		

Yet these times were achieved largely because competitors resorted to the use of motor-cycles, helicopters and unconventional forms of ground transport. And for the most part they carried only hand baggage or 'post entered' their suitcases, which enabled them to be cleared leisurely through customs by an agent. Times of 20 minutes from the Post Office Tower to sitting in the plane were not exceptional, though they were often achieved by breaking road speed limits. In New York, by a miracle of organization, with young workers pointing his route with paper arrows, Marvin Gathers, a Harlem ghetto worker, reached Kennedy Airport from the Empire State Building in 11 minutes. It made nonsense of the one and two hour pre-flight trips to New York airports experienced by so many passengers.

Inevitably, top speeds meant the use of helicopters. Ironically, just as in the 1959 London–Paris Air Race, the transatlantic event highlighted the total inadequacy of London's helicopter landing facilities. No progress of any note has been achieved in a decade, when it comes to obtaining access to the heart of London by helicopter. The only heliport is situated on the South Bank of the River Thames in Battersea, which cannot be reached effectively by public transport and is not near a rail or Underground station. Its remoteness makes it unattractive to the average passenger. As in the London–Paris Race, the only way to overcome this was to have barges moored in the Thames near Waterloo Bridge to act as temporary helipads. The Board of Trade did grant two exceptions, and twice allowed a riverside car park on the South Bank to be used as a helipad. But civil helicopters had to keep strictly to the river.

Unbelievably, no progress has been made on the construction of a central heliport for London. Plans are still at the talking stage. Safety has certainly been an inhibiting factor. Statistics show that, on average, for every two thousand flying hours one helicopter is involved in an accident, usually due to a loss of power. Over water or in open country, the accident is unlikely to result in fatalities. If it happened over the heart of London, it could be disastrous.

Yet, accepting this limitation—and there are risks with driving by car or coach to the airport—progress has been pitifully slow. The big Air Race breakthrough was the ability of the military, using twin-engined helicopters, to get permission to operate them from immediately opposite the Post Office Tower. This could be a precedent-setter which might ultimately lead to the construction of a helicopter terminal in the heart of London. Objections because of noise would certainly have to be taken into account, but the operation of helicopters into the St Pancras coalyard suggests the choice of a rail terminal—Victoria, Waterloo, Euston or St Pancras—for such a heliport. At least the noise factor would be reduced, for an approach over a busy rail track is unlikely to add an unbearable amount of noise to that which already exists. A route following a rail track could also be an alternative to the river for single-engined helicopters. A crippled helicopter landing on a rail track is probably an acceptable risk.

Vertical take-offs and landings by the Harriers added a new dimension for the future. In New York the Harrier was able to take off when even helicopters were grounded. The success of the exercise certainly spurred Hawker Siddeley on to announcing a prototype jump-jet inter-city civil airliner.

Until that era dawns—and this may be the only long-term solution to the city-centre to airport problem—then one has to look at current possibilities. Both London and New York have got to have either a monorail link—as proposed for London by the

Rapid Transport Development Company—or a conventional rail link between the airport and the heart of the city. But whatever the choice, action is urgently needed now, not after the snarl-ups caused by the jumbo-jet traffic. Yet improved access by itself still will not be enough. Processing passengers, their luggage and documents is a growing major headache. The Air Race certainly proved the worth of Britain's advanced self-selection customs procedure, where you go through a 'Red' channel only if you have anything to declare. If you opt for the Green channel, you risk the possibility of spot checks, but for 97 per cent of the time you can pass through quickly without being stopped. For this to be really effective, airlines have got to speed up baggage recovery from the aircraft—an operation that can often take up to an hour at both Heathrow and Kennedy Airports.

Customs, health and immigration checks are the most difficult to streamline when trying to speed up passenger handling. The United States are trying hard with their 'one stop' system, where one official carries out immigration and health procedures—including checks from the 'black book'. But is there really any reason why the checks shouldn't all be done at the point of departure, particularly when it is a non-stop transatlantic flight? There are precedents. Between Canada and the United States one country's officials often do checks for both. Occasionally this is done at a frontier bridge. Well, is there any real difference between a bridge over a river and an air bridge? Certainly the U.S. and British immigration authorities, having been able to pre-check the Air Race competitors, with few exceptions rushed them through with incredible speed. Why not treat the other air passengers in the same way? Some form of pre-examination should be possible.

In their first full year of operation, the jumbo-jet fleets are expected to generate as much traffic as that carried in the first twenty-five years of civil aviation. As PAN AM Vice-President Harold Graham says: 'As from 1970 we are all starting from scratch on a thing called an airline.'

Let's hope that this time the airlines, the airports authorities and the governments put the convenience and comfort of the world's 261 million annual passengers first. As the 1969 Transatlantic Air Race undoubtedly showed the public want fast, safe, economic trouble-free city-centre-to-city-centre travel. Achievement of this will need the full exploitation of computerized systems of documentation and automated baggage handling systems capable of operating from arrival points. Experimental systems are being installed in some American airports, and more are urgently needed.

Aviation is a growth industry of which we are seeing only the beginning of its impact on our way of life. Fifty years after Alcock and Brown made their historic flight, London Heathrow Airport handled 55,227 passengers in a single day, when 444 aircraft landed and 461 took off. In fifty years the problem has become not one of getting aircraft across the world's oceans, but of handling them when they arrive above the airports. Solutions are urgently needed for the mounting problems of air traffic control, or longer waits for landing and take-off will neutralize the advantages of aircraft development. This is a particularly acute problem at Kennedy, where aircraft have often had to fly around for two or three hours before being able to land.

The Air Race focused attention on some of these matters, but it also highlighted the intense interest in flying. More than that, as Peter Masefield, the chairman of the British Airports Authority, said: 'This gay adventure has brought out so well again something which is sometimes rather forgotten now—the sporting character of the Anglo-American people—the stimulus of challenge and the fun of the race.'

Certainly it was an event which received accolades from around the world. And Prince Charles, in a congratulatory message, said 'how I wished I had been able to go in for it'.

So did thousands of others. For it was, as the chairman of the *Daily Mail*, Lord Rothermere, said, a Race which 'grew bigger than the *Mail* itself. It became a national event which kindled the imagination of the world. An event which seemed to fulfil a heart-felt need to be associated with great achievement.'

Indeed it was. And a fitting tribute to the two lone pioneer aviators, John Alcock and Arthur Whitten Brown, who first conquered the Atlantic in a flying machine.

APPENDIX I

ITINERARY OF NICK KLEINER
'Mr Average Air Traveller'
London to New York

TRAVEL MODES	ELAPSED TIMES	ACTUAL TIME
Depart GPO Tower		12.55 p.m.
Boarded taxi	2 minutes	12.57 p.m.
Arrived TWA Terminal, Kensington High St	23 minutes	1.20 p.m.
Departed from Terminal in TWA bus	30 minutes	1.50 p.m.

(Note: Reporting time at TWA Terminal—80 minutes before scheduled departure, 3 p.m.)

Arrived London (Heathrow) Airport	25 minutes	2.15 p.m.
Boarded TWA 701	25 minutes	2.40 p.m.
TWA 701 departed gate	58 minutes	3.38 p.m.

(Note: Mechanical fault delayed departure.)

Take-off	26 minutes	4.04 p.m.

(Note: Delay between gate departure and take-off due to heavy traffic.)

Total ground time in London—3 hours 9 minutes

		NEW YORK TIME
Touch-down at Kennedy Airport, New York		6.00 p.m.

Total flying time London–New York—6 hours 56 minutes

Arrived at Gate	16 minutes	6.16 p.m.
Disembarked from Aircraft	3 minutes	6.19 p.m.
Completed Customs and Baggage	11 minutes	6.30 p.m.
Departed airport by airlines bus	28 minutes	6.58 p.m.
Arrived Airline's Terminal in Manhattan	29 minutes	7.27 p.m.
Departed Terminal by taxi	3 minutes	7.30 p.m.
Arrived Empire State Building	11 minutes	7.41 p.m.
Arrived finish line	3 minutes	7.44 p.m.

Total ground time in New York—1 hour 44 minutes

Total ground times in London and New York (32 miles)
                                        4 hours 53 minutes
Total flying time London to New York (3,500 miles)
                                        6 hours 56 minutes
Total Overall Time   **11 hours 49 minutes**

ITINERARY OF NICK KLEINER

'Mr Average Air Traveller'
New York to London

TRAVEL MODES	ELAPSED TIMES	ACTUAL NEW YORK TIME
Departed Empire State Building		5.30 p.m.
Walk to 6th Av. 34th St Subway	11 minutes	5.41 p.m.
Wait for IND 'F' train	10 minutes	5.51 p.m.
Subway trip to Kew Gardens (Cost 20 cents)	26 minutes	6.17 p.m.
Wait for Q10 Green Lines Bus	3 minutes	6.20 p.m.
Bus trip to JFK PAN AM Stop (Cost 20 cents)	43 minutes	7.03 p.m.
Arrived PAN AM Check-In	6 minutes	7.09 p.m.

Total travel time—1 hour 39 minutes

(Note: Kleiner's actual reporting time was 51 minutes before take-off, against PAN AM's stipulated 60 minutes.)

Boarded Scheduled PAN AM flight 2	27 minutes	7.36 p.m.
Aircraft departed from Gate	25 minutes	8·01 p.m.
Take-off time	19 minutes	8.20 p.m.

Total ground time—2 hours 50 minutes

(Note: Times now converted to London local time.)

		ACTUAL LONDON TIME
Touch-down time, London Airport (Heathrow)		6.51 a.m.
Arrived at Gate	4 minutes	6.55 a.m.

Total flying time—6 hours 31 minutes

TRAVEL MODES	ELAPSED TIMES	ACTUAL LONDON TIME
Disembark from Aircraft	2 minutes	6.57 a.m.
Completed Customs and Baggage recovery	12 minutes	7.09 a.m.

(Note: As a Race competitor, formalities were kept to a minimum.)

Departed on No. 91 bus	6 minutes	7.15 a.m.
Arrived Hounslow West Tube Station	14 minutes	7.29 a.m.
Piccadilly Line to Leicester Square, thence Northern Line to Warren Street	42 minutes	8.11 a.m.
Walk to Finish Line. Arrive GPO Tower	15 minutes	8.26 a.m.

Total ground times in New York and London (32 miles)
4 hours 25 minutes
Total flying time New York to London (3,500 miles)
6 hours 31 minutes
Total overall time   **10 hours 56 minutes**

APPENDIX II

LEADING TIMES: LONDON-NEW YORK

Position	Day	Name	Town	Aircraft/Airline	Hrs	Mins	Secs
			SERVICE AIRCRAFT				
1	5th	Sqdn Ldr TOM LECKY-THOMPSON	Salisbury, Wilts	RAF Harrier	6	11	57·15
2	6th	Flt Lt ERIC HEMSON		RAF Victor	6	16	54·72
3	4th	Flg Off. BILL FULLER		RAF Victor	6	28	09·01
4	5th	SIMON LANGDON	Kingswear, Devon	RAF VC 10	7	17	39
5	5th	Sgt HEATHER ROBINSON		RAF VC 10	7	17	52
			CIVILIAN AIRCRAFT				
1	6th	RICHARD SELPH	Sandy Hook, Conn.	PAN AM Cargo	7	6	26
2	5th	Miss VALERIE ROSARIO	Bombay, India	Air India	7	21	39
3	4th	DAVID KOLOZY	New York	Capitol International*	7	23	23
4	4th	J. A. GANET	Netherlands	Capitol International*	7	23	35
5	4th	M. M . KOSTER	Netherlands	Capitol International*	7	23	40
6	4th	TONY DREWERY	Orpington, Kent	BOAC VC 10*	7	25	14
7	4th	JAMES BAILEY	New York	PAN AM	7	28	23
8	6th	Capt M. R. SASTRY	Bombay	Air India	7	28	37
9	4th	JAMES ZOCKALL	London	Scheduled Flight	7	30	20

*Chartered Flight

Position	Day	Name	Town	Aircraft/Airline	Hrs	Mins	Secs
10	4th	STIRLING MOSS	London	BUA VC 10*	7	31	45
11	4th	RUDI CARRELL	Holland	Capitol International*	7	35	19
12	5th	RUPERT LYCETT GREEN	London	BOAC VC 10	7	35	31
13	4th	Lt SAM SMITH	Royal Marines Reserve		7	36	34
14	4th	MARY RAND	Roxbourne, Herts.	BOAC VC 10	7	37	23
15	4th	EDWIN POTTER	Sevenoaks, Kent	Capitol International*	7	38	17
			VIA SHANNON	PAN AM			
1	7th	CLEMENT FREUD	London	Aer Lingus–Irish	8	4	18
2	7th	EDMOND FREUDMANN	London	Aer Lingus–Irish	8	4	21
3	7th	DOMINIC FAULDER	London	Aer Lingus–Irish	8	4	40
4	7th	Leading Mech. HOWARD EVANS	Royal Navy	Aer Lingus–Irish	8	5	56
5	7th	JOHN KELLY	Dublin	Aer Lingus–Irish	8	15	18
6	8th	L/Seaman STEWART DOW	Royal Navy	Aer Lingus–Irish	8	17	24
7	7th	LORD MONTAGU of BEAULIEU, Hants		Aer Lingus–Irish	8	19	41
8	7th	ANTHONY APPLETON	Chelmsford, Essex	Aer Lingus–Irish	8	22	30

*Chartered Flight

Position	Day	Name	Town	Aircraft/Airline	Hrs	Mins	Secs
9	8th	DOMINIC FREUD	London	Aer Lingus–Irish	8	24	19·58
10	8th	CLEMENT FREUD	London	Aer Lingus–Irish	8	24	19·59
			LIGHT AIRCRAFT				
1	4th	STEPHAN WILKINSON		Beagle 206	20	23	31·48
2	4th	ANTHONY CAPPER	Appleton, Cheshire	Piper Aztec	21	48	12·20
3	7th	WILLIAM GUINTHER	Kutztown, Penn.	Beach Bonanza	22	13	18·31
4	5th	SHEILA SCOTT	London	Piper Comanche	26	54	01·81
5	11th	MAX CONRAD	New York	Piper Aztec	27	17	28·86

LEADING TIMES : NEW YORK-LONDON

Position	Day	Name	Town	Aircraft/Airline	Hrs	Mins	Secs
			SUPERSONIC				
1	11th	Lt-Cmdr PETER GODDARD	Royal Navy	Phantom	5	11	22·98
2	7th	Lt HUGH DRAKE	Royal Navy	Phantom	5	19	16·93
3	4th	Lt PAUL WATERHOUSE	Royal Navy	Phantom	5	30	24·43
			SUBSONIC				
1	11th	Flt Lt DEREK ALDOUS	RAF	Victor	5	49	28·81
2	9th	Sqdn Ldr GRAHAM WILLIAMS	RAF	Harrier	5	49	58·52
3	8th	Flg Off. S. STEVENSON	RAF	Victor	5	55	31·33
4	10th	Sgt HEATHER ROBINSON	RAF	VC 10	6	29	11·03

Position	Day	Name	Town	Aircraft/Airline	Hrs	Mins	Secs
			SCHEDULED SERVICES				
1	11th	Dr Ken Holden	Dublin	TWA	6	48	33·88
2	11th	Peter Hammond	Pinner, Middx	BOAC	6	54	00·07
3	5th	Peter Hammond	Pinner, Middx	BOAC	6	54	56·00
4	9th	Susi Scribner	Garden City, N.Y.	PAN AM	6	55	48·00
5	9th	Bob Ottum	Sports Illustrated	PAN AM	6	57	24·39
6	10th	James Bailey	New York	PAN AM	6	57	27·21
7	11th	Helen Lysaght	New York	QANTAS	6	58	21·19
8	9th	Jerry Cooke	Sports Illustrated	PAN AM	6	59	01·27
9	11th	Rupert Lycett Green	London	PAN AM	7	01	28
10	11th	Allen Sturges	Bedford	PAN AM	7	02	19
11	11th	James Bailey	New York	PAN AM	7	03	00·94
12	11th	Tony Drewery	Orpington, Kent	BOAC VC 10*	7	03	05·01
13	11th	Peter Shilton	New York	QANTAS	7	04	30
14	10th	William Allen	New York	PAN AM	7	07	31
15	11th	Lt-Col H. R. A. Hunt	Oxshott, Surrey	BOAC	7	09	37
			LIGHT AIRCRAFT				
1	11th	Mike Fallon	Rickmansworth, Herts.	Twin Comanche	21	31	57·36

*Chartered Flight

Posi-tion	Day	Name	Town	Aircraft/Airline	Hrs	Mins	Secs
2	11th	TONY SAMUELSON	Totteridge, London	Twin Comanche	21	32	09·04
3	11th	KERWIN KELLY	Quakertown, Penn.	Riley Rocket	22	31	48·61
4	11th	NANCY KELLY	Quakertown, Penn.	Riley Rocket	22	31	57·55
5	8th	ANTHONY CAPPER	Appleton, Cheshire	Piper Aztec	22	50	14·09
6	10th	MAX CONRAD	New York	Piper Aztec	23	13	32·63
7	9th	BRIAN KAY	Elstree, Herts.	Twin Comanche	23	23	04·13
8	9th	D. J. T. PARSONS	Elstree, Herts.	Twin Comanche	23	25	03·13
9	5th	VLADIMIR KAZAN	Wellesley Hills, Mass.	Piper	23	35	58·18
10	5th	WILLIAM GUINTHER	Kutztown, Penn.	Beach Bonanza	24	01	01·34
11	11th	MARIE-LOUISE COHEN	Roedean, Sussex	Cessna	24	32	08·69
12	5th	ROBERT SNYDER	Moorestown, New Jersey	Cessna	26	45	36·08

APPENDIX III

PRIZE WINNERS

LONDON TO NEW YORK	NEW YORK TO LONDON
Shortest time overall	**Shortest time overall**
£5,000 *Daily Mail* and £1,000 British Aircraft Corporation	£5,000 *Daily Mail* and £1,000 Vickers Ltd
Sqdn Ldr TOM LECKY-THOMPSON Salisbury, Wilts (6 hrs 11 mins 57 secs)	Lt-Cmdr PETER GODDARD Yeovilton, Somerset (5 hrs 11 mins 22 secs)
Subsonic Aircraft £4,000 Rothmans of Pall Mall	*Subsonic Aircraft* £4,000 Rothmans of Pall Mall
RICHARD SELPH Sandy Hook, Conn., U.S.A. (7 hrs 6 mins 24 secs)	PETER HAMMOND Pinner, Middlesex (6 hrs 54 mins 0 secs)
Scheduled flight via Shannon £5,000 Aer Lingus-Irish	*Direct passenger flight* £5,000 BOAC
CLEMENT FREUD London (8 hrs 4 mins 18 secs)	Dr KEN HOLDEN Clontarf, Dublin (6 hrs 48 mins 33·88 secs)
Personal attempt via Shannon £2,500 *Daily Sketch*	*Unsponsored personal attempt* £2,500 *Daily Sketch*
EDMOND FREUDMANN London (8 hrs 4 mins 21 secs)	Miss SUSAN SCRIBNER Garden City, New York (6 hrs 55 mins 48 secs)
Chartered Business Jet £500 Castle Britannia Group	*Chartered Business Jet* £500 Grovewood Securities
Sir WILLIAM BUTLIN, M.B.E. St John's, Jersey (11 hrs 30 mins 41 secs less 6 hrs handicap time)	TONY DREWERY Orpington, Kent (7 hrs 3 mins 5 secs)
Light Aircraft—man £1,000 London *Evening News*	*Light Aircraft—man* £1,000 London *Evening News*

STEPHAN WILKINSON
New York
(20 hrs 23 mins 31 secs)

MICHAEL FALLON
Rickmansworth, Herts
(21 hrs 31 mins 57 secs)

Light Aircraft—woman
£1,000 London *Evening News*

Light Aircraft—woman
£1,000 London *Evening News*

SHEILA SCOTT
London
(26 hrs 34 mins 1 sec)

Mrs NANCY KELLY
Quakertown, Penn., U.S.A.
(22 hrs 31 mins 57 secs)

NON-WINNING MERITORIOUS AWARD

LONDON TO NEW YORK

NEW YORK TO LONDON

Commonwealth entry

Commonwealth entry

£2,000 Brooke Bond Tea Ltd

£2,000 Brooke Bond Tea Ltd

Miss VALERIE ROSARIO
Bombay, India
(7 hrs 15 mins 31·34 secs)

NEIL CAMPBELL STEVENS
Vancouver, B.C., Canada
(108 hrs 14 mins 38·67 secs)

Best performance in a light aircraft under 5,000 lb.
£1,000 London *Evening News*
MIRA JOHN SLOVAK
Santa Monica, California, U.S.A.
(175 hrs 42 mins 7·11 secs)

British entry
£5,250 Butlins Ltd
shared by:

DAVID A. WYNNE-DAVIES
Bath, Somerset
(44 hrs 3 mins 10·43 secs)

Mrs JULIA TURNER
Cheltenham, Glos.
(33 hrs 34 mins 13·07 secs)

Miss PATRICIA JOHNSON
Ripon, Yorkshire
(27 hrs 29 mins 45·69 secs)
representing MacIntyre Schools
for the Mentally Handicapped.

American entrant
£5,000 Ziff-Davis Publishers
WILLIAM GUINTHER
Kutztown, Penn., U.S.A.
(22 hrs 13 mins 18 secs)

Fastest Swiss National overall
£1,000 *Blick*
BERT STUDER
Zürich
(7 hrs 45 mins 45 secs)

New York State Resident
£1,000 Empire State Building
NICHOLAS A. KLEINER
Hicksville, New York
(10 hrs 55 mins 20·92 secs)

On 17th July 1969 the Postmaster-General, John Stonehouse, with Philip Kaiser of the American Embassy, unveiled a plaque marking the check-point at the Post Office Tower to commemorate the Race and the competitors. It reads:

Transatlantic Air Race. This plaque marks the starting and finishing point of the *Daily Mail* Transatlantic Air Race, 4th–11th May, 1969, in which 360 competitors travelled between the Post Office Tower and the Empire State Building in New York. The Air Race commemorated the 50th anniversary of the first Transatlantic flight in 1919 by Captain John Alcock and Lieutenant Arthur Whitten Brown.

On 30th August, 1969, Gail Shepherd received a surprise £350 ($840) consolation prize at the Top of the Tower from another Race competitor, Swiss businessman Heini Spillmann. He had learned of her desire to buy a guide dog for the blind if she won a prize (p. 181). Though she failed in her attempt, the money raised by Spillmann and a group of friends made it possible for Gail to realize her ambition. And as a result of their interest, the Swiss group are founding Switzerland's first school for training guide dogs for the blind.

HISTORICAL

Conquering the Atlantic was a difficult and incredibly dangerous task, and many pioneers died attempting the crossing.

Here are some of the milestones which paved the way for the present transatlantic invasion, in which 1,300 passenger and freight aircraft cross between Europe and America each week, offering 85,000 seats for sale.

1919

MAY 16–27 FIRST ATLANTIC CROSSING: After eleven days and four stops, U.S. Navy Lieutenant-Commander Albert C. Read and a five-man crew completed the first crossing of the Atlantic in a Curtiss flying-boat NC4 which arrived in Lisbon on 27th May. Two other flying boats had to give up.

MAY 18–19 Harry Hawker and Lieutenant-Commander Mackenzie-Grieve set out to attempt the first non-stop crossing but after 1,400 miles—within 500 miles of success—had to ditch in the sea beside a merchant ship which rescued them.

JUNE 14 FIRST NON-STOP CROSSING OF THE ATLANTIC: Captain John Alcock and Lieutenant Arthur Whitten Brown made the crossing from St John's, Newfoundland, to Clifden, Ireland, in 16 hours 27 minutes; their coast to coast time for the 1,890-mile flight was 15 hours 57 minutes and it won for them Lord Northcliffe's £10,000 prize.

JULY 2–6 FIRST NON-STOP CROSSING BY AN AIRSHIP: The British
9–13 R 34, commanded by Squadron Leader G. H. Scott with a crew of 30 and 1 stowaway, crossed from East Fortune, Scotland, to New York and returned to Pulham, Norfolk, on 13th July.

1924

SEPTEMBER FIRST WESTBOUND CROSSING OF NORTH ATLANTIC: Four U.S. air crews flew Douglas Amphibians as part of the first round-the-world flight.

OCTOBER The former German airship taken by the Americans as war reparations and called the ZR 3 flew from Europe to America via Azores and Nova Scotia.

1927

May 20 FIRST NON-STOP SOLO CROSSING: America's Charles Lindbergh, in *The Spirit of St Louis*, crossed from New York to Paris taking 32 hours 32 minutes for the 3,610-mile flight.

MAY Clarence Chamberlin and Charles Levine flew 3,930 miles non-stop from New York to Eisleben, Germany.

JUNE 29 Commander Richard Byrd and a three-man crew crossed from New York to France, only to ditch in the Channel after over-flying Paris in bad weather.

JULY 27 Edward Schlee and pilot William Brock, in the *Pride of Detroit*, flew from Harbor Grace, Newfoundland, to Croydon, England, on the first leg of an 18,000-mile trip in 990 actual flying hours.

1928 Crossings made by the *Graf Zeppelin* and Britain's R 100 airship.

1932

MAY 20–21 FIRST SOLO CROSSING OF THE ATLANTIC BY A WOMAN: Amelia Earhart became the first woman to fly the Atlantic solo.

1933

FEB. 6–9 FIRST EAST TO WEST SOLO FLIGHT OF SOUTH ATLANTIC: James Mollison flew from Lympne, Kent, to Port Natal, Brazil.

JULY 15 Wiley Post crossed the Atlantic in *Winnie Mae*, a Lockheed Vega, at the start of the first solo flight around the world, which took 7 days 18 hours 49 minutes.

1936   Germany's airship *Hindenburg* begins scheduled transatlantic passenger services. But on 6th May 1937 she was destroyed by fire after a crossing from Frankfurt to Lakehurst, New Jersey, in 65 hours.

1937

JULY 5   FIRST NORTH ATLANTIC COMMERCIAL SURVEY FLIGHTS by Imperial Airways and PAN AM flying boats.

1939

MAY 20   FIRST SCHEDULED TRANSATLANTIC PASSENGER FLIGHT: PAN AM initiated the first scheduled transatlantic service with the 74-passenger, four-engined Boeing 314 seaplane. Initially only freight was carried until 28th June.

AUG. 5–6 BOAC inaugurated first British air-mail service across the Atlantic. No passengers were carried.

1940

NOV. 10–11 FIRST FERRY FLIGHT OF TWIN-ENGINED LOCKHEED HUDSONS: The first seven Lockheed Hudsons with a 3-man crew took off from Newfoundland for Aldergrove, Northern Ireland under BOAC Captain D. C. T. Bennett, to inaugurate the World War II Ferry Service.

1941

APRIL   Captain D. C. T. Bennett in a B-24 Liberator carried out the first 'top of the world' Atlantic route survey.

MAY 4   A westbound ferry flight for returning ferry crews to Gander was inaugurated.

1946

FEB. 4   PAN AM introduce Lockheed Constellations on Atlantic route.

MARCH 10 BOAC withdraws its Atlantic scheduled services.

JULY 1   BOAC begin operating Lockheed Constellation 049s
          on the London–New York run.

1958

OCT. 24   FIRST PASSENGER JET SERVICE ACROSS THE ATLANTIC:
          BOAC inaugurates the first pure jet Comet 4 on the
          London–New York route.

OCT. 26   PAN AM inaugurates its pure jet Boeing 707 service
          across the Atlantic, carrying 180 passengers, twice the
          number in the Comet.

1966   First stretched Douglas DC8-61, capable of carrying
          251 passengers, flew across the Atlantic.

1968   5,913,245 passengers flew between Europe and U.S.A.

1969   1,750,000 passengers flew between Britain and cities
          in the U.S.A.

MAY   The 490-seater jumbo-jet Boeing 747 prototype flew
          the Atlantic to appear at the Paris Air Show prior to
          its inauguration in Atlantic service with Pan American
          early 1970.

          At the same Air Show, two prototype supersonic
          Concordes were airborne. They are capable of flying
          130 passengers between London and New York in
          under 3½ hours at 1,450 miles an hour.

INDEX

Sponsors

Historical